THE HOMERIC

IMAGINATION

A Study of Homer's Poetic

Perception of Reality

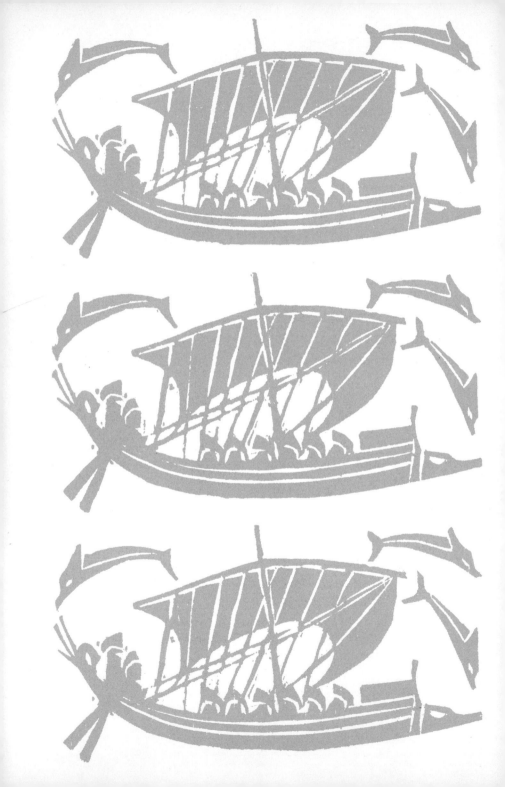

Paolo Vivante

THE HOMERIC
IMAGINATION

A Study of Homer's Poetic

Perception of Reality

INDIANA UNIVERSITY PRESS

Bloomington / London

CONTENTS

ACKNOWLEDGMENTS

Chapter I, "Homer and the Aesthetic Moment," and chapter III, "On the Representation of Nature and Reality in Homer," appeared in the Autumn 1965 and Summer 1966 issues of *Arion* respectively; and they are now republished, with slight alterations, by permission of the editors.

I am indebted to Professor William Arrowsmith for certain corrections of style in chapter II, "On Man and the Gods in Homer."

All the translations in this volume are my own.

INTRODUCTION

The search for the "original Homer" has become more and more a search for the originality of Homer. What stands out is a problem of values rather than of authorship and objective facts. The Homeric question has exhausted itself; we are driven to look at the poems themselves insofar as they appeal directly to our feeling and understanding.

We do not know the literary scene of the Homeric age, and the isolation of Homer at once baffles and impresses us. This circumstance, however, need not hamper us. When we are so far removed from a poet, historical knowledge falters, and criticism is bound to be less literary, more broadly human. The first problem we are faced with is the way poetry conceives and expresses things, in distinction, say, from religion, or law, or tribal tradition.

The Homeric poems are tantamount to a full-scale representation of reality—nature, animals, men. We may therefore reach the poet by inquiring into the picture he gives us—by seeing how true and imaginative it is. The world he describes is, after all, the same as ours. It is a common point of reference. By abstracting it from everything else and becoming familiar with his language, we may learn to look with Homeric eyes. We shall find different perspectives, but focused on the same objects; different modes of thought, but the same need of expression and representation. There exists, after all, a basic human fact—poetic expression; it exists at a deeper level than any particular form—oral or written, popular or literary, archaic or classical.

The imagination is a quality which lies at the root of poetic expression. By "Homeric imagination" I mean that sympathetic insight whereby objects and events were first rendered by the poet in significant and revealing outlines. What matters here is not so much the subject matter itself, nor the vocabulary which describes it, but the mode of apprehension. The question is not, for instance, what Homer says *about* animals, but how he sees them in their actual presence and movements. By looking again at nature after reading Homer we may thus see it with a fresh eyesight, with a fresh feeling for what it is and what it means.

THE HOMERIC

IMAGINATION

A Study of Homer's Poetic

Perception of Reality

I

Homer and the

Aesthetic Moment

It is in the nature of things that the achievement should stand out more prominently and permanently than its author, particularly so in works of art whose property it is to convert and embody into a self-existent form what of an individual's thought has an essential, universal validity. Such is more or less the condition of all human endeavor; but this common lot has nowhere manifested itself more completely than in the case of Homer—to the point that the glory of the work has quite outshadowed and obliterated the memory of the poet as a person who lived and was active in a certain time and in a certain place.

It has been so ever since the first recorded traditions, and each age conceived in its own way the poet's personification. In the earliest stage, while the Homeric poems were universally known and publicly recited by the rhapsodes and then officially edited in different cities throughout the Greek world, all precise information about the life of Homer was lost, his image magnified beyond the bounds of time, space, and reality: it is well known that many poems were attributed to him besides the *Iliad* and the *Odyssey*, that many places claimed to have given him birth, that the ancient "Lives of Homer" carry us into a fantastic mythological sphere. Later, when the poems were removed from their native soil and regarded as literary masterpieces rather than objects of worshipful performance, the ancient piety gave way to pure admiration, intellectual reverence, studious devotion; and Homer, no less projected into the absolute, appeared as an ideal master, a symbol of perfection, such as Dante saw him in Limbo leading the other poets, a "lord of highest song who like an eagle soars above the rest." Finally more recent times witnessed the effacement of Homer not only as a person, but as an idealized image, his name almost used as a tag to classify a poetry which defied the ingenuity of scholars and offered no other cue but that of its own intrinsic quality.

There seems to be no parallel to the underlying motives and characteristic circumstances of this posthumous fortune. What is so singular about it is that the process of idealization was prompted by a sense of the beautiful and went hand in hand with an idea of artistic excellence. In other cases of apotheosis, aesthetic reasons never seem to have played such a determining role. We might think, for instance, of Moses or Zoroaster. It was not so much the beauty as the religious value of the Pentateuch and the Avesta which gave these men a godlike fame and set all account of their lives beyond the reach of history. A similar destiny accrued to Homer, but from the sheer poetry of the *Iliad* and the *Odyssey*, not from those ultimate revelations of life and death which are most likely to lift a man to a superhuman, transcendental sphere.

Such a situation at once defines and characterizes the Homeric achievement. It marks the emergence of literary art in its autonomy, recognized and glorified for its own sake; the poems came as the revelation of the power which is inherent in the mastery of words. Odysseus is said to speak like a god, and the Phaeacians listen to him wrapt in mute enchantment. It is the effect which Homeric poetry must have had on its audiences. The poet himself betrays his consciousness of language as a self-subsisting reality: the "winged words" of his characters are like airy embodiments of thought which go their own way into the heart of the listener, driven home by the magic of their meaning. Indeed the poems themselves are conceived as a massive utterance, inspired by the Muse, following its thread independently of an author's will. No wonder that all personal trace of the poet vanished in their wake.

Homer thus represents, in a way, the triumph of expression. He does not limit himself to relating a fine story for our delight, he also gives a full rendering of his world. Unlike other epics, the *Iliad* and the *Odyssey* are not so much concerned with recounting what has happened as with expressing what is, exists, or lives in its own right: the actions of men are seen in their essential pattern and in the presence of a natural scenery which affords them, as it were, a sympathetic company. From the beginning of the *Iliad* we are made aware of this penetrating Homeric touch. For the action portrayed in the first book is plain and quickly enacted; but, as it develops, it instantly evokes in its setting the whole imagery of the Homeric world—the ridges of snow-capt Olympus whence the gods watch and descend; the loud-roaring sea and its barren foaming expanse as it washes the shore at Chryses' feet or as Achilles looks over it in his distress; the hollow, dark, curving, well-balanced ships by whose side each deed is carried out; the shadow of night and the radiant rose-fingered morn that alternately put an end and mark a beginning to the activity of men. This and much else furtively makes its way into the picture even as Homer sets before us one human act after the other; and we are unwittingly introduced into a complete representation of existence. What we find here is an exhaustive nomenclature, a whole system of attributes and qualifications, as if poetry had set out to explore the universe and render its outlines.

In this initial visualization of man and his world, the poet's mind was completely immersed in an imaginative perceptiveness. There could be no room left for any reference or allusion to himself. All his talents were brought into play by an overriding need to express the aspects of reality; and the ensuing representation could bear an individual artistic touch only insofar as it appeared harmonized into one coherent whole. In other words, the distinctive mark of Homeric authorship is revealed in a qualitative conditioning of the material. For the extensiveness of the picture had to be compatible with a refining principle, the complexities of things had to be rendered in the terms of a common essential character, the manifold variety had to be made manifest in an underlying simplicity of form. Take, for instance, the words which indicate men: they are mortal, earth-bound, widely-scattered, much-wandering, bread-eating, voice-endowed, miserable men. Compare the nurturing, life-bearing earth; or the luxuriant, high-leaved trees; or the many-fountained, ridge-forming mountains. Whatever the thing expressed—whether animal, plant, man-made object, or element of nature—the Homeric words always stress the structure, function, or condition which is essential to the object itself. Add to this the similes which seem to bring out a characterizing stress manifesting itself throughout the realm of being; add the usual Homeric emphasis on striking and significant details rather than on abstract ready-made things—so that, for instance, the limb of a man or a projection of the seashore are made to appear as elements of a similarly conceived fundamental pattern.

An extensive and essential setting wherein man and nature, animate and inanimate objects bear the mark of a common origin —this is a singular achievement of the Homeric imagination. Whatever is portrayed is necessarily cast in a certain mould; and the cumulative effect of this artistic rendering conveys the impression of a full-scale language which has been conceived and composed after a personal vision. For the poet seems to take a delight in naming objects for their own sake, in establishing identities, in defining the aspects of visible forms, in signifying the qualities and properties of what men experience in their lives;

and, in so doing, he never interprets or comments, but simply conveys meanings which abide each time in the perfect relevance of one word.

This complete absorption of all idiosyncrasies into a singular composure of expression seems to characterize Homer apart from all other poets. For never has the personality of an author worked itself into the subject matter so extensively and, at the same time, so deeply, so subtly, so elusively. The smoothness of a pervasive and self-consistent style gives us the illusion of a work of art as impersonal as nature itself; and yet generations of listeners or readers, ever since the earliest times, must have felt the charm of an art which would have craved to be associated with the name of a certain author, even if such a name had not been handed down by tradition. It is hard to account for such opposing impressions. All we can say is that, in this vindication of linguistic expression as a fully autonomous art, poetry found its fulfillment in the objectivity of the image, and no one-sided concern was allowed to curtail the wholeness of the picture. With other poets it is never quite so. The wistfulness of Vergil, or the irony of Ariosto, or the pathos of Tasso, or the moral tone of Milton introduce into the subject matter a partial trend which somehow dislocates the existential order of things. Even the forcefulness of Dante or Shakespeare seem a strain on the serenity of nature. In Homer the most violent emotion immediately becomes a phenomenon of existence, something that happens, that is, and must therefore be represented as a natural, transparent recurrence, no less than a flood or a wave of the sea.

It follows that so singular a work should pose critical problems of a singular kind. In these last two centuries which have seen so much ingenuity in the field of criticism, Homer has proved to be a stumbling block. The work of no other poet has been the object of such opposing theories as those that go under the heading of the "Homeric Question": for instance, Lachmann's hypothesis of sixteen anonymous primitive lays constituting the original *Iliad*, and Paley's notion of a Homer belonging to the height of Greek civilization—the Athens of the sixth and fifth centuries. It could

hardly be otherwise with poems that have the straightforward-
ness of a popular ballad and the high-wrought beauty of a classic.
For modern criticism, accustomed as it was to retrace literary influences and to study a poet in relation to his milieu, found itself
at loss before a kind of poetry so utterly self-contained and free
from external allusions. The task of reaching the author appeared
quite impossible, no convenient point of reference being available
to find a connection and explain the artistic process in terms of
cause and effect. Historical situations were thus imagined or built
up on scanty evidence to account for Homeric poetry; and what
must ultimately have been the fruit of the subjective imagination
was parceled out and regarded as a growth sprung from a certain
environment. The literature of the "Homeric Question" is therefore no mere display of scholarly ability; it is, rather, the expression of a genuine perplexity, a sign of the critical hesitation we
must necessarily feel when the problem of authorship is laid before us in all its baffling bareness, and we consider it unaided by
any external evidence, left alone to our solitary discernment.

The problem which I have in mind is, then, simply this: is it
possible to discover the poet's subjectivity beneath the compact
surface of the poems? Is it possible, in other words, to place ourselves in the perspective of his own imagination and thus appre-
hend from within his experience the ways and means of his
seeing, feeling, thinking? We may do so, I believe, insofar as we
are able to perceive how the Homeric art holds its own ground,
how it attunes to its own rendering of reality the traditional,
mythical representations whence it drew its theme. For however
original was the basic conception of the poems and the perception
of nature which pierces through them, they deal with a subject
matter which sinks deep into the past. Homer himself no doubt
felt a deep reverence for Mycenae, for its historical relics, for its
legendary memories, for its religious associations. The heroes of
whom he sings belong to that age. They must have been up to his
time hallowed figureheads, composite images produced by the
confluence of various sources—history, folklore, myth, religion;
and their heroic labors must have been handed down as taking

place in a semi-divine, unreal setting. In the Homeric poems themselves we may catch a glimpse of what that epic tradition must have been like whenever the poet mentions the background of his heroes, as in the sagas related by old Nestor. But it was a mark of his genius that he struck upon an event which "rang most novel in the ears of men," and its inherent human interest tended to overshadow the inherited fictitious surroundings, bringing with it a scenery which was similarly new, lifelike, drawn from nature.

The initial intuition had to be followed up. Not only was there a vast subject matter to be mastered, but the poet had to work in depth: what inspired him was going to be transformed in its very nature, as each image presented itself still embedded in myth. This was a task of intellectual insight and sympathetic feeling at the same time. How it was carried out we may surmise from the details of the execution; but it is clear that it required all the qualities most intimately associated with individual poetic genius: a strong sense of the real as well as a wonder for distant mysterious things, a broad receptive nature as well as a discriminating taste formed by the consciousness of an artistic ideal.

Homer, we may observe, was placed in an excellent situation for such a task. In the rising civilization of Ionia, after the destruction of the Mycenaean centers and the turmoil of the great migrations, everything seemed to start anew. Here the religion of nature was giving way to the scientific spirit, the tribal gods were being humanized, and the old royalties disappearing before the growth of the city-states; here the times were ripe for the myths to be seen in a new light, brought into harmony with a fresh view of the world. The awe for legendary glories, no doubt, still remained, but suffused with a desire to perceive, to know, to individualize. Now poetry could instill into the opaque mythological representations the spark of personal awareness. It was a disruptive and, at the same time, creative element. The traditional material was thereby given a new spell of life, but cleared of all that was not pertinent to the imaginative principle of the author. What stood out was the truth of the picture, as the heroic apparel became more and more a transparent screen and the way was laid open for the experience of reality to enter the realm of poetry.

2

Ever since Aristotle, Homer has been admired for gathering the whole subject matter around the significance of one central action rather than describing events which followed one another in a mechanical and purely chronological sequence. This penetrating appreciation stresses an essential characteristic of the poems, but it does not go beyond the statement of a fact: the unity of the composition is postulated as something excellent in itself, as an organic quality which is inherent in the artistic achievement.

If, however, we try to visualize the artistic process rather than the completed form, we must try to trace the objective values of the text back to the moment of their original conception; and we may restate the Aristotelian idea in these terms: Homer reduced the conglomerate of myth and tradition to a form which, in its unity, had for his imagination the appeal of a transparent human meaning.

It was, in fact, a value of perspicuity which touched a sympathetic chord in the Homeric mind; and the same spirit of truth revealed itself in the rendering of each act and natural feature no less than in the conception of the plot. A unifying impact was thus contained in the very simplicity of the vision which fathomed a human occurrence in its necessary development from a certain beginning to a certain end. Hence a highly intelligible story broke through the conventional heroic imagery, and, in the process, the crystallized figureheads of myth mellowed into the features of delicately conceived men and women living in a world which we might recognize as our own.

The poems themselves, right at their very beginning, illustrate how the clear perception of a deep human interest works up the unity of the plot. In the *Iliad* the wrath of Achilles is immediately apprehended in the power of its motives and in the magnitude of its consequences, so that the whole subsequent action is somehow foreshadowed and gathered around an absorbing reference point. In the *Odyssey*, no less so, the intimate state of Odysseus who desires to die unless he can return to his home is immediately presented as a fundamental human need, as a most urgent concern, such as gods and men can no longer ignore, such as to draw to itself the trend of all the ensuing events. In both cases there is in the theme itself a pregnant value whose implications run through the poems giving an intimate motivation to the action and forcing it to a distinctive course.

This is not only true of the plot as a whole, but also of the various concomitant episodes. What we have before us is not simply a felicitous idea or intuition which the poet has succeeded in realizing and carrying through, but rather a mode of conception and expression which appears inherent in his mind. For in each instance, in each scene, the same treatment is applied. The narrative is never allowed to proceed in a merely descriptive, prosaic sequence. Whatever the occurrence, there is always an issue at stake—an issue which must be clarified and explained. Thus, after the opening theme of the wrath, the rally of the Achaeans in the second book of the *Iliad*—with Agamemnon's dream, his speech, his testing of the army, Thersites, etc.—is so represented as to lay bare the human motives of the enterprise, its vanity or its justification. Similarly, the ensuing duel between Paris and Menelaus, or the later one between Hector and Ajax, are presented as moments of crisis winding up the reasons of the struggle, as ultimate tests of opposing feelings and resolutions, as actions taking place amid the whispered wishes and imprecations of a whole people. Even such an episode as the Doloneia is not simply intended as a display of bravery, but as an initiative dramatically conceived in an exchange of anguished counsels. The same might be said about Pandarus shooting his arrow, or Sarpedon's onslaught on the Achaean wall, or Aeneas' stand against Achilles— scenes and situations which are quite different from one another, but all coming as the realization of a psychic process that must necessarily follow its course, whether it be a sudden temptation

11

or a disenchanted reflection. The general battle itself appears reduced to the most forcible terms: a bid for survival locked between the hill of Troy and the sea, an effort whose strokes and counterstrokes often come with words of extreme exhortation, so that the most massive encounters appear relieved of their heroic connotations by the impact of a human cry which conjures up the chances of life and death. Likewise in the *Odyssey* the episodes bear the same pattern as the main action. For in the Telemachia everything happens as if it gathered shape from a state of mind: the inspiration of Athena and the taunts of the suitors work upon the brooding thoughts of Telemachus who is instantly stirred to move and take the initiative for a vital cause.

What is so remarkable in each case is the motivation of every deed in terms which are broadly human and universally significant. The events are never taken for granted. They are made to emerge from within the poem itself. However fateful or inevitable, they must be experienced to the full, accounted for, realized under the stress of a passion or a conviction or an intimate need; and, in the hands of the poet, the material thus acquired a dynamism of its own, as the story moved forward on the strength of its inherent values rather than along the path of traditional data.

The narrative element was thus superseded by a qualitative characterization of the action, the subject matter was reduced to a drama of converging individual experiences. Viewed in this light, the unity of the plot is but an aspect of a more essential unity which is one and all with a certain persistent poetic form. What might appear at first sight as a feat of ingenuity in the art of composition was really the effect of a creative insight whereby actions and situations could only be rendered according to an ideal pattern. It was in the nature of such a formative process that an identical touch should be brought to bear upon the general plan of the poems as well as upon the details, upon the whole as well as upon the parts; and, as a result, all the concomitant scenes seem to rehearse the same fundamental keynote which rings most powerfully in the central action.

3

As we read we become aware of this coherent mode of representation. The same basic structure recurs from one crucial instance to the other, as each time the human motivation of an act
must be persuasively expressed. A dialogue most often serves this
purpose. As the action normally implicates more than one individual at once, a relation is established which instantly defines the
position of each speaker. The characters thus become immediately
alive, as the dramatic context forces them to a quick responsiveness in words and deeds.

It is so in the first mighty scene of the *Iliad* and in its repercus-
sions in the latter part of the poem. Here the principal theme sets
the tone, Agamemnon once for all introduced in his frail willful-
ness and Achilles in his passionate temper. Again, in the second
book, the chiding of Thersites and the rebuke of Odysseus voice
the conflict of irreconcilable dispositions which is simultaneously
echoed by the swaying of a home-sick army stirred by its leaders
to fight anew. On the Trojan side the same drama is enacted. In a
sudden confrontation, Hector and Paris at once emerge as characters on the strength of a quick, essential exchange—Hector's
earnest will "cutting like an axe's edge," at odds with the disarming
self-conscious levity of Aphrodite's fondling. At the same time the
major warriors appear as massive embodiments of strength who
gradually acquire a personal physiognomy by being involved in a
dialogue with friend or foe. Ajax, for instance, might seem at first
sight a scarcely individualized image making almost one shape
with his towering archaic shield, were it not that his peers are there
beside him to crave for his saving hand and that he can expound to
them his sense of human limitations when no alternative is left but
to die or survive by a last effort. Such is Idomeneus who seems to
reveal himself to his friend Meriones with a sort of apophthegm
on the difference between the weakling and the brave; such is
Diomedes whom the words of Glaucus restore to a sympathetic

humanity. Similarly, amongst the Trojans, sobering voices emerge beside the self-reliance of Hector—as Polydamas who is the spokesman of reason, or as Sarpedon who, addressing his friend Glaucus, shows no illusion of glory, but only a will to play valiantly the tragic game of mortal life. In the *Odyssey*, even more, the characters emerge and develop in each act and situation through an exchange of questions and replies, protestations and rebukes, demands and refusals. Before it becomes an actuality, the return of Odysseus is present in the minds of everyone either as a fear or a desire, a foreboding or a hope—an issue upon which moral values are speedily engrafted; and in reference to it distinctive attitudes gather relief, even the vociferous choir of the suitors lending itself to sharp individual articulations, to undertones of irony and shifts of meaning.

We thus might say that a dialectic strain runs through the Homeric poems. The dialogues are like a keen edge piercing through the traditional story, continually transposing it into the sphere of consciousness, bestowing upon it the nimble movement of drama and the clarity of an implicit psychology. As a result the massive mythical material is loosened, thinned down, reduced to a matter of experience. All that is left of it is then the distant wonder of an action which is imagined as having taken place in a remote age at the hands of mightier people. But the action itself is at times quite forgotten or placed in abeyance when—as in the scene of Hector and Andromache or that of Helen and Priam— nothing subsists but an intimate communication of feelings and thoughts.

No drama, however, could subsist without a proper setting; and, now, if we turn to the narrative itself, we find that it is a groundwork for the dialogues, a bare and essential outline of the material structure which gives a body to the interplay of personal attitudes. In the first book of the *Iliad*, for instance, the quest of Chryses to recover his daughter, the punishment inflicted by Apollo, the restoration of Chryseis and the propitiation of the god, the taking of Briseis from Achilles, and the intercession of Thetis are capital events, indispensable to the plot, but dealt with in little more than fifty lines, as a sequence of movements instantly accomplished rather than phases of a situation ripening in the course of time. For the dynamic impact forcing new developments comes from the dialogues; the actual occurrences only have to take place, and, accordingly, they are presented in a sort of terse fulness, in their physical features, as proceedings that develop each in its isolated relief and not elaborated, explained, subjected to the link of cause and effect. Thus we see the indignant stride of Chryses along the shore as he broods upon his prayer to Apollo, Agamemnon's emissaries walking unwillingly on their thankless errand, the bereavement of Achilles as he sits on the lonely shore looking at the sea, Odysseus' ship carrying back Chryseis with the winds swelling its sail and the waves seething at its keel.

The same mode of representation prevails throughout. What we find in between the dialogues is a simple relief of form, or else, the ebb and flow required by the action: a ceaseless coming and going, a meeting and parting, a movement represented in its solemn culminating points. Even the crucial moments which bring about the intervention of Patroclus and of Achilles are rendered in a similar way. No need is felt to expatiate upon the circumstances. The arresting sight of wounded Machaon as he is swiftly carried away is enough to produce a change of mood and of atmosphere; later a sudden glow of fire on the ships adds a sense of irresistible urgency. Hence the impassioned inquiries, the hasty appearance of Patroclus in Nestor's tent, his subsequent onset, and finally the tragic message to Achilles borne by swift-footed Antilochus. Each movement, simple as it is, comes with a fateful impact; each image is there for a moment and then disappears in the execution of a task whose significance is persuasively proclaimed, while its proceedings are only represented in their necessary and fleeting occasion.

In such a narrative the subject matter is immediately transposed into a certain mode of expression. For it hardly exists outside the immediate dramatic requirements. It only has a function insofar as it subserves the action, insofar as it is a medium of representation. As the story itself is continuously dramatized, the description is resolved in a simple notation of accompanying movements. It is thus most naturally worked into a certain mould, into a certain cadence, into a certain rhythm. Accordingly each act falls into an imagery which cannot but repeat itself in each relevant instance. This is nowhere seen more clearly than in the battle scenes of the *Iliad*. Their extensiveness need not mislead us. For, every time, it is the actual clash which is portrayed as a recurrence of the same basic reality, reduced once and for all to a homogeneous normative form: the onrush, the blow that strikes a distinctive part of the body, the crashing fall. The similes, for all their variety, always lay stress upon an essential movement or position, underlining the moments of advance, or retreat, or resistance. Even where a particular encounter occasions a more complex situation, we find the insistence on a certain pattern. Thus the major drama of slain Patroclus avenged by Achilles seems mirrored, on a minor scale, in numerous examples: over and again we see the image of a man encompassed by the shadow of death; the amazement and grief that seize his friends; their effort to retrieve his body and to avenge him (cf. such sequences following close upon one another in 13. 384–403, 410–420, 427–469, 518–526, 576–583, 650–662; 14. 442–452, 453–460, 462–475, 476–489).

Such actions appear fixed in a sort of absolute form. Homer lets them develop in a way that seems essential to their nature and remains unchanged by circumstance. It is not that he is insensitive to the realities of time and space: he marks the fall of night and the break of day, he mentions certain relevant landmarks of the scenery; but the actions or situations are never strictly localized in a certain place, their duration is never expanded upon. We are never given, for instance, a complete picture of the battlefield at Troy, we are never informed about the antecedents or the aftermath of what is actually happening; and, when we take these matters into account, we discover with surprise that the action of the *Iliad* or the *Odyssey* lasts so brief a time and that its setting is so simple.

It is this reduction of the material elements which makes up, from one passage to the other, the artistic unity of the poems. A certain coherent representational form is thus laid over the variety of experience. It does not matter where or when an act has taken place: once it has struck the imagination of the poet, it must be rendered in the outlines of the same essential type. In a world so conceived Trojans and Achaeans must necessarily behave alike, and, for all their diverse scenery, the narrative parts of the *Odyssey* present the same features as those of the *Iliad:* sequences of images set in the simplest relief of recurring acts and attitudes and portrayed, therefore, in a persisting similarity of form. In the *Odyssey*, indeed, such a simplicity of outline appears quite marvellous. What strikes us is the fact that it should be so pervasively self-consistent: always essentially the same over such widely scattered areas as nearby Ithaca, Pylos, or Sparta, and legendary Scheria and Ogygia. Athena in the guise of Mentor appearing in Ithaca, Telemachus in the houses of Nestor and Menelaus, Odysseus in that of Alcinous are introduced in the same fashion—strangers instantly acknowledged and associated to the libations, the offerings, the banquets in a sequence of acts which, making up as they do the hours of daily life, follow one another with the solemnity of ritual and the naturalness of common experience. Everywhere a similar apparel sustains the scene; and it is as if a universal contour held in its frame the dispersed activities of man, making familiar even the most distant and mysterious places. Here an instant meeting, an instant coming and going suffice to keep the threads of the plot together; here the words of a newly arrived guest find a ready audience and a sympathetic echo. There is no need for lengthy introductions. The identity of almost every person is known beforehand and transpires from his very image. Like the characters of the *Iliad*, those of the *Odyssey* need but the slightest background—what is enough to set them in a certain significant posture: such as Odysseus sitting wistfully on Calypso's shore, the suitors all intent in their boisterous wanton play, Penelope standing in beauty against a pillar of the hall or reclining under the impact of the sleep shed upon her by Athena.

The process of simplification may thus be seen at work in the mere structure of a single scene; and in both poems the unity of the plot is the outcome of a creative movement which, having its roots in the simplest perceptions, is developed to the full extent of its ultimate implications. Were we to define it in its literary aspect, we might say that it consisted in a dramatization of the material and an effacement of all prosaic description, so that nothing remained but the portraiture of characters absorbed in their destinies and their images set in an environment which the genius of archaic poetry represented in a few essential outlines.

4

Dramatized as they are, the Homeric poems leave little room for external references. The events of the Trojan cycle are only recorded insofar as they have a direct bearing on the action at hand. Thus we learn nothing, or next to nothing, in the *Iliad*, about such heroes as Philoctetes, Telephos, Protesilaos, Palamedes. Likewise in the *Odyssey* the return to Ithaca is the unique absorbing theme; and we are told nothing about the previous life of Odysseus, except for such occurrences as have an immediate dramatic pertinence, like the story of the wound on Mount Parnassus.

That the poems refer so seldom, or not at all, to events of the very cycle whence they drew their theme is a fact which has often been remarked upon. It is a natural consequence of the poetic process we have tried to elucidate. How could otherwise the bulky material be so reduced and transformed?

But, over and above the particular subject matter, mythology existed in its own right as the representation of an idealized and hallowed reality. It was for the ancient mind a system of hieroglyphs charged with a suggestion of human values. In its wide range it contained an imagery whose rich symbolism made up for the lack of a clear moral content. As such it served as a sort of raw material for poetry, conditioning it to its own traditional patterns. A more superficial poet than Homer would have succumbed more often to its spell. As it is, we may gain some idea about the nature and power of the Homeric imagination in seeing how it did not yield to this temptation, but rather turned to account and fashioned to its own purposes any myth that might have come its way.

The longest mythical digression in the poems is the story of Meleager in the ninth book of the *Iliad*. But is it really a digression? Used as it is by Phoenix in a passionate effort to persuade Achilles, it presents the experience of Meleager as a parallel case of pointless and baneful wrath. It is thus a large-scale simile; and the traditional account is therefore altered and reduced by a compelling subjective interest. Nothing is said about Atalanta, nothing about the fateful fire-brand whose burning purported death to Meleager. The common story is left out or mentioned most vaguely to make room for an eventful moment in the strife over the spoils of the Calydonian boar. The hero is for some reason incensed against his mother and all his kin; he will not help them fight against the attacking Curetes; he withdraws and is proof against all prayers and offers. Only at last he intervenes to ward off a general ruin; and then he is obliged to do so regardless of any reward. The Homeric version is hopelessly obscure as to the sequence of events, but quite clear as to the issues involved. What it stresses is not a myth, but the onset of ruthless enemies and the doom of defeated peoples, an obdurate heart that will not yield, and the vain entreaties of friends. Such relief given to a single significant moment in the saga of Meleager seems to be a miniature rehearsal of the whole *Iliad*.

The myth of Niobe recounted by Achilles to Priam is likewise a simile. What is remarkable is that it is not a mere comparison between two parallel griefs, but is occasioned by Achilles inviting Priam to eat. "But now let us think of our meal," he says, "for even lovely-haired Niobe thought of food" (*Il.* 24.601 ff.). This motive is more significant than it might seem at first sight. It conjures up a deep Homeric theme. For, even when he depicts the intensest moments of the fighting, Homer finds the way of giving to the acts of eating and drinking their rightful share. Time and again the heroes are represented as "putting forth their hands upon the laid out repast" and "satisfying their spirits with an equal portion."

Under the impact of distress this seems the last refuge. So Odysseus counsels Achilles who grieves for Patroclus. It is that in Homer the taking of food is not simply an indispensable routine: it is a moment of peace, a pause between one crisis and the other, a vantage point in which to dwell for a moment in order to draw upon the sources of life and restore the wholeness of existence. Picturing as he does a vitality which is body and soul at the same time, Homer must necessarily stress the physical process which is its medium, he must tell us how the heroes renew their strength from day to day. In the same way, Priam must pause, and thereby renew his capacity for tears. In the same way, after nine days Niobe could weep no more, she took food, and then was turned into a stone to shed eternal tears, for only a stone could do so for ever. The myth is so told as to reflect a human process, a human vicissitude continually represented in the Homeric poems; and, in so doing, it also transcends it, it submerges it into the tragic reality of things, in that the weeping rock of Mount Sipylos seems to symbolize a grief beyond redemption.

Similarly a Homeric touch runs through the account of Heracles' birth as told by Agamemnon: how Hera prevented the hero from being born at the allotted time and hastened instead the birth of Eurystheus, thus duping Zeus who had solemnly pledged that anyone of his blood begotten on that day would rule over the nearby people. For the chief personage is here neither Heracles nor Hera nor Zeus, but the power of delusion or infatuation, the personified Ate, a newly conceived goddess, who struck Zeus as she did Agamemnon. Again, it is in the spirit of Homer to refashion the myth by using it as a simile and impressing upon it the mark of thoughts which are intrinsic to the poems. The unpredictable and ruinous moment of distraction was, in fact, such a matter as to engross the Homeric mind. It suggested a divine influence, the idea of an irresistible spell or temptation which was necessary to the conception of the characters and their actions. Agamemnon in particular is often made Ate's pawn and more than once he blames her for his misfortunes. We may well wonder whether this divine personification had any place in the cult, in popular religion, or in mythology. It is, rather, a poetic image which proved congenial to the Homeric view of reality. As such, it is not only present in the central theme of the *Iliad*, but it penetrates into the borrowed mythical material bringing it into unison with the spirit of the poem.

Elsewhere the mythical allusion is so stripped of all literal and mythical connotations that nothing is left but an imagery which can only be explained on the strength of the Homeric context itself. When Penelope compares her varying painful moods to the warbling notes of the nightingale that is Pandareus' daughter still grieving for her son Itylus, the bloody tale of the metamorphosis is forgotten, lying as it does outside the scope of the simile. Or, when again she evokes Pandareus, praying that she might perish like his daughters, what we are presented with is hardly a myth at all, but feelings which find in certain mythical images their adequate expression. No factual account, no digression is needed except the picture of girls grown to womanhood with the blessings of the gods and, on the eve of their marriage, ravished away by the storms. "The Harpies snatched them away," we are told, "to be the handmaidens of the loathsome Erinyes" (*Od.* 20. 66, 78). But in the language of the poet the Harpies are nothing else but storm-winds, "snatchers away" according to the etymology of the word, and the Erinyes play no other part but that of dark nature-goddesses placed beyond the pale of human life. The imagery thus opens up to Penelope a scene of wide, remote extrahuman spaces where to vanish far away from the importunity of her hateful suitors; and the myth becomes the very stuff of her emotions, of her desire "to be wafted by a hurricane along misty paths and be plunged into the outlets of Oceanus' revolving stream." What seems striking about such passages is their complete absorption into the general context. For Penelope's inner life is continually pictured as responsive to the suggestion of omens, dreams, visions; and it is as if the myth existed only for her own sake, to translate into solid form the evanescent outlines of a mental state. Even the usual parallelism of similes is done away with; we do not have a comparison of actual facts or situations, but rather the representation of inner movements all turned to an indeterminate future and seeking analogies in the world of existence.

Other examples are too brief or too obvious to require any comment (cf. the list of the gods who suffered at the hands of men in *Il.* 5. 385–400, Dionysus and Lycurgus in *Il.* 6. 130–140, Peirithous and the Centaur Eurytion in *Od.* 21. 295–304). In each case it is remarkable how rigorous a measure is set upon the expansive tendency of Greek mythology in which one legend entails another through an extensive chain of natural affinities. Here Homer is quite different from the lyricists, from Pindar and Bacchylides, for instance, who are often allured by the charm of mythical by-paths. The allusion is never allowed to overstep its bounds, to deviate from its immediate function and encroach upon the essential theme. This is generally true quite apart from the similes. Persons, places, things are all bound to the main action by a relation of actuality. Their past associations are absorbed, as it were, in their present relevance; and any antecedent event that may be mentioned only adds to the spell of what is actually portrayed. When, for instance, we read that Athens is the town of Erectheus "who was reared by Athena and begotten by the bountiful earth," such an attribute is little more than an expanded epithet, a qualification designed to set its object in the fullest relief. Thus Dorion conjures up most briefly Thamyris and the Muses; while such objects as Agamemnon's scepter or Odysseus' boar's tusk helmet are traced back to their first owners, to enhance their significance as wonderful or singular things. It is likewise with people. If a hero's forbears are mentioned, it is as a foil to the crucial and fleeting occasion of his presence. Achilles, we are told, attacked Asteropaeus "born of broad-streamed Axios and Periboea . . . for with her was joined the deep-eddying stream" (*Il.* 21. 141 ff.). Or, again, Paris killed Euchenor "who well knew his doom of death when he boarded the ship"; for often his father, the seer Polyidos, had told him "that he would either die of grievous disease in his home, or amid the ships of the Achaeans he would be slain by the Trojans" (*Il.* 13. 665). Such examples are frequent (cf. *Il.* 4. 474 ff.; 5. 543 ff.; 6. 21 ff.; 16. 174 ff.; 5. 50 ff., 60 ff., 612 ff., etc.). In each instance the brief evocation of the past serves to build up the image of the dying hero. His birth, however mythical, when mentioned, sets off the present human reality in which no divine or semi-divine parent can be of any help; and his subsequent fortunes (a family feud which drove him away from home to his doom or a happiness which was but the prelude of ruin) are not presented as biographical data, but as occurrences which are inherent in human life, inevitable features of man's nature. All previous incidents thus point forward to one final, momentous occasion which, in turn, is reflected upon them. No wonder that the pleasures of illustration could find no place in such a reduction of the descriptive matter. It is so even in the genealogies. Only once, in the case of the seer Theoclymenus, does Homer turn to a narrative genealogical digression of some length; but, even then, the wonderful exploits of Melampus are passed by in silence, and all we have is a bare account of visionary qualities as transmitted from father to son. Elsewhere it is the characters themselves that at times look back to their background. They seem to do it most reluctantly. It is with a pang and with a sense of futility, after comparing the generations of men with the leaves of the forest, that Glaucus discloses to Diomedes the myth of his ancestry and the adventures of his grandfather Bellerophontes. It is with unbelief and lofty disdain that Aeneas, confronting Achilles, tells him about his lineage from Zeus and compares his birth with that of his opponent, until he breaks off the account, unwilling to pursue a children's tale. We thereby gain the impression that the Homeric world is suspended, as it were, in a moment of extreme human relevance, hanging in between an unbelievable past and the approaching shadow of death. Even the gods partake in it in their own way. Their power is newly acquired. The older deities of nature lurk beneath Olympus or on the further edges of the world—like Night, the Erinyes, Oceanus, Tethys, who are silent presences. The Olympians are aware of them as of the past from which they have emerged; they mention them at times with dread or with awe; while, on the other hand, a blank immortality stretches before their eyes.

Myths are hardly myths any more when they are so reduced to a form of expression and representation. Genealogies then become mere scourings which leave bare the core of a personal identity, similes pure reflections of a feeling or a thought. It is significant that such mythical allusions mostly recur in the dramatic parts, in the speeches of the characters. In such a way the whole factual material—whether mythical or otherwise—acquires a characterizing pertinence. Legends sympathetically conjured up or past experiences passionately recorded are merged into the same actuality. At times we can scarcely distinguish between the two. Nestor's recollections, for instance, reach back to a fabulous age, whereby Heracles and the two divine Moliones are made to stand out in comparison with the living, within the compass of the same experience; and, in such a process, they are somehow removed from their extrahuman sphere. The details of their actions can hardly arrest our attention, related as they are to the fervor of an exhortation or a warning. It is the character of Nestor that springs into relief from such accounts. How could he be, otherwise, what he is—a pathetic witness of past and present, an old man for whom heroic prowess is but a memory or a dream?

Such myths detached from their former context and transposed into the Homeric present are striking instances of a general process. The whole unity of the Homeric poems rests upon an imaginative absorption of alien material. This is nowhere seen more clearly than in the account which Odysseus gives of his adventures. The ten years wandering is condensed into a few culminating events which are represented as taking place between the dawn and sunset of a few memorable days; and as the story unfolds what strikes us most is not so much its episodic display as the character of Odysseus himself which grows in stature on the strength of its human qualities. For the fact that such an account comes from the lips of Odysseus and not in the order of a straight narrative is, here, no literary device; it is, again, essential to the Homeric representation: the descriptive matter is made to pass through the filter of experience, and the account of the past becomes a feat of self-revelation, an immediate happening rather than a recollection of what has happened already. So that the image of Odysseus might emerge in its full value, everything in the story had to have a bearing on his character; and, once more, we see how the exuberant and incongruous features of myth or fable are subdued and reduced for the sake of a present personal concern. What is unwieldy in its multiplicity is brushed aside or dispatched in a few lines—like the Cicones or the Laestrygonians of whom it suffices merely to mention the enormous size or the countless numbers; elsewhere that timeless reality of fabulous beings is represented only insofar as it faced Odysseus and concurs to his present spell as a man who knew it and resisted its threats or seductions in the passion of his return to the native land. Thus we do not see the Lotus-eaters, but we are only told about their food whose magic all but thwarted his purpose and thus conjures up the issue which is at stake at that very moment, while he speaks. Similarly, of the Sirens we are only allowed to hear the beautiful voice. The enormity of the Cyclops is ridiculed; what is really stressed is the feat of wit and inventiveness which contrived the escape. Circe is turned from a dark enchantress to a genial friend: how could Odysseus love her otherwise and make her help him in his homecoming? In the *nekuia* the celebrated heroines of myth are pale phantoms withdrawing into the night; Odysseus, significantly enough, will hardly let them taste the blood of life. Only Anticleia stands out—a mother who died in regret for her son, missing his "pithy thoughts and his gentle heart." This and much else that Odysseus says becomes part and parcel of himself; we never forget that he is speaking. Each fact, as he recounts it, gives shape to his image. What stands out is an account of experience rather than of fabulous happenings.

5

In the same way as all that happens in the poems is made transparent by a feeling or thought that interprets it, so is the visual scenery made articulate and familiar by an eye that perceives it.

Even the most marvellous spectacle is thus given a human dimension, and all manner of things, insofar as they are described, become an impression, a vision, objects of understanding and wonder, immediately transposed into the sphere of the Homeric experience. Consider, for instance, the garden and palace of Alcinous: each detail, magnificent as it is, is represented quite objectively; the poet does not add any praise of his own. The wonder is all implied in the admiring gaze of Odysseus. Similarly significant is the look of Telemachus in the house of Menelaus. Even more remarkable is the way in which Homer expresses the beauty of Calypso's island. Here, again, trees, vines, meadows, springs are simply mentioned according to their basic nature. No predicate magnifies the picture of a luxuriant vegetation interspersed with bright, streaming waters; but, at the end, we find these words: "Even a god, if he came, would look and gaze and rejoice in his heart" (*Od.* 5. 73–4).

It is the same mode of expression that can convey all the somber gravity of a dramatic scene. For, at times, though rarely, we are given a brief picture of the battle as a whole, apart from the single encounters. It is when the fighting is supposed to be most intense; but the imagery is then reduced to a minimum, and the general effect is condensed in such phrases as: "No man who came and walked unscathed in the midst led around by Athena . . . would belittle this toil." Or, elsewhere: "Over-bold would he be who looked at the struggle with joy and did not feel pain." These words, again, reduce to a matter of perception an unusual scenery. The description is cut short, and what remains implies the rest, maintaining it within the sphere of a possible recognition.

The same principle obtains in the representation of people. They are never described at length. Whenever Homer wishes to render the beauty of a person, he never indulges in any embellishing description: it is enough for him to convey the wonder in the mind of the beholder. In such a simple way the beauty of Helen has been immortalized. Agamemnon and his men, Menelaus, Odysseus, Ajax, are imposing figures as they stand below the walls of Troy; but their features are only portrayed insofar as they meet the curious and wondering eye of Priam, so that each material detail is immediately translated into the terms of subjective admiration. Similarly Priam and Achilles stand for a moment enraptured by each other's presence, and no descriptive virtuosity is needed. Again, the figure of Nausicaa is suggested by the imaginative gaze of Odysseus who compares her to a magnificent palm which he once saw in Delos: the simile does not give us any clue of her particular traits, but suddenly conjures up a beauty which can only be measured by the spell which it works upon the admirer.

Objects, whatever their splendor, are treated in the same way. Whether belonging to gods or men, their reality is one—such as it can be fathomed by perceptive eyes. No magic properties can enhance them. The wheels of Athena's chariot, or Arete's wool, or the walls of Scheria are a "wonder to see"—an expression which recurs frequently in Homer, conveying a singular effect (in the word "wonder") and, at the same time, containing it within the world of experience (in the word "to see").

Such modes of expression stress the perspicuity which, we have seen, is inherent in the Homeric rendering of reality. For the transparent quality of the imagery is here realized by the characters themselves. They seem to experience the aesthetic feeling which the reader too experiences on a different, detached level. Existence thus finds its acknowledgment in the act of contemplation, and the massive subject matter seems dissolved into the levity of a vision.

The cumulative effect of these contemplative moments affects the whole development of the poems. Even the intensest actions must be relieved of their stress so that they may be visualized for what they are. The darkness that enshrouds the fighting over the corpse of Patroclus must be broken at last, so that even death, as Ajax says in his prayer, may be suffered in the open. For it has to be seen and witnessed; it has to bear with it its message. And as the death of a man makes an alarming void, so is his living presence an overwhelming sight: see how forcible and variously significant are the mere appearances of the various warriors, how each individual identity seems established by the feelings it inspires.

The general effect of such a treatment is to simplify and qualify the subject matter by gathering it within a certain perspective. What happens is at once an event and a vision, a destiny and an experience. Nothing is allowed to recede into a neutral, meaningless obscurity; nor can anything incompatible with this transparency find room in the field of vision. The general scenery is thus held together by the link of a common visual significance; this is not the least element of the Homeric unity.

6

Also the gods in Homer look at the human action. When they are not implicated in it, they gaze at it as if it were a spectacle. Zeus, rejoicing in his glory, enthroned on the peak of Ida or Olympus, watches the city of Troy or the ships of the Achaeans, the glitter of bronze and the bloody turmoil (*Il.* 11. 82; 8. 51; cf. 4. 4; 20. 23; 16. 644; 22. 166; 24. 23). Athena and Apollo sit on a tree enjoying the sight of fighting men (*Il.* 7. 61). So does Poseidon from the top of Samos (*Il.* 13. 12).

Through the cold eyes of the gods we see the scenery from a different angle. Even the most violent encounter can be viewed with distant detachment. For the gods can only identify themselves with a human situation up to a certain point: however much they may desire to assist this or that hero, at a certain moment their immortal nature bids them turn away from a man's plight and look at it from above. On Mount Olympus they seem to forget the earthly affections which pitted them the one against the other. What a moment before, at the walls of Troy, appeared as an exclusively absorbing issue now becomes something remote and negligible. At the beginning of the *Iliad*, Hephaestus puts an end to the human dispute between Hera and Zeus saying: "A dread, unbearable thing will it be if the two of you will quarrel for the sake of mortal men and stir strife in the midst of the gods: no sweetness shall we reap of our feasting if the baser prevail." And he presently moves limping to serve the nectar, while an unextinguishable laughter rises from the gods. Time and again, the interest in a human cause gives way to divine solidarity (*Il.* 4. 68; 5. 904; 8. 40; 15. 78; 21. 463); and we wonder at the light-heartedness of the Olympic scenes: how they contrast with the gravity of the main action, how the gods themselves can be so frivolous in heaven and so earnest on earth.

Does such a contrast impair the general unity of the picture? Are these divine scenes an alien element laid over it, an unnecessary superstructure? We are made aware that this is not so by that distant gaze of the gods which scans painlessly the world of man and presents it *sub specie aeternitatis*. For once the gods are removed from the human action, this is all they can do. The momentary drama which sets them by the side of man has in Homer an all-encompassing effect; beyond there is nothing but a shadowy destiny which deals death; and a god—insofar as he exists immortally by himself and in himself—can only appear as a witnessing presence, as someone who surveys an event without conditioning it and without suffering it, his life stretching immune beyond it. We are, then, at the margins of existence. Detached from their human experience, the passions lose their primal intensity and become frivolous, capricious, desultory. Such are the gods to one another when left to themselves in their Olympian abodes. It could not be otherwise. They cannot but lose in keenness what they gain in duration; and their view of human affairs becomes consequently absent, neutral, dispassionate.

The light-heartedness of Olympus is, therefore, justified from a poetical point of view. It projects the human action to a point in time. Visualized in this way the battle of Troy or the return of Odysseus acquire a different dimension—as of an event which, for all its momentary magnitude, recedes into the void of eternity. The frivolous attitude of the gods implies, then, the irony of existence itself: how the greatest ideal may suddenly appear a delusion or a dream, a mere moment in a repetitive sequence which stretches through indefinite time.

The human action is then laid bare in its solitary contours. Stripped of its grandiosity, it appears in a sort of lucid objectivity.

In moments of distress the Homeric characters themselves realize the essential purport of this isolation. Agamemnon, for instance, more than once reflects: "Such is somehow the wish of mighty Zeus who in the past has destroyed many citadels and many more will destroy." Compare the words of Philoitios when he sees Odysseus in rags: "O Zeus, no god is more ruinous than you; you do not have pity of men after you beget them yourself, you do not shrink from plunging them into evil and woe" (*Od.* 20. 201 ff.). In such expressions the god almost loses all personal connotations; he becomes an embodiment of time's destructive power; he assumes the image of a creator and destroyer in contrast with the conventional idea of a Greek divinity. It is that in these instances what stands out is not any individual image of god or man, but symbols of mortality and immortality—a stage with changing scenes and above it, a permanent vantage point.

Accordingly, when the gods talk to one another about the fortunes of man, their attitudes (with a few exceptions) are such as to justify the cry of Agamemnon and Philoitios. The divine conversation in the fourth book of the *Iliad* is the most significant in this respect. Here Zeus would save Troy from her doom, but yields to the destructive will of Hera who, on her part, promises that, if he so desires, she will not begrudge him the destruction of such towns as are dearest to her—even Argos, Sparta, or Mycenae. The fall of the Mycenaean centers is thereby foreshadowed: many other cities will fall besides Troy, many other heroes will die besides Hector and Achilles. Neither Zeus nor Hera could have it otherwise. Their decisions are an adjustment to the vicissitudes of fortune, not the outcome of maturing counsel; and, on the level of immortality, they can be lightly made—just as one strikes a bargain or measures a present loss against a future gain.

It will now be seen that the Olympic scenes, far from complicating the picture of the human action, contribute to its simplicity. They do not ascribe to it any ulterior motive or providential aim; they simply register it as an isolated event, as a moment in the infinite lapse of time. We are thus brought to a point in which the glory of men or states does not count any more—or, at least, does

not have any effective relevance. There is here no feeling of progress from one general condition to the other, no idea of a fundamental cause exerting its impact upon the course of events. Past
and present, memories and hopes, are all absorbed in the present
moment insofar as they have an actual bearing on an individual
character; they never concur to form a collective set of values
which might enlist for its sake the collective human effort. What
stands out is, therefore, the action in itself and by itself. Its antecedents and its consequences are passed under silence. It emerges,
as it were, in a void. Before and after it, the chain of historical
sequences is broken; and the gods tell us nothing about the general destinies of the age.

It is as if heaven were there merely to mark the timing of a
striking event. The wrath of Achilles and the return of Odysseus
are events which reverberate throughout the universe; but only
for a moment. What they lack in chronological extension they
gain in self-contained magnitude. The gods look at what is happening, and thereby pay homage to its gravity; but, even insofar
as they look, they imply their ultimate detachment and indicate
that the present will soon be forgotten. The lack of moral principle in their mutual dealings concerning this or that hero, this
or that city, leaves the action to develop on its own strength,
unburdened by any superimposed judgment. Whatever a god may
do for a man becomes one and all with that man's exertion and
the divine agency is presented as merged with the human act;
while the gods as such form a distant divine assembly whose im-
munity must necessarily offer ample scope to callous self-assurance
and irony. The plot of the poems could not otherwise retain the
human coherence which sustains its unity and, at the same time,
appear so charged with a divine influence. For, insofar as it is
perceived from afar, the most earnest drama seems a momentary
act having its beginning and its end; while, insofar as it is experienced in its immediacy, it seems to be the only reality. Accordingly, the same gods now look at it with derision and now feel
identified with it. What to many scholars has seemed the evidence
of diverse religious attitudes leaving in different ages their im-

press upon the poems is really the mark of a feeling for life's essential ambiguity.

7

Experienced as it is by the human characters, seen, pondered upon, intimately realized, and, at the same time, looked upon by the gods, the action of the poems is scrutinized in its depths. Light is projected upon it from many angles. Each deed, as it is carried out, is thus instantly dramatized; each event is not only something that happens, but a vision, a thought, a cause, an issue. The objective and factual elements of the story are plain and trite enough; what makes them so rich in purport is this constant mental participation which converts them into significant psychic terms. The unity of structure is brought about by a coherent mode of thought and expression.

Considered in its motives and purposes, the plot is a simple human drama; but, being at the same time the focus of universal attention, it seems an overwhelming reality. The bareness of it stands side by side with its magnitude. Gods and men are aware of what they are doing or looking at, and yet the event itself defies all explanation. Scrutiny cannot reason it out, but, on the contrary, reveals its inherent enigma. The outburst and subsequent self-restraint of Achilles before Agamemnon, the self-surrender of Helen—are these movements prompted from above, are they marks of fate, are they personal initiatives? Over and again the Homeric representation is such as to bring out the complexities which lie embedded in actuality. A questioning intellectual wonder runs through each scene. It spells out an unmistakable Homeric atmosphere: everything is at once persuasive and mysterious, natural and marvellous, human and divine.

The action, thus perceived in its real dimensions as well as in its underlying mysteries, could not but be conceived as the work of men who were equally true to nature and yet endowed with baffling powers. Such are the Homeric characters—images cast in a common mould, giving out a sort of natural spell whatever they say or do. They are at once human and godlike. Their mortal help-lessness is so portrayed as to be consistent with a miraculous re-sourcefulness, and the gods are spontaneously present in their solitude.

It will be seen that an imaginative unity is thus produced. In-tellectual curiosity broke the mythical structures, letting a co-herent world of images arise from the sediments. The plot could not be conceived without the characters, nor the characters with-out their destinies, nor their destinies without the gods; and each object of representation was necessarily conceived in accordance with a particular view of reality.

Aristotle's idea of an organic unity is thus very rich in its im-plications. It throws light on the whole creative process. No aesthetic theory could do without it. Even today whenever we judge a work of art we still cling to a certain principle of unity, though not necessarily in the Aristotelian terms. It is naturally so. A poem, for instance, whether short or long, must bear a distinc-tive coherent touch, a certain form which results from the indi-vidual distinctive quality of the thought whence it sprang. In this sense, the unity is an aspect of the artist's originality. Insofar as he does not compile or draw on diverse and confused data (whether conceived by himself or by others), insofar as he pur-sues a certain vision, there must be a certain unity in his work. What Aristotle perceived in the plot we may rather perceive in the imagery, in the style, or, indeed, in pure imagination; and, in so doing, we may even discard the need of a plot or a story or any definite subject matter. But we still require a sense of unity, the sense of an underlying value sustaining each part. It is that we cannot do away with the reality of feeling and thought whose roots lie in individual consciousness and, as such, must emerge in the most varied and unpredictable forms of expression.

The Homeric poems presented all at once the realization of artistic unity in the wide compass of its many aspects. As they suggested to the ancients a unifying principle of composition, so they still exemplify for us the way in which the subjective imagination imposes its own rhythm upon the most disparate objects. Seen in such a light, the emergence of this richly composed unity is paramount to the emergence of an overriding aesthetic principle forcing to its own laws the rendering of gods and heroes as well as of reality. In so doing, it had to break many an old allegiance. Its logic, concealed behind the baffling spell of poetry, could not be immediately discerned. But the strictures of Plato no less than the allegorizing interpretations of the ancient scholiasts or the modern speculations on "Homeric man" pay homage to the magnitude of the issues it set forth to resolve.

II

On Man and the
Gods in Homer

In Homer the nature of man is not taken for granted, but is presented as a fountainhead of sudden and unpredictable activities. It is as if its constituent elements had not yet been neutralized and subjected to a predetermined economy, but still retained a primal, spontaneous power of their own.

In the Homeric language there are no such abstract terms as body, soul, individual, person, character. What stand uppermost are the organs which appear most active in their several functions. Accordingly, for Homer, the feet, the knees, the hands, the eyes are not simply parts of the body, but instruments or agents charged with an overflowing energy, and single acts are often represented as self-developing processes almost independent of a person's control: it is then the feet that step out, the knees that move and carry away, the hands that crave for action, the eyes that look and gaze (cf. *Il.* 6. 514; 17. 700; 18. 148; 9. 610; 11. 477; 16. 244; 17. 679, etc.).

This spontaneous quality is particularly striking in connection with the emotions. Joy, grief, anger, hope, fear, wonder, desire, reflection are constantly localized in the heart or in other organs which are for Homer the centers of psychic activity. In such cases the impression of an autonomous movement is naturally much greater: the inward process, apprehended but unseen, suggests the presence of a power working in the depths (cf. *Il.* 1. 103, 188, 193; 2. 36, 171; 3. 31, 395, etc.).

The inner being seems to vibrate on its own account. Similarly, the feeling itself often envelops the individual. It thus happens that the Homeric characters can at times hardly master the passionate life astir within them, so that their personalities seem to break apart, were it not that these inner movements are really the pith and marrow of their physical frame. A black cloud of grief encompasses Achilles when he hears the news of Patroclus' death (*Il.* 18. 22), dark night shrouds Andromache when she witnesses Hector's fate (*Il.* 22. 466); such is the love that envelops the mind of Paris in seeing Helen (*Il.* 3. 442), such is the joy and the anxiety which beset Euryclea when she recognizes Odysseus (*Od.* 19. 471), or the wonder and awe which seize Odysseus at the sight of Nausicaa (*Od.* 6. 161), or Achilles' amazement on seeing Priam in his tent (*Il.* 24. 480 ff.).

The feeling itself becomes, in such instances, almost an image, an apparition. It lies deep within the individual; and yet it takes him by surprise, as if it came from without, like a natural phenomenon. Unlike the movement or resilience of the body, which for all its vividness must necessarily remain contained within the visible form, the emotions seem to project themselves out of the individual and encompass his whole being. They have the effect of an external, impersonal, elemental agency whose sway is passively received. Yet frequently localizing them in certain crucial organs,

Homer lets them emerge in an almost material consistency. Hence their massive impact, rendered like a blow that does not strike upon the surface but on the inner core. Because it ignored the dualism of body and soul, Homeric poetry could represent the actuality of feeling and magnify it into a transcendental force without breaking into any abstraction, only stressing the natural implications of the psychic process.

Shattering or quickening feelings can hardly be narrowed down to traits of personal behavior. They are all one with the pulse of life. As he gives them free rein, Homer moulds the existential texture of his heroes. What must first be accounted for is the actual makeup of a man. No moods and tempers are ready at hand to be mentioned and described. The characters must grow out of the very material which composes their physical existence.

In the same way as he represents the impact of feeling, Homer represents the ebb and flow of life in a man. He often dwells upon the fall and subsequent resurgence of a hero. Take, for instance, Sarpedon almost wounded to death by Tlepolemos. We read: "From him did the soul depart; and over his eyes fell darkness; then he breathed again, and around him the breath of Boreas, breathing, revived his badly gasping spirit" (*Il.* 5. 696 ff.). It is as if, out of subliminal darkness, Sarpedon were restored to himself by the very elements of nature. The wind's breath passes into his own and transmits to it its power. Homer has enabled us to recognize the truth of this airy identity: breathing, blowing are felt as the same, and the might of a man is often compared to that of the elements. There is nothing mythical in the imagery. We are not told that Boreas resurrects a mortal; but we are made aware of a healing power which is present in nature and no less wonderful than a miracle.

We may compare Hector wounded by Ajax, or Odysseus washed ashore in Scheria (*Il.* 14. 436 ff.; *Od.* 5. 456 ff.). They are both reduced to the barest human condition, stripped of everything but a flickering personal identity. Again the breath, gathering at some sensitive spot of the organism, produces consciousness and the power to move, the power to see through the deadly darkness which a moment before shrouded the eyes; and the faltering spirits, newly finding their passage, seem to recreate the obliterated individual image. "But when with breath his consciousness returned and the spirit clung again round the midriff" we are told, for instance, about Odysseus; and the materialization of a psychic process as well as the quickening of the body are suggested by these weighty Homeric words which at the same time indicate breath and consciousness, organic matter and life, a material movement and a vital function. The representation is so graphic and its implications so rich, that the literal meaning, for all its precision, conveys a sense of miraculous revival. It is as if the bare account of the occurrence explained its cause, since each objective element appears endowed with a motivating power of its own. But, in fact, no explanation can be given; and what we see is, again, a sense of wonder for a material so productive of life.

Once saved and made whole, a hero seems to stand on top of the world. After his recovery, Hector steps out with the magnificent buoyancy of a long-pent horse that, having drawn new strength from a rich feed of grain, breaks his fetters and gallops away exulting in his freedom (Il. 15. 263 ff.). A pithy sap seems now transfused into each limb, prompting each movement. How can the change come about so quickly? The effect is at once stupendous and convincing, as if Hector's bearing gathered momentum from some protoplasm whose wonderful resourcefulness was entirely contained within the properties of nature. Natural vitality fills the scene. We forget the relations of cause and effect. These heightened powers are native potentialities realized in their fulness, and the natural seems prodigious.

Homer sees an elemental force at the roots of feeling, thought, action. The very fiber of a man or woman is continually at stake. The effect of Andromache's grief is represented in very much the same way as Hector's or Sarpedon's almost mortal fall. It is so throughout the poems. In their concentrated existence, the characters have no time for perfunctory occupations. Whatever they feel or do comes as the manifestation of a sustaining power that wanes or rises according to circumstance, and each instance affects their lives like a stroke of fate. Their moments of faintness are like downfalls into the underworld of existence, their moments of recovery are like triumphs over matter; and hope or despair, joy or grief, courage or fear are aspects of this massive vicissitude, purified into feelings but still suffused with the materiality of nature.

2

The scenes of individual action or movement are set by Homer in strong relief. They often spell wonder or dismay among those that witness them. The reader himself is struck by the incisive rendering of limbs that move and of feelings that sway one way or the other under a sudden, unaccountable stress. Everything is precisely and forcibly drawn; but the power at work in a hero appears none the less mysterious for being so clearly conceived.

To the Homeric mind the very transparence of reality had a baffling spell. That human vitality, so vividly displayed, had the natural evidence of daily experience; but what was it that uplifted it, sustained it in the moments of particular tension? Was it the will of a man? Was it the will of a god? The question hardly presented itself to Homer in these terms. His way of visualizing animate processes enabled him to ignore any clear-cut distinction between the natural and the supernatural: it was the spark of life, rather than any extraordinary object, which arrested his attention and presented to him an intimation of the divine.

Thus, at a turning point of the battle, when only a redoubled effort can save them, the two Ajaxes are quickened to new vigor by the touch of the god Poseidon. The one says: "My spirit within me drives on more strongly . . . a greater eagerness is in my feet below and, above, in my hands" (*Il.* 13. 73 ff.). The other replies: "Also my dauntless hands are more eagerly set on my spear, and my spirit is all astir, and a force drives me in my feet below" (*Il.* 13. 77 ff.). A heart that stirs, feet and hands that move possessed with a resilience of their own—these are normal occurrences in the poems. What stands out is, once more, the native vitality which Homer always stresses when he portrays any living creature. We are shown the wonder of nature at work rather than any heroic accomplishment. A god finds here his proper function, as the ideal embodiment of natural forces; and his touch simply bestows increased momentum upon a ferment that is already there.

The recovery of Hector is another instance. As he renews his onslaught, one of the Greeks says: "Not without Zeus does he stand foremost with such fervor" (*Il.* 15. 292). In fact Apollo has endowed him with new strength. But, in reality, the presence of a god is suggested by the fervor of the hero, and not the inverse. Hector is a dauntless and intense nature in his own right. He appears driven by divine power even before Apollo comes to his aid. When, on the first day of the fighting, he comes forward to rally his men, it is thought that a god has come down from heaven (*Il.* 6. 108). His might is compared to that of fire, or of a storm, or of a lion at bay (*Il.* 17. 565; 12. 40; 16. 823). And yet that human might, being mortal, is necessarily brittle. If it is divine in its resilience, it is nevertheless all too human in its distress. It then seems to cry for a saving hand to sustain it; and there, as far as it is possible within the limits of nature, a god appears to uplift and magnify it.

It is the immediate action itself which in Homer is the greatest concern for any particular god. The death or survival of a man, on the other hand, lies beyond any divine control. An allotted measure—which we may call fate—here takes the place of the gods. Homer does not probe into fate and its motives. He certainly feels it as an unquestioned power; but its vague, blank, unfathomable domain did not appeal to his imagination which could only feed on the fulness of form. It so happened that blind fate was nearly identified by him with the inscrutable stroke of death; while the gods descended from heaven to sanction and make whole what appeared divine in life itself.

The Homeric rendering of the human action in relation to the gods is thus parallel to that of nature in general. A wind is simply a breath of air, but it may suggest an animate power; a wave or a flood is simply water in motion, but a sea- or river-god at times seems to drive it; storms are commotions of the sky, but Zeus is a weather-god and is often said to control them. The bearing of men in their most intense moments similarly suggests a hidden but effective power. For what takes place in such instances is a tension of each fiber, the psychic and physical faculties converge into one vital effort, and spirit is a stress that asserts itself through every pore. What is such a spirit, such a power? It cannot be abstracted into a separate entity. If externalized at all, it can only be envisaged as an object of wonder—a divine influence, whereby the human element is projected into a wider sphere and somehow identified with the general wonder which underlies the life of nature.

We may well suppose that such a vision of human actions first suggested to the poet the image of a god extending the range of a man's capacities and granting momentary fulfillment to his yearning for a heightened existence. The god would then appear as a sort of *alter ego,* the embodiment of what a man might be if his potentialities were wholly realized and his attainments made permanent. Such is Apollo by the side of Hector, breathing into him relentless life and opening him a passage through the obstructions of an adverse world (*Il.* 15. 262, 307, 355). Elsewhere Diomedes, Sarpedon, Glaucus, Aeneas, Odysseus are similarly in spired by a sustaining god (cf. *Il.* 5. 1 ff.; 12. 292; 16. 527 ff.; 20. 110; *Od.* 18. 69). Each occasion marks a fresh onset. All weakness disappears. The divine influence seems to do nothing but restore each organ to the integrity of its native function.

3

A man completely absorbed in a supreme effort merely suggests power. His self-assertion hardly amounts to a personal feat. The god that presides over him ministers to an instinctive force which is at work in all life. But it was more particularly the task of Homer to convert the trends of nature into forms of human behavior.

Sheer vitality had to be transfused into feeling, thought, consciousness. Accordingly a more intimate appeal had to come from the tense heroic image, and a clearer response from the god.

Homer was admirably placed to present the relations between god and men in a spiritual light without losing any of their force. As he did not know of any opposition between the mind and the body, he could present the activities of both as aspects of the same animating power. No less than in the might of limbs, a god might seem at work in feelings and thoughts that suddenly emerged and hardened into steadfast resolutions or materialized into full-blooded deeds. A timely counsel, or a rash decision, or a bold desire is represented as stealing into the hearts of men, suddenly altering their views of reality and their standards of behavior. The characters themselves can at times hardly account for such experiences: Agamemnon can no more rationalize his folly than the two Ajaxes can explain in human terms the sudden quickening of their limbs. Even a passing impression might seem to have something wonderful, unpredictable about it. "He had a suspicion himself, or a god put it into his heart," says Odysseus about Polyphemus (*Od.* 9. 339). Any spontaneous initiative is in itself remarkable enough to suggest a divine agency.

The movements of the mind could not be arrested, however, in a momentary wonder. They had implications whose significance went beyond one initial occasion, conditioning and moulding a man's temperament. Here the gods had to be made conversant with the reasons of emotion and reflection. For the Homeric hero is a vigorously composed individual whose urge toward self-determination makes him what he is. He will not be a blind instrument of superior powers; and if he cannot be the master of his own fate or even of his own decisions, he will at least make every attempt to draw the divine influences into the path of his own interests and ideals. The gods, on the other hand, may or may not answer his prayers; but only insofar as they are concerned with human life do they have any meaningful purpose; and the instant fortune of a city or of a man is the constant reference point to their loves and hatreds, to their inclinations and aversions. It is this dedication to momentary causes which turns their power into a capacity for sympathetic feeling and suffuses their being with the light of a personal identity. In the Olympian abodes, their capriciousness appears a distant reflection of the earnest passion which encompasses the brief and intense life of mortals; but when placed on earth face to face with an immediate human issue they are unmistakable presences exerting a personal spell. Human feelings are then brought to bear upon them and in that common experience they have to assume familiar features, gathering in themselves a man's inmost yearnings, identifying with him in his plight.

The participation of the gods in human affairs does not work mechanically as something that must necessarily happen whenever a crisis occurs. Nor does it appear in the form of casual, occasional prodigies. It is rather presented as the proof of a deep, continuous concern for a man's life. A god so attached to a man assists him in all the crucial moments of his experience; he stands by him or accompanies him without being seen; his presence is an immediate resource and a hope for the future. A continued relation thus develops. In the process a man has time to reveal himself, bringing to bear upon the god the full weight of his human appeal. Strong, richly composed human personalities thus emerge, communicating their warmth to the wan, ethereal, receptive image of the deity. What matters is, again, the full-grown image of a man whom the gods embrace for his prowess and mourn for his inevitable transience.

The close relation between a god and a man ultimately rests upon a mutual influence whereby they characterize each other. Thus Apollo presents himself to Hector saying: "I am he who is ever defending yourself and your city" (*Il.* 15. 256). What is the reason of so persistent a union? Homer does not trace back to any particular occasion Apollo's favors or Hector's deserts, nor is there any specific cause that may account for them. The reason must be found in a qualitative predisposition of the material—that is to say—in a basic affinity which associated the images of the god and of the hero. Is not Hector the most truly human among the

Homeric warriors, and Apollo the most compassionate among the gods?

Let us look at this kinship more closely. Hector is the character in whom life shines out most richly and most briefly. He knows crippling weakness no less than exulting self-assertion; he is stirred by a sense of immediate glory as intensely as he is haunted by the thought of impending death. We can watch him living, dying; and not only as a warrior, but as a man: he fondly smiles and laughs with his child; no loyalty can match his love for Andromache; no bitterness can make him forget the charms of Helen. Complete as he is, he burns himself away—too courageous to seek shelter, too weak to win. No wonder that his god, Apollo, broods with deep sympathy over the condition of man. To Poseidon who asks him why he takes so much to heart the cause of Troy in spite of past wrongs suffered at the hands of Laomedon, Apollo cannot give a factual explanation, but momentarily withdraws from the battle saying about men in general: "Miserable ones, like leaves now do they glow with life while they eat the fruits of the earth and now do they waste away into nothing" (*Il.* 21. 463 ff.). Such is preeminently the lot of Hector whose fervor is always over-shadowed by a feeling of transience.

Further, Hector is a highly flexible character. Reckless as he is in moments of triumph, he is also very sensitive to reproach—as when he is chided by Sarpedon (*Il.* 5. 472 ff.) or by Glaucus (*Il.* 17. 142 ff.). He rebukes Paris most bitterly, but is also ready to forgive him (*Il.* 3. 39 ff.; cf. 76; 13. 769 ff.; cf. 788). He brags with Diomedes (*Il.* 8. 161 ff.), but he is at once defiant and modest with Ajax (*Il.* 7. 234 ff., 288 ff.). In short, there is in him each time a supple, versatile spirit, in harmony with itself. Such are the qualities which Apollo seems to have in mind when he taunts the other gods for their hardness in allowing the mutilation of Hector's corpse. The fates, he says, have given men a patient and tolerant spirit, so that they know how to yield and relent; but Achilles does not have pliant thoughts, he cannot be moved, he lacks all pity and reverence (*Il.* 24. 39 ff.). This is essentially the same reproof which Hector, at the moment of his death, addresses to Achilles (*Il.* 22. 356 f.). Apollo echoes it again. His sympathy with mortal life has given him a sense of human tenderness. That "patient and tolerant spirit," those "pliant thoughts" which he upholds among the gods seem to mark the quality of the human as opposed to the mythical, articulating the primitive nature of man with an intimate and supple responsiveness.

Apollo and Hector must have been conceived by the poet with the same feeling. Just as the hero at the end is singled out in his solitary doom, so does the god stand aloof from the other Olympians. He does not descend from heaven in any equipage, but haunts alone the city and plain of Troy, receptive to the cry of any man in pain (cf. *Il.* 21. 515 ff.; 16. 515 f.). He seems a nimble spirit—like Hector—appearing suddenly, fitfully in the battlefield, with full-blown but elusive power.

A god thus sheds part of his radiance upon a striving and vanquished man; and the mortal effort, though doomed, is blessed with a divine halo. Apollo's role signifies a new and crucial phase in the relations between gods and men. Attacking him Hera points out the absurdity of rating Hector as an equal to Achilles: one is the son of a goddess, the other a mortal suckled by a mere woman. The conventional view of religion clashes here with a new feeling for life and its values. It is a feeling which Homer made his own insofar as the real, the natural, the human, appeared to him in a native fulness and wonder, suggesting the presence of the divine.

The relation between Athena and Odysseus is similar in its motives to that between Hector and Apollo. It does not have the same breadth of human implications, resting as it does upon qualities of a more particular import; but for this very reason it is more precisely drawn and followed up more closely.

Again, no specific motive is given for such an attachment. It must contain its own justification. It is Athena who enlightens us when she says to Odysseus: "You are the best among men for wisdom and words, and I am famous among the gods for my mind and my wiles" (*Od.* 13. 297 ff.). And elsewhere: "I can never abandon you for all your wretchedness, because you are well-spoken, quick in mind and in feeling" (*Od.* 13. 331 f.).

A natural and ideal affinity binds Athena to Odysseus. It is effective, persistent, right from the beginning of the action when, in the opening book of the *Odyssey*, she pleads for him on Olympus. Henceforward, near or far, she accompanies him step by step to his final victory. For the *Odyssey* is concerned with the destiny of one lonely man. The fitful scenes of the *Iliad* are now far away. A mellower mood has set in. What matters is a complex personal enterprise which requires a long train of thought. Each initiative, as it comes, affects the course of events; and the hero's mental resourcefulness is a central force. Athena is thus an indispensable agency by the side of Odysseus. She presides over his capacity for thinking and acting.

The aid of Athena is, therefore, unobtrusive. No more than Apollo does she manifest herself in overpowering, fantastic ways. Her presence simply accrues to the native faculties of Odysseus. Because of her spell he appears more beautiful and mighty to the eyes of Nausicaa and the Phaeacians, more formidable to the suitors of Penelope; but both beauty and strength are intrinsic to his character. Also his striking transformation into an old beggar is convincing: it might be taken as an extension of his power to deceive. But what is most remarkable in this respect is the nature of his mental activity—how subtly and naturally Athena works in the process of his reflections and decisions. Even his solitary brooding is sometimes represented as a conversation with the goddess (cf. *Od.* 13. 303 ff., 362, 376 ff., 421; 17. 360; 20. 30 ff.).

The participation of Athena gathers momentum once Odysseus is back in Ithaca. This circumstance helps us appreciate the way Homer conceives divine influences concurring with human efforts. For now Odysseus is alone, drawing all his powers into one great action; and so singular a character suggests the help of some god.

The loneliness of a remarkable man at odds with the world is in itself something that makes us wonder. Such is the plight of

Odysseus, whom the Phaeacians have just laid ashore in his sleep. Why does Athena envelop him at first in a cloud so as to make him blind to the very identity of his native land? While in other places —on the island of Circe or of the Cyclops—he pictured himself as boldly finding his way by himself; here in the land that he knows so well he is completely at a loss. The reason is, no doubt, that he is no longer the proud expounder of his own life, filled with the conviction of his high quality. The poet now represents him as a man exposed to the blows of chance, only endowed with his marvellous resourcefulness. He may be mistaken for a beggar or for a god. Within a few days he must emerge triumphant from his destitution; and we must be made aware of the distance between the starting point and the goal, of the discrepancy between the means and the achievement, so that we may wonder the more.

The qualities and achievements of Odysseus can thus be seen from two different angles, the human and the divine. They are human insofar as Odysseus thinks or speaks of them subjectively; they are divine insofar as they are events which take their place in the world of nature. It is interesting, in this respect, to compare the passages in which Odysseus gives an account of himself with those in which he is represented in the third person. In the former he dwells upon his own presence of mind and hardly ever mentions any god; while in the latter Athena often intervenes. The power shown in both cases is the same. But what is a personal glory to the hero concerned appears as a miracle to all others— something that would not be possible without the inspiration of a god.

What the genius of Odysseus really is may best be learnt, of course, from his own account to the Phaeacians. Each passage of his narrative is interspersed with introspection and with a self-conscious feeling of personal resourcefulness, as though the mental faculties were fathomed for the first time as constituent elements of a man's prowess. They emerge with the fresh energy of a newly discovered power. Inward spontaneous movements though they are, it is a practical need that enhances and spurs them. Even understanding, knowledge, wisdom are felt as active capacities, inseparable from their immediate application. The mind is here intelligence in action; it is ingenuity, inventiveness, skill, and craftiness as well as thoughtfulness. A man so endowed must appear a marvel of versatility. Such is Odysseus; and he sometimes seems to wonder at himself, as when, in a famous soliloquy, he mentions his own flawless judgment, admiring its past achievements and hoping that it might again prove its worth (*Od.* 20. 20).

His fame stretches far and wide. Even Circe and the Cyclops know about him before they see him; but then they are surprised that he is an ordinary human individual, having expected him to be some portentous creature in appearance as well as in fame. Their expectations are somehow justified; for his glorious qualities might well seem incompatible with his human frailty, and, in a world of gods, divine accomplishments could not be admitted to contain the seeds of decay and death. It was the task of Odysseus to reconcile the terms of this disparity. He could foster a sense of glory even in mortal resignation. His experiences and achievements, after all, could only be what they were by being exposed to deadly dangers.

Thus complete in himself, Odysseus makes his grand entrance into the world. Men and gods watch him. He wanders far afield working his way; and he is a challenge to the primordial deities of nature that all but engulf him. Will he be saved? Will he perish? The issues of his destiny bewilder the Olympians. So subtle and bold an individual cannot pass by unheeded. His spirit exerts a rightful claim to have its place in the order of the universe. It projects itself into the sphere of the divine. It is Athena that gathers it to herself. She is moulded in the likeness of Odysseus and reverberates upon him, with an intensified glow, the light that emanates from his being.

4

Over and above individual cases, there is a natural kinship which unites the gods and men of ancient Greek poetry. "One is the race of gods, one is the race of men; and from the same mother we both draw the breath of life," says Pindar. That common mother is the earth. The myth of creation plays no great part in Greek religion; and the sense of a divine origin appears scattered in the life of nature, not symbolized in the creative act of a god. All animals, even plants, may have a sacred character and attain divine status.

The common origin of gods and men lies deep in Greek myth. It is implied, for instance, in the tale of the Golden Age and in the genealogies of the heroes. The Mycenaean kings claimed divine ancestors; and Agamemnon thus traces his lineage back to Zeus, Nestor to Poseidon. All these stories of a divine birth are not just distant memories for the Homeric characters. Several of the heroes are themselves sons of gods or goddesses—Achilles, for instance, and Aeneas, or Sarpedon.

To be born of gods, and yet to be human—here was a disconcerting ambiguity. Homer must have felt the problem of this divine association. He had to take it into account, and yet bring out to the full the humanity of his heroes—insofar as they had to be real characters and not mythical figures. The mythical past could not be discarded, it was part and parcel of the subject matter; but the claim to a divine descent could be stripped of its literal meaning and converted into an actual possession of divine endowments. What in the myth was a factual intercourse thus became in Homer an ideal relation. What was handed down as a kinship of blood was transformed into a feeling of kindred qualities on levels standing far apart in the hierarchy of existence.

Such a change in the conception of men and gods and of their mutual relations did not, of course, come about easily. The Homeric characters with their divine epithets are still soaked in mythical associations. They are still haunted by the thought of a past fellowship with the gods, as when Glaucus speaks about his grandfather Bellerophon, Diomedes about his father Tydeus, Nestor about the Moliones and Heracles. The burden of such a past weighs heavily upon them. It is as if they had been dashed into the sphere of bare mortality and their dauntless tempers could not be resigned to this precarious state.

Characters like Hector or Odysseus, as we have seen, are perfectly human. The crude element of myth seems cast out of them completely. There is no discrepancy between what they are and what they do. The divine is resolved into a personal spell; and if they yearn for a higher existence, they can find release in an ideal communion with the gods who protect them. But in others the divine ferment is still seething. Humanity is not made aware of its limitations—at least, not right at the beginning. In a clash of opposing values only sobering blows can bring about an inner reconciliation. In such cases the gods are at the same time an inspiring and a curbing influence.

The fifth book of the *Iliad* shows most dramatically, in the character of Diomedes, this interplay of human and divine motives. Diomedes is at pains to find his bearings, oscillating between the restraints if his earth-bound mortality and the movements of a pride that would assail the heavens. But he must be checked in his overwhelming impulses. It is the goddess Athena who initiates him to a new self-awareness by dispelling from his eyes the dark mist that mars his lucidity so that he may be able to distinguish between gods and men. That deluding cloud was like the continued spell of the Golden Age, a lingering twilight still enshrouding all things, blurring each particular contour and destined role, confusing human and divine attributes. Diomedes, whose genealogy told a tale of cruel excess, needed to be shaken by the impact of actuality and brought back to the world of man. He is enlightened; but now this very awareness bewilders him. How will he be able to act in a world which is still so fraught with heavenly presences? The encounter with Aeneas protected by his mother Aphrodite complicates the situation. Athena does not resolve the difficulties by telling Diomedes that he must keep away from all other gods, but not spare Aphrodite. Human and divine are here inextricably mingled in the bond of mother and son; violence to the one must also fall on the other; and Diomedes attacks the goddess. She is wounded and driven back to Olympus by Iris. There Dione, her own mother, consoles her telling her of Otus, Ephialtes, Heracles—gods who suffered at the hands of men. Diomedes is the last one of that line, and appears the one survivor of a world as yet untamed by human experience. Indeed he is the only man in the Homeric poems who consciously attacks a god. "Reckless, overbearing, unscrupulous worker of evil, not knowing in his heart that brief are the days of whoever fights against the immortals," concludes Dione (*Il.* 5. 403 ff.). But Diomedes does not stop, not even when Apollo takes his turn in defending Aeneas. He bears no reverence, he continues to fight. Three times he attacks, three time he is struck back; and does not yield until the god tells him: "Beware, o son of Tydeus, and yield; do not have the spirit of a god; for the race of gods is not equal to that of men who walk on the earth" (*Il.* 5. 440 ff.).

At last Diomedes steps back. Apollo is there, Ares is there, gods taking an active part against the Achaeans. He steps back and commands his companions to do likewise. Later on, we find him removed from the battle, stanching his wounds; whereupon Athena again incites him, this time to defy any god whatsoever. Her might concurs with that of the hero. It is she who drives his spear against Ares. The god is overcome. Like sultry mist in a summer storm swept by the winds he vanishes, a cloudy phantom, into the sky.

This last scene, with its overpowering simile, gives us a glimpse of elemental forces, or inchoate essences, passing into one another and scouring the universe. Ares is not simply compared to a storm; his actual outline seems to melt into the elements. It is a metamorphosis that takes place quite naturally. In a world where such things happen there are no separate spheres pertaining to separate beings. The gods themselves cannot keep up their own distant loftiness. They are driven into the same struggle as men, merged with them into nature; and uncontrolled force holds the field.

Diomedes has now had a last illusion of divine power. But he is a man. The intense experience has bewildered him, but cannot alter his nature. His unclouded eyesight might have been dazzled; but the words of Apollo have struck deep. What Athena gave him was a capacity to distinguish between gods and men. But this capacity was not a true insight into the essential difference between divine and human nature. In order to be really human, he now needs knowledge with resignation, a sense of the limitations which are inherent in each form, a consciousness of conditioning values, prowess bearing in itself an awareness of its own measure, a sense of humility.

Diomedes, we may suppose, goes through deepening stages of introspection. The terse, concrete style of Homer conceals a refined psychology. There is, therefore, no contradiction in his attitude now and later: on the one hand, his conscious defiance of the gods in the fifth book of the *Iliad*, and, on the other, in the sixth, his modesty and avowed ignorance as to who is a god and who is not, in spite of the discriminating power previously bestowed upon him by Athena. In the latter book, in fact, his role is inverted. He who was driven to assail the gods now refrains from assailing mortals, since they may be gods.

To the eyes of Diomedes the object of discrimination has now changed. It is no longer a question of telling a god from a man on the strength of some external identity. The divine has become for him a quality, an aspect of all living things. It colours the mortal complexion of a man just as much as it flashes out in the epiphany of a god. Insofar as it can be perceived, it is nothing but a bright, immediate presence; and only a shattering experience or a careful inquiry can reveal it as the sign of an actual god. A man must, therefore, walk through the world discovering for himself the disparity between gods and men—not by means of some magic device, but guided by a sympathetic and questioning eye. This is why Diomedes asks Glaucus, who is now his foe, whether he is a god or not; and he approaches him with open-minded admiration, like one who takes a fresh view of the world, wondering and trying to understand.

The reply of Glaucus follows in the same spirit. It is to Diomedes, significantly enough, that he addresses the famous passage which compares men to the generations of leaves. "Why ask my ancestry?" he protests (*Il.* 6. 145); but then he surveys it briefly; and the exploits of his grandfather, the divine Bellerophon, carry us back to an age of superhuman achievements when there were no limits set to the blessings of heaven. Bellerophon appeared to defy the sway of death, like Heracles, or Melampos, or even Diomedes' own father Tydeus. In this context those words about the fleeting successions of men's generations are particularly appropriate. They do not fall on deaf ears. As he hears them, Diomedes seems to have gone through the whole experience that separates the age of demi-gods from that of men.

Diomedes realizes his true nature through a maturing awareness of mortality and of the human condition. The shattering experience related in the fifth book of the *Iliad* has been enough to release him of all burdening delusions. We later find him as a man at peace with himself—brave and temperate at the same time (cf. *Il.* 9. 32 ff., 697 ff.; 14. 110 ff.). His ordeal makes us think of Achilles. There is between them a likeness in the mode of self-realization. Achilles' identity is also painfully established. Again, in his case, the divine element must come to terms with the human in the shaping of character; again overbearing emotions must lead to a clearer insight into the values of life. But the complexities of Achilles are far greater. We watch him develop from the beginning to the end of the *Iliad*. An inner drama is enacted before us; and Zeus, with all the gods, participates in its phases.

As the son of a man and of a goddess, Achilles can hardly resolve the contrasts of his dual nature. How could he, when the opposing strains exert such a pressing claim? He knows that his life will be short; and, at the same time, through the bond with his mother, he feels part of a divine world where Zeus listens to his wishes and the sea-nymphs echo his griefs. The blood of the gods runs in his veins like a powerful ferment. It seems to produce a vitality which is all the more intense since the days allotted to it are so short.

The condition of his birth thus works on his character. The divine which he could not inherit as immortality accrues to him as a primal exuberance of feeling that can scarcely be contained within the patterns of heroic behavior. A powerful, seminal spontaneity marks each of his attitudes, whatever their occasional purport. According to the varying friction with the environment, the tide of his affections swells or recoils upon itself; but it is always the keen edge of the same passion which stirs him and prompts him, in his repinings no less than in his reckless ways. He is, accordingly, extreme, abrupt, unpredictable. He can weep like a child, show the fury of a lion, be as insensitive as a rock; and carry into all these moods the whole weight of his being. In his case, variability does not mean fickleness or weakness, but a capacity to sustain successive and differing states of mind with a single persevering intensity. It is as if the sea-goddess Thetis had transmitted to her son something of the restless power brooding in her element.

We first see Achilles in the opening scene of the *Iliad*, in which Agamemnon unjustly deprives him of his girl-slave Briseis. Any man, any animal would feel strongly. But the wrath of Achilles, the *menis*, breaks out with the impact of an elemental power. It is, as its name implies, a divine, not a human emotion. It works havoc among men. It cries out to heaven. Thetis immediately flies for help to Zeus who nods assent; and Mount Olympus shakes, the whole world of gods is set in deep commotion.

If left unchallenged, such a hero as Achilles would have indulged his prowess, like a god. But the quarrel with Agamemnon, with the consequent loss of Briseis, involves him in the logic of a personal drama. Henceforward an overriding interest will absorb his emotions; his actions will be pertinent to it; his days will brighten or darken according to the fortunes of his cause. He can no longer stride scatheless from one triumph to another, scouring over the paths of existence like a mythical hero or a demi-god. A deep earnestness will now cover his luxuriant and wanton nature, as he passes from the barren multiplicity of repetitive exploits to the simple reality of one engrossing experience. A godlike temper is thus humanized. A primeval, vital material here falls into a form, into a way of life. The divine element is still present; but only insofar as it sharply brings to a head certain basic proclivities of a human character.

So did the poet, no doubt, first conceive the image of the hero—

all one with the wrath that so encompasses him. We find here a total commitment. Character, life, fate hang on the thread of one great passion. What is at stake is Achilles himself. From now on each failure or each achievement must either shatter him or restore him. His wrath is thus a feeling of life made hollow and a tremendous craving for recovery, a debasing torment and a restless claim to self-assertion. He is coming into his own as a man rather than a hero—not conquering the world, but subjecting it it to his own personal perspective. Recalled from a dream of eternity to a point in time, he seems to retrieve his fall by attaching an absolute value to issues which are but momentary.

A wrath of this kind brooks no compromise. All that Achilles can do is to withdraw from the army and refuse all allegiance. We next find him, in the ninth book, aloof in his tent, rejecting all entreaties and reparations. He will not return to the battle and help the battered Achaeans. The fiery anger of the first scene is now spent. He is no less uncompromising, but solitude has fostered in him new depths of feelings. As his friends try to win him back, he presents to them unexpected alternatives. The wide world lies open for him, not only the miserable Greek camp. Why fight? Why slay a people that defends its city? The choice offered him between a long and a short life stirs his mind with a sense of elusive and yet possible blessings. He can now visualize distant scenes of happiness—domestic joys and basic human goods. He can, above all, cry out the praises of life which is dearer than honor or gold, and he can vindicate the rights of individual existence extolling them above all other loyalties and interests. It is as if the moment of truth had broken out in all its simplicity marking Achilles as a man. No wonder that this supreme hero uses the same language as Thersites in denouncing the war; no wonder that this half-divine newcomer into the world of mortals will say, when he is a shade in Hades, that it is better to be the serf of a pauper than a king among the dead.

The thoughts of Achilles are deeply human; but his aloofness is superhuman, more like that of a god than of a man. The days pass, the battle rages, the Trojans set fire to the ships of the

Achaeans. Not even then does Achilles move. He sends, instead, his friend Patroclus who momentarily saves the Achaeans, but is slain by Hector. Now at last Achilles is stirred out of himself. He again joins his peers—not for compensations received in accordance with heroic custom, but for possessive feelings which are strong enough to alter his nature.

The death of Patroclus is a summons to a yet wider reality. Grief strikes deeper than anger. It also stirs a sense of human sympathy. A mind so affected naturally presents a richer mould, a greater breadth. It is as if to give further scope to the human side of Achilles that the poet has placed Patroclus beside him. Patroclus is indeed wonderfully suited to the purpose. Unlike other heroes, he is unencumbered by that starkness which comes of family pride. He seems to lack a tribal or divine background. We know nothing of his ancestry except that as a child he came with his father, as a fugitive, to the house of Peleus. No glory works on him retroactively; it is his association with Achilles that gives him splendor. By his side Patroclus is a calming presence, a friend who speaks timely words of persuasion and wisdom. Accordingly, he is renowned for his kindness; "he knew how to be sweet to everyone" (*Il*. 17. 671), and Briseis mourns him for his compassion. His warlike exploits, mighty as they are, are speedily accomplished —an inroad just in time to rescue the Achaeans, cut short by death.

The interplay of divine and human values is again reflected in the relation between Achilles at Patroclus. Compared with his friend, Achilles has the dark inscrutable temper of a god. His aloofness is quite awesome. But in the company of Patroclus he can freely indulge his human longings. The sweep of overwhelming emotions here subsides into a mellower measure.

Thinking of his own imminent death, Achilles sees Patroclus as a father to his son, as an *alter ego*, as a depositary of all his affections; and, in so doing, he recognizes in him a kindred being, a receptive counterpart, someone upon whom he could bring to bear the capacity for expansive and communicative feeling pent up in his nature. This relation is not casual, not arbitrary. There is at at its root the fundamental need of a response to solitary assertiveness, a striving for recognition, a bid to find a place in the human world. Achilles is thus drawn into the circuit of mutual experiences. His proud feelings are released from an exclusive self-absorption, are enriched with a sympathetic strain. In the presence of another he finds no antagonism, but a reflection and a proof of his own identity.

Achilles' attachment to his friend is a condition of his human makeup; it is inevitable, irreversible like any phase of a vital process. His dedication must again be total, peremptory, exclusive. He is like a god who, in a sudden humanization, cannot but see his preferences and ideals in the light of an absolute and reckless realization. It is in such a spirit that he says to Patroclus: "Would that all the Achaeans, that all the Trojans should perish, and that the two of us alone escaped death" (*Il.* 16. 97 ff.).

The loss of Patroclus is, therefore, a death-blow to Achilles, the support of his human existence suddenly giving way. He feels like a vain burden to the earth. He wants to die. It is to his immortal mother that, significantly enough, he declares his desire of death. The taste of human affections has led him to disown all other allegiance. Like Odysseus, he has chosen the world of man. He would not have immortality, we may suppose, if it be at the cost of parting forever from his friend.

Achilles, on the shore, learns that Patroclus has died from Antilochus (*Il.* 18. 1 ff.). His great cry is heard by Thetis in the depths of the sea. With the sea-nymphs she joins him in his grief; but she is really weeping for Achilles himself who is fated to die soon after Patroclus. The divine and the human must here part company. The great scene of mourning marks the irrevocable break: Achilles dying, the proudest of lives forever cut off from its divine background. "Alas for my woe in begetting the best of all men," Thetis cries out (*Il.* 18. 54). The act of giving birth, a glorious offspring, an inevitable doom—all this is implied in the extraordinary word *dysaristotokeia* with which she describes herself. She is at one a goddess and a woman, placed at the crossroads of mortality and immortality. Achilles is a "young plant," a "tree on a hill-top" which she has mothered. Through her words nature herself seems to mourn over the plight of her best fruits.

Thetis now weeps, but will pursue her immortal life. Achilles, on the other hand, is resigned, even eager to die. His humanization is spontaneous, intimately realized; it is not a doom imposed upon him from without. He has by now outgrown the crude urge for self-assertion. When he tells his mother: "Would that you had dwelt with the immortal deities of the sea, and that Peleus had taken a mortal wife" (*Il*. 18. 86 f.), his heritage means nothing to him any more. He has developed in his own way. All the vehemence of his exalted nature has gone into anguish for someone that has just died. Here is a hard-won lucidity, a liberation from all vanity. There is no room for self-pity. Achilles grieves not for himself, but for the downfall of an earthly joy that was his reason for living. He thus breaks away from his immortal mother of his own free will: the divine and the human might coexist and intermingle in the wholeness of nature or in the momentary zenith of fulfillment, but not when a god is all gathered in his immortality and a man has accepted in full his human attachments. The individualizing process forces an insoluble split.

Left to himself, Achilles lives only to avenge Patroclus, and to die soon after. The vengeance taken on Hector rekindles his ancient ruthlessness. We see him wantonly maiming Hector's corpse and slaying some Trojans to burn them on the pyre of Patroclus. But this final action brings him into a drama which is not only his own. The desperate plight of other people is shown all around him. A wider reality opens up before his eyes. When, in the last book of the *Iliad*, Priam appears on his threshold to kneel as a suppliant and ransom his son Hector, Achilles seems far removed from his previous cruelty. Priam is there before him as the image of a kindred pain, of a whole world which is similarly outraged.

The change in the feelings of Achilles is nowhere explained or traced. It is the actual scene that accounts for it. The very images, focused as they are on each other, suggest the interplay of sympathetic emotions: Hector is to Priam what Achilles is to Peleus; the death of Hector is no different from that of Patroclus or from the imminent one of Achilles. There are neither friends nor enemies, only men. A common doom hangs over all alike. Achilles and Priam feel an inevitable solidarity.

Everything in the scene is immediate, freshly conceived, realized before our eyes. The amazement of Achilles on first seeing Priam breaks through the crust of convention, prejudice, hatred. Hence his receptive mood, his gentle hand, his tears that mingle with those of the old man. Then the grief subsides, and he dwells on the vanity of tears, on the vanity of life, on the gods, on the world. He sounds like a sage; and yet he is not. A sinister impulse of anger seizes him again when Priam insists that his son be restored quickly. Almost fearful of his old self Achilles rushes out like a lion, to compose Hector's bier and propitiate Patroclus' ghost. In that interval his finer feelings prevail. When he returns, he seems to have passed from the sphere of surfeiting emotions to that of lucid perceptions. He is gathered in a high, contemplative calm. The human scene that surrounds him is no longer a challenge to his feelings, but a world to be scanned and understood. He now not only broods on life, but reflects on the ages and recounts the tale of Niobe in a spirit of universal sympathy. Similarly he can find peace in the pure spectacle of things, he can indulge in self-oblivious silences and in mute delight contemplate the noble features of Priam.

Achilles acquires a human physiognomy step by step, until at last we see him at his ease, in the unconstrained composure of his being. His image is conjured up at each moment. Thoughts, words, acts come suddenly, freely. Each phase is as unpredictable as it is forcible. Nothing is taken for granted; and yet nothing is arbitrary or casual. A refining influence is unmistakably at work, as fresh strains of feeling emerge and come into their own, drawing from the ancient fire a powerful quality. It is as if incandescent materials now instantly cooled into articulate and significant forms. A quicker rhythm sets in, as the poet brings to an end the task of shaping a character out of primordial matter.

Every mood of Achilles is a new start in the art of life—quite natural, and yet brought about as if by magic. We are reminded of other scenes in which a hero is engaged in a supreme effort and a god is supposed to stand by, increasing his strength. In Achilles it is a new mode of being which is driven to quick maturity. What elsewhere is a momentary increase of energy is here a heightened capacity for feeling and thought. The wider scope of Achilles' expanded faculties stirs a greater wonder, the power that sustains him appears more momentous; and the voice of all the gods is placed behind his bafflling spontaneity.

The Olympians, in fact, prompt the ransoming of Hector and inspire Achilles to kindlier feelings. But this in no wise affects Achilles' freedom of initiative. The influence of the gods is, rather, complementary—a heavenly participation in the wonder of psychic developments which are so real in their occurrence and so mysterious in their ultimate causes. Similarly it is the behest of Zeus which speeds Priam on his way to Achilles, but it comes as a sanctioning sign to an intense and intimate desire. Again and again Homer renders the activity of men as a present wonder by stressing a sense of power in each relevant moment of initiative. The divine is thus integrated into the human as a leaven that increases its potentialities. It is especially so in the case of Achilles. All the gods are concerned with his destiny, and Zeus himself so sways the action as to reflect his inmost desires, fears, and hopes. But, above all, human and divine are intimately entangled in his nature. Men and gods exert opposing influences upon him; and he must find his own harmony—in a life which is at once so haunted with death and so filled with moments of absolute self-realization.

5

A character challenges our interest. We do not take it for granted; rather we trace qualities and experiences which gather into a personal physiognomy. So Homer sees in a hero's life the work of heaven and earth. But, for the most, we only see people in general, people that come and go. What then matters is the mere appearance of a man or woman; acts just witnessed, words just heard. The complexities of experience and character are left out, but the fresh impression of life is none the less striking. Any existing form claims recognition. Here is a puzzling identity for eyes that can see and wonder.

Homer was a keen and sympathetic observer. Any colourful object—even something ordinary like a chariot or a tripod—is visualized in the poems with a strong feeling for its structure and perfection. All the more so living persons. No craftsmanship could compose them, no mechanical design conceive their organism. Here again, just as in the case of the heroic characters, some less obvious power seemed at work. What was it? Not, in this case, a particular god appearing on a particular occasion, but an influence vaguely scattered throughout the world of living beings. The lives of men were thus seen in the integrity of nature—that is to say, exposed to the gods that dwelt in the elements, in the passage of day and night, in the surrounding universe. Divine and human appeared interwoven in the very fact of existence.

"The mind of man," says Odysseus, "is like the day that Zeus sends over him" (*Od.* 18. 136). In these words Zeus is hardly a single well-defined god. He is a power both internal and external —at work in the individual and in the outside world. The days which he sends bring storm and sunshine, fortune and misfortune, good and evil. Men suffer or rejoice accordingly. The same stress falls upon nature as a whole. Personal experiences are thus resolved into general conditions of existence and of fate. At a distance, everything that is peculiar falls out of the picture; what remains are basic dispositions of mind and body, which seem allotted as heavenly gifts.

Virtues like wisdom, courage, beauty, strength are often attributed by Homer to the dispensation of a god, (cf: *Il.* 1. 178; 3. 64 f.; 5. 51, 61; 7. 288 ff., etc.). "Not to all men alike," says Odysseus to Euryalus, "do the gods bestow the grace of their gifts. . . . One may be unsightly in features, but a god so crowns his words with beauty, that people gaze at him with joy; he speaks with force and gentle reverence standing out amid the crowd, and if he walks along the streets all look upon him as upon god" (*Od.* 8. 167 ff.). What inspires this passage is the sense of a native and mysteriously present quality—at once a personal talent and a divine gift. Stable characteristics, no less than changing moods, seem to be brought about by a power that quickens them. However human, they belong to a sphere of their own, they are as inevitably present as the light of day or the shadow of night. He who possesses them is at the same time possessed by them. Hence the radiance of the man portrayed by Odysseus. The gods have graced him, and he is himself like a god. As he speaks, a divine influence converges with his human talent. He stands transfigured, his own words reflecting upon him an unearthly glow. We are not merely told that the man is a wonderful speaker. The gods, the admiring listeners, all conspire to make him what he is; and the significance of a glorious moment is cast into a permanent image.

All excellence in Homer presupposes a god. Even if the god is not mentioned, he is felt as potentially present. On the other hand, gods so conversant with human attitudes are deeply humanized; and their influence ceases to be purely external, it becomes part and parcel of a person's faculties. So a good craftsman is inspired by Athena, a minstrel by the Muses. All men and women in Homer seem to have a full capacity for whatever they happen to do. They cannot help being what they are. Even doubt is an inspiration. We might object that this is not the way people behave. But a sense of wonder makes up for the lack of realism. This wonder is the divine element at work in their actions.

Furthermore, a human individual taken in itself and by itself may seem wonderfully alive. Homer sees something remarkable in its mere presence and countenance—in that it exists, it grows, it develops. The epithets give us a cue. About a woman, for instance, we find: "white-armed," "lovely-cheeked," "divine among women"; about a man, "swift-footed," "faultless," "godlike." Such epithets have more or less the same esthetic value, the same resonance: the sense of a human or animal quality melts into that of the divine. People are thus endowed with a natural spell. As soon as mentioned, they seem suspended between the world of

gods and that of ordinary reality. It is not because they are miraculous, but because they are so composed by nature. Newly introduced into the human world, they gather into their limbs the
draught of life as something naturally divine.

The influence of a god on the mere task of living is sometimes
rendered in detail. It is so in the case of Nausicaa. We first find her
sleeping in her room in Scheria. Athena stirs her, bidding her go
wash her clothes so that she may meet Odysseus on the shore and
show him the way to her father; he will then obtain the help required to go home. But it is not the manner of Homer to arrange
things so mechanically. The goddess tells Nausicaa that the time
of her marriage is approaching, that she must wash her linen and
prepare her wardrobe. The dramatic moment thus coincides with
Nausicaa's coming of age. No expedient motive prompts her, but
a vision of love and life.

Athena lies at the source of Nausicaa's awakening consciousness. She is the divine touch in the flush of puberty, in the tingle
of ripening powers. Once awake from her heaven-sent dream,
Nausicaa is filled with a new vitality. She must immediately arise
and ask her father's permission, no less keen in her bashful
reticence than in her avowed desires. She is free, alert, delicately
articulate and forcefully self-assured. We next see her at work,
playing, singing with her handmaids by the river that flows into
the sea. When Odysseus emerges from the bushes, naked, be-
fouled with brine, fearful to look at, she does not escape in fear
like the others. Her boldness is inspired by the goddess; but it is
all one with a natural confidence, all one with the strength of new-
blown feelings. She is not described. Her very beauty is the impact
of her presence. What Odysseus admires is no particular outline,
but a being wrought in the fulness of life. He says:

> I pray you, O queen are you god or mortal? . . . If you are a mortal,
> thrice blessed your father and mother, thrice blessed your brothers;
> they surely must always rejoice and feel warm in their heart for your
> sake, when they see such a flower walking into the dance; but he
> above all the most happy who will prevail with his offers and have
> you in his home. Never my eyes ever saw such a being; a great won-

der is mine as I look. Only once have I seen something like you, in Delos by Apollo's shrine—the young branch of a palm tree arising up to the sky. (*Od.* 6. 149 ff.)

We may remark how Odysseus uses images of plants for Nausicaa's beauty—a flower, a palm tree. The whole scene is quite real, such as might happen even today; but Nausicaa has a spell which is more than human.

Youth is an age of transformation. A god, we might think, taps unsuspected potentialities. Adolescence, maturity certainly appealed to the imagination of Homer. All forms of vital self-realization delighted him. He often dwells on feelings that suddenly fill the heart, or on the increased energy of certain moments. On the same account he portrays individuals in their first youth: here again a new power possesses body and mind, just as much of a wonder, just as much a sign of the gods. Such is the state of Nausicaa. Such is the state of Telemachus.

We first find Telemachus as he sits in the midst of his mother's suitors, "grieved in his heart, seeing his father with his mind's eye" (*Od.* 1. 116 ff.). He is melancholy, resigned to his loss, indulging in mere hope, too weak for action. But he has now grown to maturity; and Athena appears on the spot to bring about, as it were, the hatching of his manhood. She encourages him; and he boldly challenges the suitors. She bids him go to Pylos and Sparta to inquire about his father's return; and he is filled with personal initiative. "If the great might of your father is instilled into you," she says, "such as he was in the shaping of action and thought, then not in vain will you go on this journey" (*Od.* 2. 271 ff.). But the journey is actually useless in terms of the plot. Its point is the glory of the effort itself. It is a test for Telemachus' self-assertion. The world is now open to him; wherever he goes, he stirs curiosity, wonder, praise, soon overcoming his lack of experience, his initial restraint. So, in Pylos, he is too shy to approach Nestor; and it is again Athena who quickens his senses, standing beside him in the guise of Mentor. "How shall I go? What shall I say?" he asks, "No knowledge have I of cunning words." And the goddess replies: "Some words you will think yourself in your mind, others a god shall inspire; for I do not think you were born and grew without the will of the gods" (*Od.* 3. 22 ff.). Athena is a *kourotrophos*—though Homer does not call her this—a goddess rearing the young, anxious lest the promising seed be thwarted in its growth. She is a power of nature, but spiritualized, refined into a subtle influence which penetrates the mind. Life thus becomes an inspiration; it is full, confident, responsive to each need. Telemachus, like Nausicaa, might well seem a god insofar as he has perfectly grown into his own image.

6

The characters and the plot are inconceivable without each other; but each may be viewed independently. I am thinking of the action itself which gathers momentum and has its own drift over and above what any particular actor may think or do. It is so in a novel, in a play, or in history, or even in life, insofar as events and circumstances concur to a certain end. We see a complex interplay of certain forces, everything driving toward a catastrophe which nobody may expect. Chance, fortune are called into account to explain the unexplainable.

If we knew exactly what we were doing and if everything happened according to schedule, there would be no problems. There would be no thinking either. The more consciously a man acts his part, the less mechanical seems his course of action. The urge for achievement is itself imponderable. The march of events is equally so. It is quite understandable that the decisive phases of any enterprise and its final outcome be ascribed to some unaccountable power. This view of man's activity is abundantly illustrated in Homer. It is not conceived in any crude fatalistic way, but through the continual relation between gods and men. We see how, step by step, important acts are inspired from above. It is a dream sent by Zeus that bids Agamemnon rally the army; it is Athena that influences Achilles not to kill Agamemnon or Pandar to shoot a fateful arrow; it is Aphrodite that fills Helen with desire. These people act with full conviction, and yet hardly know what is at stake.

The poet who perceived wonder in the simplest acts and feelings could not but follow up this basic perception and work into the general plan of the action the same intimation of the divine. The god imagined to be present in one single deed would naturally extend his agency, in increased proportions, to the collective enterprise and to the whole course of events. What appeared to be true in one case had to be true in all others. Here no exception could be suffered. This relation between gods and men came to be regarded as an aspect of reality; and, coherently, the Homeric imagination fashioned after it its own world.

So it is throughout the poems. At the beginning of the *Iliad* the prayer of Chryses sets heaven and earth in commotion; at the beginning of the *Odyssey* the plight of one man cries out for redress, and the eyes of the gods are all turned toward him. In both cases a human yearning brings Olympus down to earth, and the drama is quickly enacted, sped to its conclusion through efforts wherein a heavenly influence joins a human will.

This interdependence of gods and men is so intimately conceived that it does not result in forms of cooperation or in sequences of cause and effect, but rather resolves itself into the unity of one compact action which is human in its intellectual transparency and mysteriously powerful in its massive sweep. Hence, although the plots of both poems are prefigured in heaven, the gods share in the enterprises of men as if they did not know their outcome. Zeus gives his sanction to whatever is going to happen; and each event is rendered in its actuality, not as a result of supernatural decisions. The human predicament motivates the divine machinery rather than the reverse. As the prompting of a god was recognized in a solitary feeling or deed, a more generalized influence could likewise be suggested in a broad sequence of acts developing from a certain beginning to a certain end.

The representation of an event in itself and by itself is therefore quite compatible with the idea of a superior agency that plans it. The divine influence in no way diminishes the value of the human effort. On the contrary it is this effort that ultimately draws the gods to participate in it; and the gods are at home throughout the poems, present in any remarkable occasion, as companions rather than arbiters. Their participation adds to the dimension of the action, without altering its human purpose. They identify themselves so deeply with it that they hardly look at it as outsiders. Critics have remarked that even without them the plot of the poems might have had the same course, that they thus appear as an unnecessary addition; and they have considered this an anomaly. But the gods are the personified projection of a wonder embedded in the nature of things—in this case, in human nature. As such, they are not a superfluous, but an integrating element, required by the action as Homer conceived it.

Religion, initially, idealizes natural powers. In Homer it becomes more intimate, spiritualizing certain relevant human faculties and projecting them in heaven. In a world like the Homeric where the characters are so majestic and yet burdened with mortality, the gods represent an ideal fulfillment of human potentialities. They seem to beckon the striving nature of man toward a sphere where even the boldest exertions can instantly attain their goal. Here the gods are for men reference points to their highest yearnings, and men are for the gods objects of exclusive care, as if eternity could not find for its sustenance any motive worthier than a frail human being. Such a relationship is therefore maintained by the sympathy which joins to one another the separate scales of a common existence; and it is quite natural that, in its spirit, the gods should have ceased to relish human sacrifice, and that men should regard all excess as a trespass over the cosmic ordinances of the world. It is significant, too, that no offerings, no hecatombs are mentioned where this kind of relation binds a man to a god—as Hector to Apollo or Odysseus to Athena. Cattle are offered, for instance, by Nestor to Poseidon or by Agamemnon to Apollo and Zeus, to appease their wrath or win their favour, according to traditional practice. But it is not so where the goodwill of a god does not have to be bought, where it comes spontaneously from an intimate, personal interest. Nothing else, then, seems to prompt it but the silent appeal of a human figure that stands out bearing in its existence and in the very fact of its individuality the cause of its deserts.

Such a communion of gods and men is at once tragic and wonderful. Magnificent in its ideal significance, it offers no bulwark against fate; and it suggests a sense of human solitude in a world haunted by the suggestion of a divine, unattainable life. The picture is quite different from that of a mythical Golden Age. Men are here castaways from divine society, doomed to toil and grief. What is remarkable is that, even so, by stressing the bare splendor of certain vital moments, Homeric art somehow recomposes a human-divine reality. Its inspiration is freely imaginative rather than religious; and yet an ancient piety sustains it. For nature is still represented as lavishing all sorts of omens, good or bad; and the ritual accompanying certain occasions, the statements of soothsayers, the intimations of dreams are all things which are very meaningful for the poet or, at least, for his characters. The human action remains what it is; it breaks through these religious signs, but it is somehow permeated with their presence and derives from them a mysterious weight. Here a word is but a word, but it comes as an inspiration from above, stirring the listeners, purporting good or evil; here a deed is but a deed, but it is enacted as if the elements of nature conjured to bring it about. At the same time no uncanny intrusion is allowed to force the actors in an unnatural way. The human quality of each act stands out unimpaired; and all forces concur in its fulfillment, as if the power of remote and invisible agencies had been transposed into the actuality of things.

A similar godlike solemnity could not but be worked into the characters themselves; and here again an ancient awe helped to foster the divine illusion. For in composing them the poet took advantage of their legendary associations, accepting into the body of the poems the memories of the Mycenaean royalty and its sacred prerogatives. But what was a traditional datum resolved itself into its inherent values, and the tokens of exalted dignity, detached from their conventional surroundings, became elements of personal characterization. For in the action of the poems the heroes are confronted with the issues of life and death: of their sacred character nothing remains but a majestic bearing, while their humanity breaks through the blazonry of ancient attributes.

The gods too have their place in this transformation. They still retain, of course, the power which they derived from their association with nature and local cults; but in the imagination of the poet what stood uppermost is their interest in the fortunes of individual human beings. And, by being thus removed from their static positions, they appear as nimble agencies ready to assist a man wherever he might be. Here too accretions of power fell in abeyance or were converted into a capacity for immediate, self-conscious action: the gods seemed to forget their hallowed haunts in order to pursue any object that might appeal to their sympathetic will; and from figureheads in charge of a tribe or a mountain they became personal agents responsive to individual needs.

Nature too was gathered in the same vision, as a pervasive animate presence; and poetry still found sustenance in religion. The imagery of natural objects was conceived: all the striking features of land and sea as well as of animals, men, gods. The various parts of the living world seemed placed in a mutual interdependence by an innate kinship, by a common source of life. But at the same time no superstructure, no metaphysical system was allowed to overlap the objects of experience; and the vantage points of reality were so maintained in their respective positions that no one-sided or arbitrary alteration could encroach upon the prevailing harmony. The gods, far from disturbing this equilibrium, appeared to corroborate it, as presences in whom the energies of nature could converge and be made articulate in the language of man, as links between the various scales of existence, as intermediaries between one end and the other of the empirical world.

A pervasive interplay was thus set afoot. There is in it a persistent pattern, a compelling poetical logic: the human effort, in its fervor, evokes the presence of a god; the god, on his part, in order to be made intelligible and convincing, must assume a human physiognomy; at the same time, men are part of nature, of an animate world which suggests the presence of other gods; and these gods of nature speak to man no less than those who are more intimately connected with his life. The most personalized deities—like Athena or Apollo—are constantly present in man's crucial experiences, but also those that lurk in winds or rivers or the sea occasionally respond to his call; and the sun, the earth, the waters are invoked to bear witness in the most solemn moments.

This world, however, is no fairyland for the people who inhabit it. Mortality and immortality confront each other at its opposite poles; and dissonance breaks the divine spell. For an action of men stands at its center; and not the sympathetic will of all the gods can redeem it from following its own mortal trend. In such a perspective, the scenery of nature must be looked at with disenchanted eyes. Man is, indeed, part of its wonders; but, once individual conscience is awakened, this participation ceases to be an end in itself; and the wonderful enclosing spectacle recedes, becoming a background to the human drama.

With self-awareness a new lucidity sets in: not only the surrounding world, but also the role of man is laid bare in its objective proportions. The transience of life is then realized in all its implications; and, in the mind grown death-conscious, the feeling of a divine presence becomes a distant dream, an ideal, an image of absolute fulfillment suggested by mortal longing. The belief in the gods, therefore, is never allowed to be crystallized into a doctrine or diluted into an airy fancy. It resides in a vital apprehension of what existence might hold in store; and, as such, it passes into the very stuff of the emotions which accompany the shifts of fortune—into the hope of achievement, into the despair or grief for what might have been and is not, into the joy for present good.

Ready as they are to read into the animate world the signs of divine favor or disfavor, the Homeric characters have a deep sense of what is inevitable or impossible. Their most far-flung hopes are also the most human, inspired by perceptible and recognizable goods. Hence each Homeric situation, unpredictable and wonderful as it may be, develops according to the measure of human expectations. Even a miracle must be convincing; it must manifest

itself in a singular concurrence of possibilities suddenly materialized, and not in the promise or the realization of impossible blessings. Even such events as Paris wafted away by Aphrodite or
Aeneas by Poseidon do not alter the general picture. They seem
to symbolize the unaccountable touch of chance, salvation, or
death coming when least expected; and they are exceptional episodes which leave the human actors bewildered for a moment,
the action pursuing instantly its human course. Moreover, such
things might seem plausible where the surrounding forces of
nature are endowed with sentience and possessed of power. It is
significant that the device whereby a god saves a man is no stag-
gering epiphany, but an enveloping cloud. In the same way, lightning, thunder, and storm signal some momentous turning point;
winds become effective agencies; the night puts a stop to the fighting. These are portents of a crowning touch, not signs of ultimate
deliverance.

A sense of mortality permeates the Homeric world. It also
quickens it with the sting of life. A world of gods and demi-gods,
on the other hand, would be timeless, removed from all culminating experiences. But here heaven and earth seem stirred out of
their changeless eternity to witness a human deed and participate
in its consummation before it is too late. A pressing anxiety brings
men and gods together: here is a movement running toward some
ultimate issue, an effort or pursuit turned to its unique momentary
occasion, an impulse which must work its way before its energy
peters out.

In these circumstances, the assistance of the gods comes with
the same urgency as the need of men. As regards its general and
ideal purpose, it restores a man to the wholeness of his native vitality; and, indeed, it momentarily relieves him of his burdening
solitude, integrating him into the surrounding universe. It is as if
the divine found its proper place in the warmth of an earthly
solidarity, while the human cry reverberated through the elements with the appeal of feelings, qualities, values which would
otherwise seem hopelessly confined to a weak mortal organism.

III

On the Representation of
Nature and Reality in Homer

The representation of nature in Homer follows the same lines as that of human actions. As he discarded or transformed historical or traditional data in the portrayal of an essential drama, so he ignored any local or predetermined landscape in picturing the places in which that drama was enacted. Only once, and in a simile, do we find a place described in a way that suggests personal knowledge—the Asian meadows on the bank of the Kaystrios, haunt of geese, cranes, and swans (*Il.* 2. 461). Nowhere is there any attempt to reconstruct a scene literally. The earth is a bare foundation on which to stand and move, or occasionally, in the *Odyssey*, a spectacle to be seen and admired, never a general background or environment objectively described.

Nor is there, on the other hand, any conventional setting. Such landmarks as the mound of Ilos or the hill before Troy "called Batieia by men, Myrine by the gods" or the grove of the nymphs in Ithaca were probably handed down by tradition, but they do not play any significant part in the landscape of Homeric poetry. What stands out is simply a walled city, a rugged island overshadowed by a mountain and surrounded by smaller ones.

No less than the action, the landscape in Homer is so conceived as to appear equally removed from descriptive imitation and from the imagery of myth. What struck the Homeric imagination was neither the peculiar quality of a certain site nor the wonder of distant mysterious regions, but, rather, nature itself in the variety of its elements. Places, no less than people, are conceived in their essential outlines. They are there insofar as their striking identities seem to have a function and a meaning to the eyes of man. Thus we read, for instance, that Achilles, in his grief, "sat on the shore by the foaming water, looking over the boundless sea" (*Il.* 1. 350), or that Odysseus, in his weariness, rested in the shelter of two trees interwined "which neither the might of damp-blowing winds could penetrate, nor the shining sun could light upon with its rays, nor rain could pierce" (*Od.* 5. 478 ff.). When at last he lands on Scheria or Ithaca, he kisses "the bountiful earth." A spring surrounded by poplars stands out most conspicuously—a happy halting place and a haunt of nymphs or gods. Similarly a mountain is a majestic presence in itself—like Mount Ida, "many-fountained," "mother of wild animals," from which Zeus seems to send his ominous thunder and lightning. In such passages, we hardly have a sense of landscape. Shores, seas, trees, springs, mountains do not compose one whole self-contained picture; they are represented as elements of nature, indispensable forms of existence, each present in its own right and, at the same time, vantage points for the life of man. There is nothing peculiar about them, nothing characteristic of a certain region. They could be anywhere—quite apart from the setting in which they may happen to be found.

Such a view of reality naturally excluded all partial interest in the particular localization of things or events. Homer never goes out of his way to fix in their relative surroundings the sites which he mentions. In the same way his absorption in the portrayal of action removed all considerations of chronology, so that everything seems to happen outside the course of history. As we read the poems, no other time exists but that required by the plot, no other space but that surveyed or known in its basic aspects by the characters themselves.

Countries near and far are thus essentially the same. The world appeared to Homer for what it was in the uniformity of its essence rather than in the variety of its regions. In his language, indeed, there is no general term for "nature" (the word *physis* appears only once to signify the natural potency of a certain herb), but, all the more, the existence of a common pattern throughout the world is strongly felt in its strikingly concrete forms. The lack of knowledge about the physical dimensions of the earth was thus compensated by insight into existence and into the order of things. We might say that Homer worked in depth rather than variety. As he centered each of his poems around the significance of one drama, so he turned his eye to what was typical and universally perspicuous in nature and refrained from what was strange, peculiar, anomalous, grotesque. Had he tried to tell us more about the various peoples and territories which he mentions, his account would have been largely mythical. As it is, one sole reality stands out in the poems, even though it may be set in this or that part of the world.

A wondering ignorance about the geography of distant regions was thus coupled with a deep understanding of nature. Imagination was here stimulated by experience; and, in a vision both familiar and poetic, true, lifelike images could be projected into fancied regions placed beyond the seas.

In such a spirit a world was conceived which was at once real and imaginary, well known and mysterious, precisely drawn in the detail of its features and yet vaguely surmised in its general contours. The river Oceanus flows around it, man lives in its centers, its extensions are unknown and unmeasurable; but to Homer even its remotest parts could only be imaginable in simple human terms. Thus in a black, foggy, inscrutable night, as they approach the land of the Cyclops, the ships of Odysseus are suddenly driven on an unknown shore. It seems a place quite removed from the world of man. But then, the light of day shines upon a soil which is rich and soft and mellow; there is a harbor sheltered from all winds, there is a cave with a bright spring and mighty poplars. Here wheat and vines grow in plenty, here a seaman might rest leaving his ship unmoored.

The Homeric world is full of such vantage points. They present the reality of the Greek territories which, in their incisive outlines, seem to epitomize the entire world. The island of Calypso, for instance, is conceived in this way. Scheria is like an Ionian city; and the wonder of Alcinous' garden is conveyed by nothing else but its exuberance which, though extraordinary in the rhythm of its growth, is such as the earth might produce in a happy climate. Even the extreme bank of Oceanus with its entrance into the underworld is conjured up by an imagery which is essentially well known—"a narrow strand and the groves of Persephone, tall poplars and willows shedding their fruit still unripe" (*Od.* 10. 509 f.). In the same way, wherever Odysseus turns his exploring eye, it is always a clear relief of form, of structure, of position which strikes his curiosity or his attention: the island of the Phaeacians which rises like a shield above the water, or that of Circe, a squatting shape crowned by the sea, or the cloud-colored surface of Scylla's rock. Likewise, the general scenery of the *Odyssey* could be reduced to a few basic, characteristic traits— projecting cliffs and the stillness of natural havens, the regular ebb and flow on the shore, the calm of seas at rest, swelling waves, and storms descending from heaven like night.

It is as if the true aspect of things emerged out of unknown spaces. What stirred the Homeric imagination was not so much fabulous stories like that of the Cyclops or the Laestrygones but a reality which remained what it was wherever it might be situated. Isolated in a world of unknown dimensions, the appearance of a familiar object becomes even for the reader something miraculous—so true to its own nature, so real and self-consistent in spite of its limited existence. A fig tree growing on a rock saves Odysseus from the dread whirlpool of Charybdis. It is just a plant; but here, in his mysterious spot made famous by legend, it seems to remind us of what is natural, real, intimately and constantly known. Like the intertwining olives of Scheria, it stands out with a special clarity, it grows into a striking image because of its mere presence and not because of any prodigious quality inherent in it.

We should not however suppose that this fundamental unity of the natural world was suggested to the poet by the fact that it was evident far and wide in many places at once. On the contrary, he might never have travelled, never have moved from his native village. Once perceived in their characterizing forms, objects were rendered in appropriate poetic images; and the truth of these images could not but seem universally valid. The whole world had to be submitted to their measure; and the Homeric touch seems to penetrate further and further into its different regions, clearing away the superstructures of myth. "Alas, what men, what land is this where I have come?" Odysseus asks himself more than once during his wanderings; but he soon makes himself at home as the scene grows familiar to his eyes. In the same way, as we read, places and countries—no less than human situations—reveal a Homeric quality: the mark of something well articulated and deeply intelligible in its detached, remote existence.

Now, things so portrayed seem to exist in their own right, irrespective of where they belong. They are removed from whatever is merely accidental. Each feature appears distant, solitary, homeless, being so strongly represented in its individual identity. Reality is here purified into a vision or an ideal. This is not only true of the indeterminate areas of Odysseus' wanderings but also of the more familiar regions where the action of the *Iliad* takes place. Although Homer must have had a very good knowledge of the geography of Asia Minor and of the Greek mainland and the Aegean, each place he mentions is nonetheless a center in itself. The Troad seems to concentrate in her boundaries the whole agony of the universe, and so does Odysseus with his crew, whether he is in Ismaros or on the brink of Oceanus. The location of such places does not need to be explained, seen as they are against the mere background of earth, sea, and sky. In the same way places like Mycenae or Argos or Sparta are self-contained centers of attraction in their own right, geographically undetermined. They belong essentially to the same landscape as that of Scheria and other unidentified islands of the West which are distant and mysterious, but, at the same time, familiar with the human woes of Troy. Places too, like things, have a sort of distant radiance, wherever they may be situated.

No part of the world can be mentioned by the poet without being made to participate in this imaginary reality, translated as it is into forms which he has made familiar to our artistic sense. In this respect even the catalogue of ships has its own poetry. Its fidelity to historical truth has long been recognized; but, at the same time, each place that is mentioned seems to exist absolutely. For the bare names immediately conjure up the essential image of town or country once inhabited and abandoned by its men who have gone to war; and yet this is no prosaic list of names, since the epithets scattered here and there are sufficient to place the whole series in a lifelike perspective. We read, for instance: "They that dwelt in Hyria and rocky Aulis, in Schoinos, Skolos and many-ridged Eteonos, in Thespeia, Graia, and wide-spaced Mycalessos" (*Il.* 2. 496 ff.). The literal relevance of the epithets need not detain us; what they convey is an emotional stress or a certain coloring which ultimately springs from experience and the observation of reality. Nor does a concern for the exactness of each reference trouble us; we feel that what is said is true or might well have been true. The words simply tell us what a town is, or should be, as seen and known by man. The absence of description or historical information only enhances that immediate, and yet remote, reality; and, in such a context, the proper name has in itself an evocative power, as if at one and the same time it were synonymous with such general terms as "town," "city," "country," "home." A whole world is thus condensed in a few place-names. Almost unwittingly we are led far and wide through various regions, struck by a sense of space and inhabited lands. Our impressions are visual rather than geographical or historical, suggested by epithets which offer glimpses of projecting cliffs, promontories, hills, bays, vineyards, meadows.

Such a space is naturally visualized and idealized from the point of view of the people who live in it. As the scene of human actions and events, it acquires a significance in relation to them. The earth groans under the trampling feet of the Achaeans, the water seethes around the keel of Odysseus' ship, a headland affords him refuge or sustenance, while the sky thunders or flashes with signs of good or evil, and the sun, as well as the earth and its rivers, is called to witness in solemn moments. Seen in this light, the scenery is as much of a material substance as is necessary to sustain and accompany the human process. There is always an indispensable, inevitable bond between eyes that see and the objects offered to their view, between bodies that move and the surface upon which they move. Neither can subsist without the other. Homer seems always conscious of this basic relation; and this consciousness keeps him from indulging in detailed pointless descriptions. There are no blank stretches in his poems, no intervals to be filled with realistic, imitative matter. What stands out are such things as a sea to be crossed, a shore, a land to be gained, walked, lived upon —realities most concrete and most tangible, but so universal that they seem to be placed in a world lacking all local characteristics. The action is thus conceived in the same mould as its environment —the one as essential as the other, the one conditioning the other to the same simplicity of form. This is quite different from the accounts of modern novels and other epic poems in which the action is seen against the general background of different lands and people. Everything is here conceived in a single comprehensive harmony where the landscape cannot but be a condensed expression of the world itself.

Such a rendering of reality accounts, I think, for the poetic quality which is diffused throughout the poems quite apart from the particular merits of outstanding passages. For, from page to page, we find images which have nothing else to sustain them but their solitary power and the earth upon which they stand. Chryses striding along the shore in his impassioned prayer, Apollo descending from the ridges of Mount Olympus in his fearful visitation, Achilles and Agamemnon confronting each other beside the hollow ships, Thetis rising from the depths of the sea in answer to her son's lamentation . . . : all these images stand firmly implanted as on a native soil and, from their respective positions, they seem to call into play the influences of heaven and earth. Now, this all-encompassing picture would not have been possible if the poet had set out to give a varied, picturesque account of its whereabouts. Details would have remained mere details, and the total effect would have had to be gleaned little by little, as in a long story. But, as it is, the bare outlines of an elemental reality keep the action in its proper place, in contact with nature itself.

2

This effect of grandeur is created by very simple means. The same images of sea, air, and land continually recur in the poems. Their persistence might seem monotonous to one whose ear is not attuned to Homeric poetry. But we have learnt better: for, in their repetition, they stress certain fundamental features and give us a stronger sense of reality than a diffuse description could.

The tendency to stress the basic properties and, particularly, the form of things was rooted in the language itself. This is evident in the Homeric system of epithets. When Homer says, for instance: "the high-leaved oak," "the taper-leaved olive tree," the many-ridged mountain," or "robe-stretching Helen," "wing-stretching birds," he unwittingly evokes images which, at once, convey a concrete sensuous spell and express a general quality. Such abstract characteristics as "high," "broad," and "long" presented themselves to the poet at one with the contemplated object though without in the least losing their general meaning; and, on the other hand, the object was mentioned insofar as it could be visualized and bore with it the mark of its form, property, dimension. The words were thus filled, as it were, with a plastic significance; and the language could hardly fail to suggest a picture of reality reduced to a few essential lineaments.

This habit of looking at things in their elementary appearance must have brought with it a perception of the formal relations existing between things. Again, the language may offer us a clue. When the poet says "wind-footed" or "storm-footed Iris" or "oars which are wings for the ships" or "the sea's broad back" or "the heads of cities," there emerges from the imagery itself a strong sense of wide-ranging similarities. The word "foot," for instance, naturally carries with it the idea of swiftness; and an image of wind or storm is immediately joined to it, the whole fused into one vision by a single word; in the same way other parts of the human body like "back" and "head" suggest a vital sense of breadth and height, somehow enlivening the vision of the sea or of a lofty city.

Such expressions may have been not the poet's own invention but the stock-in-trade of the language; for their steady recurrence and the constancy of their form suggest a stylistic trend that has gradually taken shape. However that may be, it is certain that in the Homeric poems they are still in the making—not a dead, stereotyped series of formulae, but recurring words and phrases possessing a poetic function. Even if Homer was not the originator of this style, he made it his own. It is quite in tune with his view of reality as I have tried to outline it. It is a style insofar as a persistent mode of seeing and thinking naturally falls into an equally persistent mode of expression.

Further evidence in the same direction is provided by the Homeric similes. They develop and expand what this poetic vocabulary merely implies. An expression like "wind-footed Iris," for instance, or "rose-fingered Dawn" is already, potentially, a simile. It shows wholly different objects in the light of a common quality, though the images are congealed, as it were, in the fixity of an epithet. What they stress is not a given point of resemblance inherent in the objects themselves (as in "rose" and "finger" or "wind" and "foot"), but the passing occasion which sets them in the same momentary perspective. A certain position or movement may thus be conveyed which subjects the most disparate elements of nature to an identical tension; and the disparities of shape or feature then appear overshadowed by the reality of one moment.

Consider, for instance, the way in which Homer represents the fall and the death of Gorgythion: "As in a garden a poppy droops its head on one side, being heavy with fruit and with the showers of spring; even so he bowed his head on one side burdened with his helmet" (*Il.* 8. 306). From a grammatical point of view, this is of course a mere figure of speech—as we might say "he trembled like a leaf." But what is so striking in the Homeric words is the full realization, from beginning to end, of an identical, significant movement in two such different, lifelike images. It is the actual drooping which makes them what they are, giving to both the same significance: two verbs meaning "to fall on one side," "to recline" stress this parallel process. What stands out is, therefore, a material position marking a fatal moment. We naturally read into it moral, human values; but in Homer there are only clearly defined natural forms.

It is as if the purpose of the simile were simply to emphasize the basic nature of the event itself. We are not told that failing Gorgythion was like a drooping poppy; nor is the poet trying to depict a heroic image by making it more convincing through analogies drawn from nature. What struck the poet's mind, rather, was the act of falling and all that it implies. It seemed a crucial occurrence not to be dismissed in one word, but to be represented in the wide range of its occasions. As such, it is visually rendered. It appears essentially the same in the hero and in the flower; even that pathetic side-drop is a mere graphic detail of what actually occurs. Man's plight is thus presented in a basic form, grounded in nature; and nature, on the other hand, assumes a human coloring. The images compared stand, therefore, independently of one another—a drooping poppy, a drooping head, both enacting the same momentous event.

We may compare with this several other similes in which the

death of a hero is compared to the fall of a tree (*Il.* 13. 178, 389; 14. 414; 16. 482; 17. 53). Here again the simile does not serve to explain anything or bring out any particular point. It is, once again, the fall that needs to be stressed as a recurring drama in the images and the occasions which are most striking; and what is more evidently so than a man brought low, or a tree cut down by foresters or overthrown by the wind? The same verbs, or verbs very nearly synonymous, mark the same crisis in both images. The idea of suffering or dying is here, as often in Homer, treated as a natural process. The poet feels no need to work up the emotional possibilities of the scene; the mere juxtaposition of such parallel instances is in itself striking enough, symbolizing the pervasive presence of a destiny which cannot be but what it is, and taking the form of an erect living shape falling low in sickness, agony, or death.

Nature is thus introduced into the picture, not as mere scenery or suggestive imagery, but to mark the full impact of an experience which is not only human. Hence the precise correspondence between the two terms of the simile; for the sense of an identical occasion in the fall of a man and that of a plant sustains the rendering of the analogous scenes and does not admit any digression. This coherence appears peculiar to Homer. We may realize it the better by comparing Vergil's imitation of *Il.* 8. 306 in *Aen.* 9. 433: "Euryalus rolls down in death and blood runs over his beautiful limbs, and his neck sinking down reclines on his shoulder: as when a purple flower dug up by the plough languishes and dies, or as when poppies, burdened with rain, bow their head with weakened neck." What is paramount in Vergil is the lovely, familiar figure of Euryalus; and the simile conveys a sense of vanishing beauty. A certain atmosphere is conjured up, blurring the significance of that solitary relief which is so important in Homer. Hence, to increase the pathos of the whole scene, the image of the poppy is accompanied by that of a ploughed-up flower, drawn from a different literary source; and the actual physical process appears outshadowed by the feelings which it evokes. In the same way, Vergil never compares the solitary image of a falling tree to that of a falling hero. There is no parallel in the *Aeneid* to these Homeric examples; only once does he use such an image, and then, significantly enough, not as a simile for the fall of one man, but for the whole ruin of Troy:

> Then indeed all Ilium appeared to me sinking in flames and Neptune's Troy thrown down from its foundation: as upon mountain peaks an ancient ash tree is hacked by iron, and the woodmen outdo one another trying to bring it down with blow upon blow of their axes, and it staggers, shivering through all its leaves, its topmost branches rocking, until little by little it is overcome by its wounds; it gives one last groan and, torn from the ridge, comes crashing down. (*Aen.* 2. 624 ff.)

These words create a powerful impression of life destroyed and of wholesale ruin, rather than marking a common trend in nature. We have here a different poetic approach. Vergil introduces a principle of human abstraction into the objects portrayed, whereas the Homeric similes stress a natural movement or a mode of being which is essentially the same in man and in any animate object— a parallelism which brings out some identical disposition or elemental quality quite apart from the requirements of a particular characterization.

The Homeric similes thus show the same breadth of outline as the general representation of nature. But they portray events rather than objects. What they stress is not so much a static pattern as the life of nature in the stress and lapse of its flux. All the more, their scope reaches beyond any particular trait, as they reduce each feature to an essential resemblance. Here an image is only itself but, at the same time, it is subjected to a certain tension, transformed by the impact of the moment which marks a phase of its natural destiny. It is so in the heightening as well as in the failing stages. A parallel natural scene is suggested by a man's effort no less than by his fall; and, in each case, it is no particular resemblance but rather the significance of a common physical movement which offers a concrete hold to the poet's imaginative rendering. We do not merely have, for instance, the comparison of a fervent hero with a hungry lion or a swift horse; it is, rather, the glowing defiant eye, or the nimble foot and the vigorous stride which are pictured as marks of an overriding reality. The images of man or animal have the same vital energy.

Consider, for instance, the famous simile of Paris and the horse (*Il*. 6. 506 ff.). The emphasis falls on the motion of knees and feet which is identical in both; and it is a sense of native resilience which relates the one to the other, giving to each act a sort of sinewy quality and outright sweep. Here boldness is natural strength, self-reliance is pure vitality, and beauty is nothing but the relevance of each feature. The parallelism of the two scenes thus springs from the perception of an existential identity and not from some literal point of resemblance nor from any vague idealization of form. Again, a comparison with Vergil's imitation (*Aen*. 11. 492) is revealing. In Vergil it is as if the bond of animal identity had been broken: Turnus is a man exulting in the pride of his might and high hopes, the horse is an animal that prances and whinnies in the wantonness of unspent vigor. Each is pictured according to his own characteristics, so that the simile rests upon an ideal resemblance rather than upon a basic natural identity. What stands out is something exceptional, a quality which all may share but which is seldom granted; and we admire its singularity rather than its adherence to the ways of nature.

Over and over again we find in Homer similes which liken the action or condition of a man to that of other animals; and each time we have an intense moment of experience rendered, as it were, on two levels—the distinctively human and the broadly natural. It is most often a vital organ which sustains the parallel actions; for instance: "Achilles . . . sprang like a lion . . . whom men strive to slay, the whole village gathered together. At first he passes on heedless, but when struck . . . he crouches gaping, foam breaks out over his teeth, the heart bursts within him, he lashes his sides with his tail and, glaring, he is driven forward by his spirit . . . even so his might and spirit stirred Achilles" (*Il*. 20. 164).

In such passages, nature—or the life of nature—is not seen as a mere spectacle whose aspects offer striking similarities to the curious eye, but, rather, it is apprehended from within, at the source of its operations, in intensive moments when what stands out is the pervasive effectiveness of one vital principle, and not occasional peculiarities resembling one another. Even the realistic details (a gaping mouth, a lashing tail) are not so much the characteristics of an animal as movements of an energy stretched to the furthest point. This is, in fact, what the Homeric words emphasize: a panting heart, an impetuous spirit, the *thymos*, the *menos*, which are the same in the lion and in Achilles, producing kindred scenes of animate stress. Such a feeling for nature and animate life seems absent in other poets. Once more, the Homeric treatment may be appreciated more clearly if we notice how different are Vergil's lions and heroes. For instance in *Aen.* 12. 4 (cf. *Aen.* 9. 339, 551; 10. 723): "As in African fields, a lion is struck by hunters with a grievous wound in his breast, and then at last he moves to war; joyfully he shakes his great mane, undaunted he snaps the robber's arrow stuck in him, and roars with his bloody mouth; even so Turnus' fury is kindled and mounts high." In Vergil the lion is somehow taken for granted as a heroic animal; and, being thus characterized, he appears humanized—warlike, defiant, fearless, joyously moving. Such analogies may indeed be read also into the Homeric similes, but in Vergil they are abstracted from the natural texture, made explicit, conceived as attributes of a certain kind of behavior rather than conditions and modes of being. (For other Homeric examples, cf. *Il.* 12. 41; 13. 471; 16. 156; 17. 109, 133, 570, 742; 18. 318; 21. 573.)

We have seen that Homeric similes express a certain identity of tension rather than objective resemblance. It follows that the subject matter of the similes is limitless. Any part of nature may be comprised in it as long as it shows some transparent from or movement which appears universally significant to human eyes. Animal life, in its wonderful flexibility, offered the poet an admirable material, for animals are subject to the same stresses as man. It is always a relation between living beings which is, thereby, portrayed: some form of opposition or support. But at times the poet feels the need to represent a position or a movement in itself and by itself; and then nature at large offers him a better point of reference, a possibility of grounding his perceptions in an element which is less specific and one-sided. Take the occasions when the advance of a hero is compared to a river. Here too, as with animals, an animate principle might be perceived, yet quite removed from any particular, arbitrary direction. For water too presents a plastic, flexible appearance; and yet it seems to follow a course which could not be otherwise, surprising and inevitable, abrupt and determinate at the same time.

> He raged through the plain like a full, winter-flowing river that running swiftly breaks the dykes; neither the well-built dykes can contain it, nor the enclosures of flourishing orchards, so suddenly it comes when the rain of Zeus falls heavily, and many goodly works of men lie shattered under its impact; thus before the son of Tydeus thick troops of Trojans were routed, nor could they resist him though they were many. (*Il.* 5. 87; cf. 11. 492)

There can be nothing here, of course, about limbs or breath or the spirit of life; but, all the more, what is conveyed is the sheer motion of a mass whose pressure cannot be withstood. For Diomedes does not have, in this instance, any particular opponent. It is simply the full weight of his advance which is emphasized, and the representation of the river brings out the sense of unswerving, almost impersonal motion. It is as if the force of gravity, or of some elemental energy, were poetically embodied in that bulk of moving waters. Accordingly the imagery follows a coherent trend. There is no descriptive virtuosity, no attempt to give us a picture of wholesale destruction, but simply the images of dams, barriers, hedges that give way. There is no landscape outside these images, and they themselves are nothing but the contour of a general phenomenon of movement in the flux of existence. This is, again, quite different from Vergil's way who in similar instances (*Aen.* 2. 304, 496) portrays the general ruin produced by the flood rather than the irresistible movement of water.

We might thus say that, in its ultimate implications, the Homeric simile disregards the particular and descriptive features of objects in order to bring out something quite basic and elementary —something neither animal nor human nor assignable to any given species. The hero is doubtless nothing but a man, the river nothing but a river, and yet what we derive from the picture is simply an impression of sheer power following a certain course. It was the genius of Homer to draw his images true to life, and at the same time endow them unwittingly with a symbolic significance. Symbolic of what? we may ask. Certainly not of any superimposed value, but of a stress or mode of being which appears native to the object themselves. It is as if the images lost their particular identity and were merged into an identity of a larger, different order. The man is no longer a person with a physiognomy of his own, the river is no particular river running in a certain place; they become typical forms of the same motion, of the same power. Diomedes and Ajax (the two heroes who are actually compared to rivers) lend themselves admirably to such a treatment. They are the sturdiest, the most hardy and rugged Homeric characters. Consciousness lights them in a few memorable instances; elsewhere a surge or accumulation of strength makes up for their lack of nuance. Being what they are, they naturally suggest a primordial, inorganic imagery.

The similes rendering the powers of nature thus recur where the individualism of the characters is less marked. It is especially so when the poet represents masses of men, as in *Il.* 4. 422: "As on the resounding shore a wave of the sea arises in its turn under the impact of Zephyrus; out in the deep it first rears its crest and then it breaks on the land with a great roar, it bulges, it arches itself over the beach's edge and spews out the froth from the surf; so in turn did the ranks of Achaeans move relentlessly into battle." "Waves of fighting men": the image has become a trope. But in Homer we find the freshness of an initial perception, as if the identification of the objects ("waves," "men") were quite secondary and what came foremost was the impression of shapes emerging out of a certain movement.

Many other similes drawn from the sea are of the same sort,

especially *Il*. 13. 795 (cf. *Il*. 2. 207, 394; 4. 275; 11. 305; 15. 381). Another example, *Il*. 7. 61, shows the same mode of representation, but with a different object in view. It renders not a movement but a momentary stillness: "They sat close together in their ranks, rippling with shields and helmets and spears. As, at the moment when Zephyrus rises, a ripple spreads over the sea, and the water darkens beneath it, so the ranks of Achaeans and Trojans sat on the field." The word "rippling," as referred to men, is inappropriate in English, but appropriate in the Greek which renders the bristling of weapons on the plain of Troy and the roughening of the water as aspects of the same phenomenon. There is no rhetoric here: what we see in both cases is a teeming emergence of forms from an undifferentiated mass.

More than once we find in the poems the rendering of this shadowy transfiguration—not only in the sea (cf. *Il*. 23. 692; *Od*. 5. 402) or in the battlefield (cf. *Il*. 13. 339), but also in a field of ripening wheat (*Il*. 23. 599). These glimpses of the scenery of land and sea are thus prompted by a penetrating perception of nature, not occasioned by any casual motive nor by any interest in a picturesque setting. Accordingly the picture is not expanded through descriptive details. It is a particular vibration—a ripple, a color, a shadow—which enlivens and justifies each image.

Such similes lead us into an imaginative world where objects appear removed from their conventional habitat and placed, as it were, in a sphere of pure existence. Stretches of scenery are placed before us insofar as they suggest a basic form or condition of being. As we read, we acquire a habit of mind both perceptive and speculative: things are what they are, and yet they seem to carry out a design which spells a certain order in the universe. If we tried to reduce such a design to certain objective data, we would not find any appropriate terms. It is ideally posited by a vision which discovers pervasive identities of form, appearance, movement. What emerges in one instance emerges again throughout nature; and, through his extensive system of analogies, Homer brings out the focal points in which such basic coincidences are gathered and made clear.

A representation so conceived for the sake of significant outlines and forms is naturally quite free in the choice of its objects.
It is not conditioned by conventions; it does not gauge things according to their greater or lesser dignity, admitting the one and
excluding the other. What matters here is an immediate visual
relevance, and not an epic or heroic quality belonging to the
subject matter. In this perspective the great could find a parallel
in the small, the extraordinary in the familiar; and it was in the
Homeric spirit to unravel the complexities of a massive scene by
reducing it to the outline of a simple phenomenon occuring in
nature or art: as when the suspense between equal, opposing
armies is compared to the balance of the scales in the hand of a
woman weighing her wool (*Il.* 12. 433) or to a straight line wonderfully drawn by a carpenter's rule (*Il.* 15. 410). In the same way
the immobility of resisting warriors is compared to the precarious
stillness of clouds when the winds are for a while at rest (*Il.* 5. 522)
or the poise of wrestlers straining against each other to that of
rafters on opposite sides of a roof (*Il.* 23. 711).

What sort of simile may occur, and where and when, cannot of
course be foreseen. And yet this freedom has its own logic; the
choices are not arbitrary. It is as if the very movement of the
narrative were so conceived as to suggest a simile: an effort, a
movement reaches its climax and must be resolved into a wider
sphere of reality in order to be sustained in its natural rhythm. A
human action thus becomes a general occurrence, an event whose
course becomes integrated with nature. A certain posture or direction is thereby imposed upon existence, and the sense of its impact
prepares us to visualize it in the terms of a broad, extrahuman
imagery.

As the poems deal so much with moments of swift transition or
of self-contained intensity, the similes must underline such moments and be dynamic in their character. The *Iliad* in particular
may be viewed as a process, a continuous ebb and flow, a sequence
of pauses and movements. The poet dwells with a sympathetic
mind upon these instances of sudden and quick realization, when
the drift of events comes to a head, altering the atmosphere or the

scenery and tracing its shadow over the field of vision. It is as if the action were for a moment arrested in an outline, as if it became an image; and we can then almost prefigure the tension of the coming simile.

Thus, for instance, snowflakes swiftly gathering, drifting, veiling earth and sky, are instantly suggested by stones or arrows flung massively through the air or by the rallying of men in an open space (*Il.* 12. 156, 278; 19. 357); and, similarly, a cloud driven by the wind upon mountain peaks (*Il.* 3. 10) or chaff blown into a white-gleaming heap when the wheat is threshed (*Il.* 5. 499) seem to enact upon different planes of reality the imagery of dust arising from the trampling feet of men. As we read, not only the plot but the occasion of the simile recedes into the background. We wonder what is this thickening of the air, this coloring that gathers into a shape; and the actual snowflakes, the clouds, the chaff emerge from the dynamic context—familiar things endowed with a fresh significance in that they seem to respond to our inquiring vision and offer a hold to our vague sense of changing appearances.

This discovery of the familiar in the most startling occurrences is an insight into the ways of nature. We are led to expect the mark of a certain measure in anything that may happen, setting aside all distinctions between what is heroic or merely human, imaginative or natural. When, for instance, we read (*Il.* 13. 588) that an arrow bounced upon a shield "as from a flat winnowing-shovel dark-husked beans or peas leap up, driven by the shrill breeze or the sweep of the winnower's fan," what strikes us is not so much a warlike action as the effect of bounding and rebounding on a hard surface under the impact of some natural force. Again, we are shown the pigmentation on the cheek-ornament of a bridle (*Il.* 4. 141) or the swift curdling of milk (*Il.* 5. 902), stones set closely together to build a wall (*Il.* 16. 212), motion of water irrigating an orchard (*Il.* 21. 257), or the live coals under the ashes (*Od.* 5. 488). The homeliest occasions no less than the broadest phenomena—all become central moments or instances showing the interplay of conditions which prevail in the flux of existence.

Confronted with the activities of nature and of man, the poet felt the need to reach out more deeply into their sources, more widely into their reality; and we learn to pause with him in the contemplation of those images which render those activities most vividly. Far or near, human or non-human—it does not seem to make any difference. If man-made objects often shine like the sun and the stars, if voices roar like the sea, this is no exaggeration; for what is conveyed is the essence of light or sound in its purest and most valid form.

It will be seen that the range of the similes is as wide as the vision which sustains them is simple and coherent. Such a vision must have been fostered in the poet by the sense of a vital unity embracing the various compartments of existence. Mere lucidity of perception would not have been enough; the pervasive analogies of the similes could not have been rendered so powerfully and truthfully without a deep sympathy for the life of nature as a whole. Hence the constant juxtaposition of men and animals, men and natural phenomena—a parallelism founded on innate harmonies and not on any artful treatment of the material.

This wide-ranging unity was, of course, grounded in the sense of a single animating principle. Even for us this is no difficult, far-fetched theory; but for Homer it was not so much a theory as a feeling. In the Greek world of the ninth century, neither religion nor philosophy conditioned the poet's mind to any clear-cut categories; no scale of values regarding the classification of species impeded his vision of existence; he was unaffected by the distinction between soul and body, spirit and matter. Thus he did not have to humanize animals when he compared their actions with those of men, nor did he have to treat natural phenomena metaphorically in order to dramatize them. Even the most fleeting feeling was charged with a material vitality, even the most massive natural upheaval seemed tinged with a transparent animation.

He was therefore well placed to see even in the movements of the psyche the effect of natural forces. Their vibrations appeared to be the same as those which emerge at certain moments of unrest in the elements: as if an intense human feeling and a tension in the outer world of nature were marks of the same vicissitude.

And this is what we actually find in a number of Homeric similes. Human feelings suggest a kindred disturbance in the world at large; a state of mind is transposed into visual terms and the external scene is caught in a moment of inner significance.

This, for instance, is how the poet pictures the desperate brooding of Nestor (*Il.* 14. 16): "As when the sea heaves strongly with the ground-swell, and rolls neither this way nor that but stays where it is until a strong wind swoops down from heaven; so the old man brooded, divided in heart." What is portrayed is a moment of threatening suspense, approaching the breaking-point. How does it come about? As an arrested movement, a stirring stillness as yet unspent but ready to explode—a swirl in the waters, a congestion in the human heart. The translation I offered cannot properly render this basic analogy; for in the original the verbs πορφύρω, ὄσσομαι, ὁρμαίνω have an ambivalent meaning that can refer both to man and to the sea, and thus suggest a physical commotion in the psyche, an animate stress in the sea. Again, then, the simile depends on the perception of a common reality, a common process; it draws its cogency from words that are sensuously expressive of feeling. The imagery is not stained by any superimposed meaning. The perceived identity is all contained in moments which convey a certain motion of the spirit. No particular contours are needed, no suggestion of a somber environment: only the sense of an inner tension working on its material sphere. It is as if feeling had found in nature a mould in which to manifest itself visually; and what we have before us is not so much a seascape as a mood of the sea.

In another instance (*Il.* 16. 297), a respite of the hard-pressed Achaeans is conveyed in this way: "As when from the lofty summit of a high mountain Zeus, assembler of lightning, shifts a dense cloud; the hill-tops and headlands and valleys suddenly appear, and from heaven on high the infinite air breaks into view; so the Danaans . . . took breath." As in the preceding passage, the scenery appears to act as the physical extension of a mental process. What goes on in the mind goes on also in the atmosphere. For what is it that happens when exhausted men revive? As the self emerges again, the breath resumes its rhythm, the eye sees far and clear discerning the landmarks of existence. It is as if an obstructing cloud had given way, as if such a moment restored to all objects their natural contours. One could not find a better way of presenting a certain pattern, or order, arising out of chaos. An objective clarity reveals itself in things, an articulate self-possession in individual beings—both being shown as moments of the same elemental process. The scene which is set before us in this passage is, therefore, not so much a landscape as an essential vision, a bright open space filled with recognizable forms. And these Homeric peaks, promontories, valleys seem to have an almost metaphysical existence. They are visually persuasive, to be sure, but at the same time they are the outlines, the symbols of a world that the human mind can comprehend and make itself familiar with.

Another example, from the *Odyssey*, presents the same relation between nature and the human mind from an entirely different point of view. The tears of Penelope in the presence of Odysseus who, in disguise, gives her news of himself, are thus portrayed (*Od.* 19. 205): "As the snow melts away in high-ranging mountains, thawed by the East wind after Zephyrus has poured it down and, while it melts, the rivers run full; so her lovely cheeks were melting in tears as she wept for her husband who was sitting there beside her." Like the ground-swell of the sea (*Il.* 14. 16), the melting snow is here the expression of an essential mood, but on the level of a more articulate emotion: a breaking-point not of rage or violence but of tenderness. For here too the simile rests upon an identity given by the nature of things. There is a sense both psychic and physical in the verb "to melt" (τήκω) which in Greek applies both to the actual liquefaction of, for instance, snow and to the pining away of the human spirit. It is easy enough to see the relation between the two terms of reference. But in our passage this connection seems to be traced back to its source, to a point where we can hardly speak of a metaphorical usage or of a transferred sense. The clogging burden of grief at a certain point dissolves into tears, as though the mental load returned to its constituent material elements and the anguish found its place in the normal process of nature.

Elsewhere (*Il.* 23. 598) the heart is said to rejoice "like the dew on the ears of corn when the crops are ripening." Again, the verb (ἰαίνω) which means at the same time "to warm," "to cheer," "to brighten" seems to reveal a primal meaning that merges feeling and appearance into one. As such, it conditions the simile in which the field becomes the momentary aspect of a pervasive mood, the translucent dew being like an animating touch. It is in the same frame of reference that the recurring outbursts of a troubled sky seem to enact the repeated inner signs and throbs of Agamemnon's raging spirit (Il. 10. 5).

The Homeric similes dealing with nature, we may conclude, present a consistent picture. In their diversity, they always stress a certain drift or form in natural events. Hence the recurrence, or even repetition, of typical scenes (Il. 16. 299, for instance, appears also in Il. 8. 557 in an entirely different context). This need not surprise us. Once a simile has been fashioned to set forth a prevailing aspect of nature, it stands out in itself and by itself as an appropriate, eloquent outline of what actually exists and is permanently relevant. As we read, our mind is conditioned to see the world as an array of prevalent forms, rhythms, sequences. What exists in its own right seems to mark, at the same time, a central moment in a general cadence. Objects, for all their solidity, are here transparent embodiments of general attitudes, modes of qualification, signals of typical events. As the story proceeds in its massive sweep, it touches on this or that moment of experience, and at its crucial points it expands into a simile as if to bear witness to the worldwide relevance of what is being said or done. The oscillations in the human action thus have their counterpoint in nature; and nature, on the other hand, appears as a series of perspectives which elicit from a man a response, a recognition, a sympathetic participation. What is seen in the outer world may be an omen, good or bad—or an analogy. In any case, a meaning emerges as a significant point of reference. If we had the similes without the narrative to which they belong, we might still be able to recompose from them a dramatic sequence—an epitome of attitudes and experiences, even if not a story.

This qualifying sense inheres in the scenery of the similes even when they seem to develop on their own account, growing into a representation of nature apparently removed from their occasion. A notable example occurs when stones are described as being thrown as thickly as flakes of snow:

> As snowflakes fall thickly on a winter's day when all-wise Zeus stirs himself to snow, revealing to men his own arrows; laying the winds to rest he pours down snow steadily until he covers the high mountain peaks and the uttermost headlands, the flowering plains and the rich fields of men; even on the white-foaming sea the drifting snow falls, and on the harbours and shores; but the wave, striking against it, keeps the snow off. Everything else is covered over, encompassed by the storm Zeus has sent. (*Il.* 12. 278 ff.)

The picture is prolonged beyond the limits required by the occasion; but what stands out from beginning to end is a sense of encompassing thickness, a blanket or layer covering all distinct features. Again, then, the poet presents a state of things whose reality could not possibly be worked out by taking into account casual, particular details; it has rather to be drawn in broad, essential outline. And here, therefore, we have once more the familiar traits of the Homeric landscape—hardly, again, a landscape at all but rather an epitome of the world: the mountains, the sea, the plains, the headlands, seen as vantage points of existence.

The similes, therefore, reproduce, as in an abstract, the imagery which we find scattered throughout the poems. In the first book of the *Iliad*, for instance: the long outline of the shore's edge, the mountain ridge whence the gods are wont to descend, sails stretched to the utmost and full-blown by favoring winds, the seething wave and its sound along the keel—all these images, represented as they are in a sort of full simplicity, set nature in a fundamental relation to the modes of human experience. That Olympian eminence bears, for eyes that can see, the fullest significance of distance, height, or simply of a form towering in the vacant air; that neat outline parting the dry land from the sea is an essential frontier in the existence of things; that wind may be felt as a natural influence for good or evil; that wave might be taken as an eternal instance of movement, sound, turmoil.

This is so even where the scene is purely human: the spirit of the similes seems to integrate man into this world of natural images. Take, for instance, such a commonplace passage as "when they assembled and all were gathered together, swift Achilles arose and thus he spoke in their midst" (*Il.* 1. 57). Or again: "Hector . . . stepped in the middle and held back the troops of the Trojans, spear in hand; they all stopped and sat still" (*Il.* 6. 103). Such typical instances are fixed in constant terms which underline the salient moments of a natural process. Their relevance transcends the compass of any single occasion, for they suggest a sequence which is native to the order of things—a figure standing out above the others, an object gathering upon itself the general attention, and event which precipitates a movement in a given direction.

The similes may thus serve as a touchstone of the poet's mode of representation. As we read, whatever is portrayed grows upon us, brought into focus by the full reality of its dimension, position, attitude, as though it assumed a rhythm or a form at once specific and yet inevitably falling within a pattern given by nature. It might be objected that it must obviously be so in any true description of phenomena and events. But what is elsewhere taken for granted is in Homer a central theme. For it is his way to stress the natural ways and means of being, happening, moving, so that a sense of sheer existence is present even in his most casual passages. It is as if the Homeric scenes implicitly contained a simile—so fraught with native power is the outline of each act as it develops, of each feature as it is set where it is.

3

Animate and inanimate objects so represented in essential postures and movements can only be situated in a space which belongs to them by a sort of natural necessity. A horse breaking loose from the stable and cantering down to the meadows and the river bank, a rock whose support is washed away so that it rolls down a hill—images of this sort serve to stress the impact of human movements; and they require for background or support only the barest outline of a cliff, a slope, a plane.

Such space is an indispensable field of vision. It provides not only a place, but a condition of existence, a measure, a dimension, to whatever happens on its surface. While it does not bear the mark of any particular landscape, it suggests a sense of near and far, of presence or absence, of height, depth, length, fulness, as the case may be. Life is harmonized to its proportions, and men's eyes color them with a human significance. A hill, for instance, or a plane, or a stretch of water trace an ideal distance which the mind fills with its projections. Any escape or pursuit, departure or arrival cannot but be imagined in the concrete setting of such natural images.

The language of the poet seems to be conditioned by this form of elementary apprehension. Thus Achilles rejects all enmity between his people and the Trojans, saying: "there lie in between many mountains and the resounding sea" (*Il.* 1. 157). In a similar way the yearning of Odysseus for his native land is conveyed by his sitting on Calypso's rocky shore and gazing over the barren waste of water. In both cases the sense of distance and separation is poignantly realized by the immediate perception of physical reality. Likewise, Hera's divine horses leap "as far as a man can discern, sitting on a hill-top and looking over the wine-coloured sea" (*Il.* 5. 770); the island of Pharos is as far from Egypt "as the sea which a ship can cover sailing the whole day if a shrill wind blows it forward" (*Od.* 4. 356); Odysseus, swimming, approaches the Phaeacian shore as near "as one can call without a shout," at a point where the waves can be heard breaking on the beach (*Od.* 5. 400).

It might be urged, however, that the use of these concrete images to express spatial measurements is normal in a poetic language which avoids technical terms. But in Homer, this is not merely a conventional device. We find the same attitude here as in the similes. Nature, or everyday reality, again appears to offer pervasive terms of reference. Stripped of all superfluities, the images are so harmonized as to fit into an ideal vision of distance. The world extends far and wide; but at the same time it seems to take on essentially familiar dimensions: what eyes can see, what hands can reach, what the mind can picture as a setting for speed or for stillness. No alien standard of measurement, therefore, is brought into play. The normal Homeric imagery affords the means of expression. When we read that the island of Pharos is as far from Egypt as the stretch of sea that a ship can cover sailing all day driven forward by the shrill wind, this imagery of distance re-creates, as it were, a day of Odysseus' seafaring. That expanse of water, that favoring wind have become the very stuff of experience. What we have before us is at once an elemental scene and a human situation, a segment of matter to which Homeric poetry has given a clear meaning.

Or again (to take an example from a completely different context), when we read (*Il.* 23. 759): "Odysseus leapt behind him as near as the weaving rod is to the breast of a woman as she stretches out the spool past the thread of the warp and holds it close to her," we can appreciate this indication of measure with a sort of sympathetic understanding: weaving women often recur in Homer, rendered once and for all in an image which is rooted in life and is, therefore, permanently valid.

These expressions of distance thus point outwards to a world which has been scanned and sympathetically explored. Like the similes, they show the raw material of reality sifted, ordered, portrayed according to a certain idea. Things are made to stand out for the sake of a relation which obtains between them; and they combine into patterns which bear a message to the mind. What emerges is a humanized space, convincing in its reality, imaginary in its idealization, responsive both to the requirements of immediate perception and to the fancy of a harmonious whole. As we read, we become more and more aware of it. We see how subtle, how penetrating is the process of selection whereby the picture of existence is reduced and simplified. Much is left out; a few basic significant elements are mentioned and emphasized and what remains bears a common stamp: images related to one another insofar as they make up the backbone of the world we see, essential objects of our recognition and understanding.

It is especially so in the *Odyssey* where the similes are much less frequent than in the *Iliad*, but, on the other hand, nature is displayed in the clear-cut dimensions and forcible patterns which the similes have made familiar to us. In the account of Telemachus' journey or of Odysseus' wanderings, for instance, nature is a presence always related to human needs—to be feared or to be trusted. a danger or a refuge. Thus the scenes of storm or clear weather are never described at length in picturesque detail, but simply outlined in the essential images of a threatening turmoil or a reassuring brightness. Accordingly, almost the same words recur in the various instances. Time and again Zeus stirs up the winds with an awesome squall, a cloudy mass darkens the earth and the sky, night emerges from heaven (*Od.* 9. 67; 12. 313; cf. 5. 291; 14. 303), or, on the other hand, the winds are set at rest, the waters are still, a bright calm is spread all around (cf. *Od.* 10. 94; 5. 391; 12. 168). Darkness, light; turmoil, stillness—this is at once a landscape and a human impression, the physical elements all merged in an encompassing condition which has a scope and a meaning.

What is true of the general representation is also true of any single self-contained scene. In the fifth book of the *Odyssey*, for instance, the storm which overtakes Odysseus is rendered as a succession of moments in which the sea continually stands out in its human relevance, an almost purposeful power embodied in the water. Hence we find no description of nature but a dramatic vision; no seascape, but an ever-enveloping wave. This may remind us of certain similes in the *Iliad:* Ajax advancing like an overflowing river, Hector falling on the Achaeans like sea water over the deck of a ship. There is no mixture of heterogeneous elements here. Homer's poetry has trained us, on the contrary, to perceive in one distinct visual form the values which have a human bearing; and it is this which makes the image so forcible. The waves which envelop Odysseus are thus like the blows of a warrior, or like the saving hand of a god. This kind of impersonation gives them a particular character. They each seem to take shape and to act in their own account—setting the raft spinning and dashing Odysseus overboard, plunging him to the bottom, lifting him up, carrying him in one swoop to the shore. Similarly the winds—Eurus, Notus, Zephyrus—seem to play with the vessel as though it were a ball, throwing it to one another. This is how nature must appear to a virgin eye—an object of contemplation, but also a challenging presence, a mode of experience, an enemy, or a friend. The Homeric imagination perceived it in this light. In so doing, it could not but take into account a relevant perspective rather than a whole landscape.

If, in the same book, we follow Odysseus on the shore, we are presented with a landscape conceived in the same spirit: not a comprehensive picture, but a series of dramatic notations. Each natural feature is essentially real in itself, inescapable, solidly entrenched wherever it is placed; and yet, at the same time, it is a helpful or hostile presence confronting human initiatives. Hence we have glimpses of landscape set in solitary relief: crags, reefs, rocks, sheer cliffs washed by deep water, and then the hospitable river mouth with its retreating beaches where the waves enter slantwise. Such landmarks, so concisely and yet so powerfully drawn, are at once translatable into human terms—as dangerous approaches where death lies in wait or as saving and sheltering havens. Transparent as they are, they might well find their place in a simile, representing the extreme circumstances in which life is endangered and rescued.

The land itself, once reached and displayed, does not present itself in the beauty of its varied scenery, as it does, for instance, to Aeneas when he approaches the mouth of the Tiber. For Odysseus the land is essentially the "bountiful earth"; and he stoops down to kiss it. What stands out is, again, the earth itself in its ideal significance, as a human value, as a goal, as a familiar reality. In a simile from the same context (*Od.* 5. 394) we read: "As welcome as the life of their father to children, after he has lain wasting in long sickness with bitter suffering and a heavy fate upon him; and then he is released by the gods from his anguish; so equally welcome appeared to Odysseus the earth and the woodland." Human emotions here converge massively upon a material essence. It is as if the whole reality of the earth were centered in one point when Odysseus kneels down to kiss.

A little later, in his exhaustion he finds shelter from the cold under the intertwining branches of two olive trees which form a thicket that neither wind nor rain nor the rays of the sun can penetrate. Again, the highest effect is achieved with the simplest means. A completely expressive symbol is abstracted, as it were, from the undifferentiated range of a general landscape. Those two trees include in themselves all the shady darkness, all the stillness of a forest. Whatever protection nature can provide in such circumstances seems concentrated in one spot. The poet has isolated a certain form, and filled it with an overwhelming significance. Hence the atmosphere of wonder and, at the same time, the truthfulness of the picture. For the object is visualized and idealized at the same time. Similarly in the representation of the waves, the sea is present in its own right and yet quite transformed by eyes that can perceive in it a human significance.

Even the representation of well-known places made famous by the story follows the same lines. Ithaca is a case in point. It is described more than once—by Odysseus, by Telemachus, by Athena (cf. *Od.* 9. 27; 4. 606; 13. 238). Different words are used, but the basic attributes recur over and again, conveying a persistent picture: an island clear in the distance, a mountain rising over the water with its quivering foliage, a rugged form, a haunt for goats rather than for horses, but a good nursing-mother, watered by springs, blessed with tilth and vineyard. It is a typical Greek island, no different from any other. As such, Telemachus contrasts it with the fertile plain of Laconia; but, beyond this, we are given no distinctive details. It is no wonder that some scholars thought that they could identify it precisely, while others denied that it could be identified at all. The point is that Homer does not insist upon minor characteristics. All that is necessary is a recognizable form, something that has become dear and familiar through seeing, knowing, living. Accordingly, the characterization of the island is broadly conceived, but deeply felt. Thought and feeling have so worked upon it that it has almost become an embodiment of human passions.

And yet Ithaca is in no way symbolic. Removed though it is from all realistic description, the island is nevertheless entirely real. There is no "patriotism" here in the modern sense, no abstract attachment: what stands out is a mountain, a tree, a spring, a house—nature and reality immediately perceived, as they strike the eye and the imagination. That epithet "rugged" points to the actualities of life—as if fertility were dearer and lovelier in so craggy and solitary a spot. It might thus appear as a wonderful refuge, a desirable halting place, a pole of attraction beckoning from beyond the waves. Homer surely speaks here from personal experience; but also in the name of our own experience: we have felt the spell of such islands sailing through the Greek seas. But Homer helps us to conjure up out of many a certain island image which seems to contain the essence of them all—a significant natural shape and, at the same time, an image of life lying out at sea.

Now, such an island as Ithaca, a place so meaningful and so real, is not only an important center, but also a strongly marked individual presence. It is with islands, cities, landmarks, as it is with persons. Homer mentions many. Even if obscure, they are never taken for granted as mere geographical data. We are always given a sense of their existence, their identity (cf. *Od.* 1. 50; 3. 293; 4. 354, 844; 5. 55; 7. 244; 9. 116; 10. 1, 135, 194; 15. 403; 19. 172). We read, for instance: "An island exists far out in the surging sea, facing Egypt. Pharos they call it" or, "there is a sheer smooth reef on the water off Gortys in the cloud-dark sea" or, "far away an island is laid out on the water, Ogygia."

Such islands, such places are thereby given, as it were, full status. Their position is accounted for pictorially, visually. They are set concretely in our mind's imaginary map, however doubtful or fantastic their actual setting may be. They are real presences immediately made familiar to us by the poet's touch, very much in the same way as a new character, like Thersites for instance, is suddenly introduced in the *Iliad*. Compare, in this connection, the whole group of islands neighboring Ithaca: "Many islands abide all around very near one another, Dulichion and Same and woody Zacynthus, but Ithaca lies sloping down to the waters in the far west, while the others look towards the dawn." The verb which I have translated "abide" in Greek poetry normally means "to inhabit" and can refer both to people and places. The word thus seems to set the tone of the whole passage. Immediately the archipelago comes alive. The islands dwell, lie, face one another, project into different directions, placed in a sort of animate relief and spaced out in a certain order, a certain rhythm. Compare the many scenes in the *Iliad* where a hero stands out prominently surrounded by his followers and friends as, for instance, *Il.* 3. 229: "Massive Ajax is there, a bulwark of the Achaeans, and on the other side Idomeneus is standing like a god amid the Cretans, with the chieftains of Crete all gathered around him." Two such examples, taken by themselves, might not mean much; but this mode of representation, in its cumulative effect, makes us look at things, as well as people, with sympathetic eyes: even a rock is given the full value of its reality.

Just as the human situation suggests analogies with the world of nature, so natural objects are related to man. But only moments of particular human intensity seem to require a comparison, an outlet into a wider sphere. Nature, on the other hand, is complete in itself; it does not need to be drawn out of its own proportions which contain the measure of all patterns. Thus, we do not find in Homer similes in which a natural phenomenon is compared to a human act. Such correspondences are implied in the mode of representation. They reside in a silent suggestion of form or position, in an articulate prominence, in a strength of relief which tends to place disparate objects on the level of the same visual value. In the passages quoted above, for instance, a wave, a beach, a tree, an island convey a host of associated ideas and feelings unaided by any simile. In their simple presence they are pregnant with meaning. Objects here becomes images, with all the significance and dignity given them by the distinction of form. The accidental material conditions are then somehow transformed; movement is power, stillness is rest and tranquil self-existence. That wave is like a hand driving to some purpose of its own; that tree, that island seem to have their own destiny in the solidity which affords life and peace.

A sympathetic vision thus presented the animate and the inanimate in the same light. Material objects found their place side by side with people, animals, on an equal footing. Faced with this perspective, we might almost forget for a moment the dramatic human issues which are the central theme of the poems. They are placed at a distance, they cease to be a pressing and exclusive concern and become part of a more general picture in which the different planes of existence seem to be interrelated by virtue of their elementary significance. Thus even in most intense passages of action we are made to stop and take into account the glitter of bronze or the all-nourishing earth or the resounding sea. It is as if what counted was a lucid reality of form insofar as it could be visualized, contemplated, admired.

This pervasive practice of setting widely differing things on a common ground required, of course, that they be viewed as aesthetically commensurate with one another. Absorbed into Homeric poetry, they were no longer mere objects, but images bound together by the link of a mutually responsive quality—possessing the same clarity of structure or design, the same visual charm. The specific features of each object according to its kind and nature were, of course, respected; but they seemed to matter less than the relevance of form common to all—as shown by the epithets which bear a common stamp whatever their particular reference.

The same attitude of mind which prompted the use of similes was at work here, in a less pointed, but more diffuse way. It might be defined, in this respect, as a capacity to feel the common consistency of things insofar as they exist in a certain fulness of form. To the contemplative perception of the poet their still composure placed them most naturally in an identical condition of being, within the compass of an identity which was native to the imagery itself. It was as if the principle of the similes was converted and extended into a mode of representation. Rather than a specific parallelism between two given moments we have a general harmony in the setting of each separate object.

Even man-made objects were similarly treated. For they are beautifully wrought and a wonder to look at. It is so, again especially in the *Odyssey*, where we are often shown houses with their interiors. In the palace of Alcinous, for instance, Athena enters the room where Nausicaa is sleeping "like a goddess in feature" and, at either side of her, two maids as beautiful as the Graces, "and the gleaming portals are closed upon them." A detail of the room is thus made a fitting companion to the human inhabitants. Similarly, in the halls, the brazen walls, the enamelled cornice, the doors with their doorposts, lintel, and handle, the chairs with robes laid upon them receive scarcely less attention than the Phaeacian elders who sit there and eat and drink. The herald ushers in the minstrel, brings him the silver-studded chair, places it against the lofty column, hangs the clear-toned lyre on a hook over his head, lays out a beautiful table with food upon it. Likewise, when a guest arrives at a house, the same array of objects is always carefully mentioned and set in its proper place: the chair, the skilfully-worked linen cloth spread over it, a footstool underneath, the lustral water brought in a fine golden jug and poured in a silver basin, the well-polished table set at his side (cf *Od.* 6. 19; 7. 84 ff.). Less princely surroundings are treated in the same way. Such is the dwelling of Eumaeus: its outstanding details gradually come into view, each in its own right—the yard, the hogs and their sties, the dogs, the herdsman himself (cf. *Od.* 14. 5 ff.).

In the portrayal of these objects there is always the sense (expressed or implied) of something good, beautiful, brilliant, well made, perfectly contrived. It is not so much that they are generally found in royal dwellings as that the poet cannot conceive anything except in full relief—just as men and animals are generally represented in their full dimensions or in the vital composition of their parts. Here again the mention of an object at the same time serves to stress some bright point of reference. Thus any piece of Homeric ware—a cup or a tripod, for instance—strikes both the eye and the imagination, suggesting a whole kindred environment. This is why houses are not described in their general plan—there is actually no common word for "house"; the significant details, set side by side, conjure up an idea of the whole.

It might be objected, at this point, that I am reading too much into a mode of representation which is but the mark of a certain style, in that Homer tends to coordinate objects in a row, each in a separate clause, rather than subordinating them in one main sentence. It might be answered that a style is the outcome, not the cause, of a certain view of reality. The main point is to see what is coordinated to what, and for what reason, and in what spirit. In Homer, it is clear, the portrayal of objects each in its own right is inspired by their relevance to an imaginative principle. He knew where to look and what to ignore—how to focus his vision upon the vantage points of reality. At the critical point of contact with the world, the Homeric imagination was able to reproduce it and at the same time reduce it to an essential form.

4

Such an intellectual and imaginative insight had its own sphere. And it gave rise to an original and autonomous interpretation of the world: things appeared in their true contours and, at the same time, brightened by the significance of their form.

But, side by side with poetry, there exists another kind of imagination working on the same object, though on a different level. I refer to the mythological imagination. It is always so, and it must have been particularly so at the time of Homer when, as we may suppose, the religion of nature still held its ground.

Here, then, is a contrast and a concurrence of values which it is not easy to disentangle and isolate. The close relation only serves to make more evident the deep divergence between the two kinds of creativity. Mythology, we might say, is a grosser product of the same mint. Natural shapes, natural events are here likewise imaginatively transformed; but individual thought, whatever was its initial role, plays little part in the further process. Some original intuition, we may guess, dramatized a certain phenomenon in terms of human behavior, as in a simile; but it was not followed up in the same vein, the hold upon genuine perception was lost, and the true vision developed into a fiction, caught as it was in the drift of a popular and hardly personal inventiveness. At such a point curious, grotesque, marvellous details must have prevailed, obscuring the essential and transparent meaning. A random fancifulness replaced imaginative insight—as when a dream develops beyond all bounds some particular feature of a familiar image, something which to our waking intelligence is quite marginal and trivial.

Many a myth, no doubt, would lend itself to such an interpretation. We might suppose, for instance, that a cloud pierced by the slanting rays of the sun was compared to a golden fleece (Aristophanes actually compares clouds to fleeces), and that, hence, in popular fancy, the cloud became a golden ram wafting Phryxus into safety and bringing about the various episodes connected with the Argonauts. Or the image of a seed imprisoned under the earth and budding through the influence of rain and sunlight might have suggested a liberating golden shower, whence the story of Danae immured in her brazen tower, wooed by Zeus in the shape of golden rain, and her subsequent adventures. In such cases a marginal idea suggested but not contained in the original imagery —a ram, an imprisoned body—would have become the central theme and developed in its own way. These particular explanations, however, might be quite wrong and absurd; I mention them merely to elucidate my meaning. Whatever may be the origin of such myths, it is certain that a wayward and exuberant fancy soon broke the lucid form in which a certain event was originally visualized. What had been imagined as a mode of being, as an implication, was now taken literally; and the mental analogies become material transformations. The suggestions inspired by the image thus replaced the image itself, and all point of reference was lost. A meandering vision proliferated in different directions —creative in its own way, but allured by the fascination of varied and distant wonders rather than sustained by the spell of a central theme. Hence the many versions, the lack of a true beginning and end which we usually find in myths.

This waywardness of the mythical mind appears not only in the account of events, but also in the representation of nature. A sense of metamorphosis must have blurred the confines between the different realms or planes of existence: mountains, springs, rivers might be conceived as one with their local gods, or simply as scenes of a divine epiphany. Thus the island of Delos, a conscious witness of Apollo's birth, is transfigured by it, and Mount Cithaeron seems to share in the revelry of Dionysus. In the same spirit, vague associations with images of an animate and personal power might give rise to the conception of incongruous shapes— as in the bull-like appearance of river-gods or the primitive horse-form of Poseidon, the sea-god. Many tales told by Greek and Latin writers have familiarized us with such a process of transformation; but they are, I suppose, reflections of a more primeval and radical vision: nature seen in the identity of a pervasive animation rather than in the distinction of each species and the isolation of each significant form.

Now, Homer, it is clear, lies at the opposite pole. He looked at nature face to face; and the animation of the elements was for him no more than a certain glow or suggestion contained within their natural features. In other words, his vision was poetic rather than mythical. The way he perceived and expressed what he saw is the secret of his art. All we can do, as we have tried, is to look at the details of the execution and mark how the evidence of reality was wrought into the imagery of linguistic expression. It is otherwise, however, at certain points where the poet, forced by the subject matter, had to deal in full with previous mythical representations. These lay outside his world, they were conceived in a spirit quite removed from his own; and, in dealing with them, the identity of his poetry was at stake. In such instances we may realize with special clarity the way in which Homeric poetry approached nature—how it maintained its own character in the face of an alien and unwieldy subject matter. We can observe what caught its interest, what it transformed, what it discarded.

Take, for instance, the Proteus episode in the fourth book of the *Odyssey* (4. 456–7). Here Homer dispatched in only two lines the mythical, flashy episode of Proteus' metamorphoses. What appealed to him was the real nature of the old sea-god conjured up by the wonderful display of the seals emerging from the water and lying down on the shore, bringing to land all the pungent smell of the salt sea. Those amphibians seemed to blend into one vivid natural form the reality of two worlds; and therein for the poet lay the true protean quality. Proteus himself is pictured as an image naturally disengaging itself from its native element, as he comes to view still overshadowed by the darkening ripple of the windswept water. To Homer the terrific transformations of the god were a barren subject, however much they might have stirred the fancy of a primitive or baroque-minded poet. His imagination went its own way, discovering a sensuous significance behind the specious features of the myth, eliciting a subtle ambiguity from the suggestions of form where others could only conceive a succession of changing shapes.

This emphasis on natural, rather than prodigious, wonders may be noticed throughout the wanderings of Odysseus. There are indeed those giant cannibals, the Laestrygonians; but they are disposed of in a very cursory manner. There is the Cyclops, there is Circe with her spells; but these gave the poet the occasion to develop, over and above them, a simple human theme. On the other hand, we are not shown the weird shapes of the Sirens, but only allowed to listen to their beautiful voices; and the sea-monsters "which Amphitrite rears in great number" are kept well under the water.

Uncanny, unnatural occurrences are thus presented almost as a foil to the ingenuity or humanity of Odysseus and his companions. But wherever the scene is set in the world of nature, what stands out is a marvel contained within natural bounds even where the myth would have it otherwise.

The treatment of Scylla and Charybdis is remarkable in this respect. These monsters were landmarks in the wandering of Odysseus; and Circe, in her directions to him, describes them in advance. She insists especially on Scylla, depicting in detail her terrific shape, no doubt following a traditional account (*Od.* 12. 85–110). But it is quite otherwise when it comes to the actual encounter (*Od.* 12. 223–259). Odysseus, expecting to see the fearful adversary, arms himself for the fight; but, standing on the prow, he looks in vain for the monster. His eyes grow weary gazing at Scylla's cliff veiled in mist. There is nothing but the stillness of the rock. Then six men are suddenly snatched away like fish lifted by the pull of a fisherman's rod: all we can see is feet and arms waving in the air, bodies dashed against the stone, hands stretched out in a last appeal to Odysseus. Scylla is, indeed, the agent; but, as a mythical figure, she is almost completely ignored. Her presence is nothing but an expectation and awareness of death; her action is a sudden jerk, a movement of bodies leaping and then falling into the waves to be devoured.

In the same way, "divine Charybdis" lies concealed in her whirlpool. Homer could not visualize her as a monster, but he created a powerful image out of the movement of the water: a seething cauldron as it surges up toward the overhanging cliff, a chasm revealing the dark sand beneath as it circles downwards. This is no fantastic posture, nor is it an ordinary description. We have nothing but a whirling motion developing into a rise and fall whose rhythm seems to acquire a bodily lineament of its own. And where is Charybdis? She is there, but not *in corpore*, only as the active subject of the sentence—a feminine power that sets these movements going and sustains them, unseen, lurking behind them and giving them their animate power.

We may well ask: "What are Scylla and Charybdis? Are they place-names? Or are they, rather, personified powers, divine beings?" None of these things, we might say, and yet all of them at the same time. Monsters do not exist, and yet Scylla and Charybdis are not mere place-names. There is in those places a threatening and deadly presence; unaccountable deities might well live in the depths. It was the poet's achievement to take the myth into account only insofar as its intimations might be absorbed in his rendering of reality.

We might find in such passages an intentional divergence from the mythical data. It is as if the traditional view had been invaded and even replaced by a new strain of feeling. We can only recover it indirectly, or by the aid of external evidence lying outside the imagery itself. But it is not always so. At times the myth was not discarded. It could be rendered in its own terms, for it afforded the poet a material which stimulated him and which, at the same time, he could remodel for his own purposes, bringing it into unison with his customary imagery. The process by which myth was formed was here reenacted, but in a clearer and more intelligible form.

This is eminently the case in the scene where Achilles fights against the river Scamander (*Il.* 21. 211 ff.). As the hero's antagonist, the river had to be presented as a personal agent, as a god engaged in desperate combat. Homer, of course, had no difficulty in conceiving an animate presence in the elements. But here the suggestion of animate power was not enough. The impersonation had to be worked fully into the material, and in such a way that the image of the god was not divorced from its natural element but rather drew sustenance from it. Even in this task, however, Homer did not have to seek modes of expression that were not essentially his own. It was his way, as we have repeatedly seen, to isolate from the surrounding mass some startling feature and let it stand out in solitary, awe-inspiring relief. And a wave was peculiarly capable of being made to appear miraculously real —something driven forward by a sort of self-contained power. Here, then, was a pliant, responsive shape which could be filled with an extraordinary resilience. In order for it to assume a personal aspect, it had to gather momentum and rise to such a pitch of intensity as to give the idea of a struggling body—a mass acquiring an articulate form in the very fervor of its effort. And this is what actually happens. The wave was no longer visualized as a momentary, transient form arising, subsiding, and vanishing into nothing. It stands, it resists, it rebounds and revolves upon itself compressing its fluid substance into a solid mass; and, in so doing, it swells and rages, it leaps and stirs, it strikes and thrusts, as if impelled by some deep-brooding resolution. Achilles is overwhelmed, and, to escape from the river bed, he reaches out to an elm which crashes and brings the whole bank down with it, damming up the water. He can then leap out; and the river overflows in pursuit. The wave overflowing its bank is now unmistakably the god himself. It darkens, it roars in anger—a somber curving shape encompassing its enemy from above and below, as it strikes against his shoulders and washes away the soil from under his feet.

It is the poet's language, no doubt, which is ultimately responsible for this dramatic effect. But the free plastic power of the mythical imagination seems to be transfused into his language. The verbs which express the connotation of the river-god convey at the same time an action and an emerging shape. We read, for instance: "He rushed forward in a boiling surge and roused all his streams in commotion . . . awful, churning within, the wave stood up around Achilles . . . the god did not cease, rose against him in a darkening crest."

The spell of words gradually conjures up the scene and leads it to its climax. Not only is the action, as it develops, instantly solidified and modulated into a sequence of images; but the variation of moods and feelings is represented at one and the same time. Here again, the Homeric verbs can be taken both in a material and a spiritual sense. Such words as "to arise," "stir," "seethe," "rage," "swell" possess vitality. We cannot distinguish in them a literal from a transferred meaning as we might do in a modern language. The motion and the impulse being equally expressed, it is easier to identify the movements of the water with phases of passion and volition, to see in these several acts the signs of a personal will. In translating, for instance, I hesitated whether to render: "He rushed" or "It rushed." No such difficulty arises in the Greek. Those acts are at once natural phenomena and divine personal initiatives.

And yet the language, of course, cannot by itself account for the nature of the scene. We may, therefore, still wonder how the story was conceived, how far the poet was drawing on a theme or a source. There was doubtless the traditional deification of rivers. There was, too, the supple nature of water images which is so appealing to mythology: the love scene of Tyro and Poseidon both enshrouded by the curving wave of the river Enipeus (*Od.* 11. 243–4) might give us a clue. But, above all, there was the reality of the Homeric image—in this case the wave as an image of power. Fashioned as it was through poetic insight, it could not be the sort of motley figure we come across in myth. It had its own form, its own coherence. In this particular case, it proved capable of assimilating to itself the fanciful fictions of myth. Thus the traditional bull-figure ascribed by popular belief to rivers might possibly have been somewhere in the poet's mind when he made the soaring wave low like a bull (*Il.* 21. 237); but for us this is no conceit, it is simply an additional touch which enchances the animate nature of the water. And, similarly, when the voice of the god surges up from the depth in human words, we are not surprised, for the poet has made the watery shape so articulate and sentient that it seems to yearn for expression.

Once this poetic image had gathered into itself the prestige of an ancient myth, it could properly appear as the embodiment of a god. It was now established in its own right; the animate figure could join the fray and face Achilles. Hence the encounter could be developed as one between two warriors, however unusual and awe-inspiring it might appear. The whole scene has the clarity of all other Homeric scenes, but suffused with a sense of mythical power.

Thus at the very beginning of Greek literature, Homer at one stride resolved myth in his own way, treating it not merely in terms of narrative but of imagery. The representation of Achelöus in Sophocles seems much more traditional in the way it accepts the mythical metamorphosis. In Homer, we notice, the river-god never takes a human shape; all we hear is a voice speaking human words—just as the resounding waters suggest the lowing of a bull but never the physical aspect of a bull. When the flood darkens and overflows, the transfiguration seems to reach a breaking point. It is only the stir of troubled waters, but we feel that the suggestion of life could no longer be contained within them and had to break into articulate form. Yet an inescapable bond still keeps the animate substance within its own natural limits—a necessity of supreme importance to the Homeric imagination. The dividing line between matter and form, between physical reality and individual self-assertion is very nearly reached, but is soon resolved into an image which participates in the nature both of man and the elements.

5

At this point the representation of nature touches on the sphere of religion. A feeling of the divine was inherent in the very perception of animate forces at work in natural phenomena; and when such a perception combined with some particular trend of the popular religion, that feeling could crystallize into a conventional belief and find its object of worship in some hypostatized symbol. Here Homeric poetry was no doubt confronted with a whole system of existing religious interpretations—not so much mythology, in this case, as religion itself. The Creto-Mycenean religion of nature—which its scarcely humanized gods and its sense of an undifferentiated natural power manifesting itself in many forms—must have been strong still in Homeric times, as indeed it was much later.

How could Homer remain untouched by it in his comprehensive representation of reality? Insofar as nature presented itself as something familiar—a shore to walk on, water to be cut by the keel of a ship or churned by oars, landmarks offering conspicuous points of reference—it could be rendered in purely visual terms. Here, as we have seen, the Homeric representation of landscape was prompted by an urge to see, to know, to possess, to relate the things perceived with human needs and ideas. But nature also presented a more distant and mysterious side—or, at least, something self-existent, unmastered, an object of awe or fear. In such cases religious belief would intervene, blurring the pure outlines of the human vision, passing them through the filter of its deeply entrenched animism.

Where the overlaid significance was purely mythical and plastically conceived, the Homeric representation could hold its own by imputing to the sensuous details of the material an animate quality. Here the religious implications, if any, were quite carried over into the wonder of forms whose appeal was rather of an aesthetic kind. It was so in the episodes of Scamander or of Scylla and Charybdis, in which the dramatic requirements led the poet to deal boldly and freely with the traditional data. But the matter was more difficult when the god appeared enshrined in his element as an overriding presence. What stood out then was a deity, not an arbitrary mythical image that could be reduced or transformed; and the religious reality had to be taken into account.

Poseidon is a case in point. He is still very close to the sea, and yet he is a major god. As such he can move anywhere and cannot be identified with any particular feature of the seascape. It is as if he had a dual nature—the one quite separate from the other. His epiphany in *Il.* 13. 17 ff. seems to distinguish between these two different aspects. Riding gloriously in his chariot he is indeed a god in human form whose pursuits carry him far away; but, as he passes, the sea opens up in delight, and the brood of the Ocean frolics in enthusiastic revelry around him. The water is struck with a sense of recognition as well as the animals. Nowhere else in Homer is a natural element imbued with so specific a human feeling. But at the same time no mermaid, no Triton emerges to symbolize the sense of an integrated life. That delight remains contained within a natural movement—the sea is gathered in a massive wave that splits the waters apart, the fish leap up as if driven by a shudder of joy.

This was Homer's way of responding to the religion of the sea. The image of water stirred by a sense of joy is not a trope. A movement of this sort is a sign of things coming alive, a pulse, an exultation. There is an almost mystical atmosphere in the picture: words like "beauty," "splendor," "magnificence" do not even occur and we are left wondering at a scene which is not described but dramatically rendered as a mysterious emergence of life.

The god himself, on the other hand, does not have any part in this commotion. He is only there for a moment. Although his traditional haunt is the sea, he is travelling way from it, engaged in a purely human quest. It is as if he had just been given human form and divorced from his primeval home. He is not quite humanized yet in character, not as articulate as Athena or Apollo; but he is decidedly a personal god who stands on his own—as he will do before long when he appears before the walls of Troy.

The perception of nature was thus followed up in its logical implications. A mind like Homer's, so keen in eliciting the structure of things, could not admit any forced alteration of natural appearances. The distinctive forms of each species and natural element appeared as a basic articulation of existence. Pervasive harmonies existed no doubt, they were just as true, but true on a different level—as essences discovered by the mind rather than literal facts. Religion, no less than mythology, had to accord with this basic attitude. Once conceived as persons, the gods could not but appear in a completely human aspect even when (like Poseidon) they were deeply associated with a natural element; and the elements, on the other hand, however penetrated with divine life, could not be visualized in any hybrid shape, but only in the shape that accorded with their nature.

This might seem a commonplace classification. But it is not really so. Even the most obvious natural objects are always mysteriously suggestive to the poetic mind; and they must have been doubly so at a time when they revealed themselves heavy with religious awe. It was therefore no small task to render nature in a spirit of truth and yet take into account the divine which lay embedded in it. How could the gods be removed from their haunts and their presence still be felt as an enriching quality?

The ground upon which the Homeric action takes place is richly supplied with such haunts. Below and around the heroes and the humanized gods, the land and sea—if we look at them closely—present scenes whose suggestiveness seems the echo of a divine presence. Thus the Mother-goddess is in Homer forgotten or ignored, but the earth is constantly represented as a divine, life-giving power. There are no mountain-gods, but a mountain is the mother of wild beasts, it shakes, it feeds its springs, it quivers in the foliage of its forests. There are no tree deities, but trees have high-wrought epithets no less than gods or heroes; and the palm tree which Odysseus once saw in Delos stands out in magnificent relief quite detached from the shrine of Apollo, but it is its sacred character which makes it beautiful and makes it a fit simile for the beauty of Nausicaa.

Moreover, Homer took over in his poetry the Mycenaean custom of open-air shrines. This is significant; for it implies the idea of a place which is naturally possessed by a god in contrast with the temple artificially designed to be his, or her, abode. Such a spot owned its holiness to some striking feature—a perpetually flowing spring, for instance, the shady depth of a grove, or the mysterious atmosphere of a cave. Homer knew the spell of such places. In Ithaca, Scheria, and elsewhere, we find caves and rocks where the nymphs rest and dance. Here the imagery of luscious trees, grass, deep hollows, ever-flowing waters is enough by itself to suggest the presence of deep-rooted pieties.

The case of the nymphs by the harbor of Phorkys in Ithaca is slightly different, for it occupies a central position in the *Odyssey* and the poet had to emphasize it (*Od.* 13. 96 ff.). These nymphs were rooted in the earth; they embodied, as it were, the sanctity of the island; and it is to them that Odysseus addresses a prayer after kissing his native soil. A kindly influence might be expected to emanate from the land itself, from powers so naturally enshrined in the mysterious recesses of a cave overlooking the harbor mouth. What would the poet do? Would the nymphs appear as goddesses in human shape, or would they be so identified with the place as to lurk invisibly behind its natural features? From the Homeric point of view there could be no doubt. It is Athena, the most articulate of goddesses, who in Ithaca as elsewhere greets and aids Odysseus. Those nymphs belonged absolutely to the place, they had to be treated as one with the cave and the rocks. Homer could not give them a vicarious life apart from their native ground; and, here again, the problem of bodily form was solved in accordance with the principles of his art.

What makes the place so remarkable and its poetry so striking is, in fact, the absence of these Naiads and, at the same time, the intimation of their imaginary presence. How did Homer achieve this effect? Not by conjuring up a dark mysterious atmosphere, but by reading into the pure shape of the stone an imagery of life. For the hollows here become mixing-bowls, amphorae; the tapering stony pinnacles become the beams of looms; the reflections of stalactites or the colorful interplay of light and shade become sea-purple robes; and the nymphs are supposed to use these implements, to weave these robes, when no human eye is there to look at them. Human objects, human activities are thus transposed and embodied into the patterns of nature; they cease to be human, they become elements in a primordial process, while the rock seems to acquire a form and a meaning. For what goes on in the cave is no casual task, but a work eternally renewed. A crowning feature is the honey stored here by the bees—again the sign of a restless production that seems spontaneously drawn from nature.

The animistic experience by which the cave became a shrine was here experienced anew, but also, somehow, surpassed. For us, at least, what matters is the beauty of the place and not its religious significance. The same might be said about the "delight" of the sea as it opens up at the passage of Poseidon. Did Homer really believe in those pieties? We cannot give an answer, of course; but there is in his attitude a sort of contemplative reverence which is different from modern aesthetic perceptiveness. It is as if he stood on the threshold of purely poetic visual experiences—like one who has discovered a new land and yet carries with him the strength of ancient attachments.

Awe and wonder thus precipitated the sense of beauty in nature. Homer felt the loveliness of a natural scene as a mysterious presence inherent in the forms of things, as a spell to be suggested but scarcely expressed. It is remarkable how he avoided coloring his visual impressions or even qualifying any general view as "beautiful." He usually applied such an attribute to man-made objects, as being well made, or to a plant for its luxuriance, and not so much to persons as to their perfect limbs and bodily features. It was otherwise when he turned his eye further afield. Here nature appeared concentrated in moments of tension to be dramatically rendered, or in silently expressive shapes to be visualized rather than interpreted, leaving no room for description.

The wider connotations of the beautiful were, therefore, part of nature—divined in its structures and not arbitrarily imputed here and there. Hence what we may call the "picturesque" was quite absent from the Homeric landscape. We do not find any grouping of charming natural images designed to evoke a certain atmosphere. Beauty was not something "given," a well-established, familiar value characterizing this or that place, this or that image. Everything, in a sense, was beautiful, insofar as it was a fully developed form. Here the real needed no setting, no environment. It appeared self-sufficient, self-justifying. A cave, a mountain, a spring —each was a self-contained vision; and no ornament could enhance the spell of its presence.

IV

Time and Life in Homer

The action of the Homeric poems takes place outside the bounds of historical chronology. A drama is here enacted whose antecedents sink back into an obscure mythical past and whose sequel bears no relevance to the actual story. The characters are thus caught, as it were, in an absolute moment of existence, their past almost forgotten, their destiny immediately at stake once and for all. To Sarpedon, for instance, neither his descent from Zeus nor the future mean anything when he tells Glaucus: "If, o my friend, away from this war we could ever live without old age, without death, neither would I be foremost in fighting nor would I send you to the battle where men win glory; but now, whatever we do, the spirits of death press upon us in thousands, not to be escaped or avoided by any mortal; let us then go, whether we triumph on others or others on us" (*Il*. 12. 322 ff.). Life here flickers for a moment and thereby forces a sense of urgency, a need to live and to act in the instant; an immortal existence, on the other hand, would stretch out in an indefinite series of days unaffected by any tension or crisis that might endanger it. Time is thus implicitly envisaged in its human dimension—as a span of individual experience, quite apart from any sublimation on a mythical level. It marks off a vital, crucial moment—a certain action that must be realized, a commitment that must be made good, an immediate achievement. Before and after hardly exist, blank ages that can scarcely be imagined or accounted for.

This position of the Homeric heroes between two voids is the symptom of a newly acquired humanity: they are children of the gods, but shut off from the divine world; they are men, but not merged as yet into the common stream of history. What is in question is not so much a trait of their character as their human identity. They are what they are insofar as they realize a present issue—how time runs short under the stress of what must be done and achieved for an overriding personal motive. It is as if their individualities gathered shape all at once from a sudden confrontation with reality and not gradually through succeeding and overlapping experiences.

It is so especially in the *Iliad*. Hector is driven to action and to death by a searching concern, his last days winding up the story of his whole life. Achilles is no less committed: anger and grief plunge him into the thick of a fatal action which, brief as it is, marks him as a man. A vital need to act speeds these dramas to their conclusion; and what happens needs no other justification, emerging on its own account irrespective of myth and history. Even the war as a whole is left out of sight, its general causes and consequences irrelevant to the poem. All that matters is the single clash, the single encounter; and such heroes as Ajax, Diomedes, Idomeneus only prove themselves in central instances where life is at stake.

So placed and contained in the actual moment of experience, an individual has no other frame of reference but that of the world at large. Ancestral glories or the thought of future generations hardly come into the picture. Achilles would disavow his divine lineage; and similarly Aeneas regards his genealogy from Zeus as a futile tale. Asteropaeus is a descendant of the river Axios; he dares withstand Achilles, and being asked who he is, "Why do you ask my lineage?" he replies with a sense of final detachment. In the same way Glaucus answers Diomedes, adding the now famous comparison between the generations of men and those of leaves. Such instances are remarkable in an age that must have laid so much store on tradition, on legendary genealogies, on tribal history. A new spirit seems to breathe here, removing the layers of emblazoned pride and baring the reality of life.

Homer thus represents the exalted heroes of a mythical past as men who are about to die. On the one hand, a divine halo; and, on the other, a helpless human brittleness. Time seems thereby set in motion to impair and recompose those compact antique images. "Nothing that the earth rears is weaker than man," says Odysseus (*Od.* 18. 130). "All too many, one after the other, day after day, they fall. . . . Bury we must whomsoever dies, steeling our heart, weeping him for one day" (*Il.* 19. 226 ff.). While the epithets of the single heroes often point to a superhuman state ("divine," "similar to the gods," "nurtured by Zeus," "dear to Zeus"), the epithets of man in general convey his ephemeral nature ("mortal," "bread-eating," "earth-creeping," "miserable" etc.). It could not have been otherwise. The underlying contradiction was implied in the subject matter—in the human theme which could not but use, to express itself, a hallowed imagery coming from the past.

Now, in the outward presentation of the characters, it was natural to preserve the heroic apparel; but this was impossible in the conception of the drama itself. Here the rejection of the mythical illusion had to be complete: how else could the action develop in its own right from beginning to end? It would have lacked its essential earnestness, if it did not proceed according to a tension of its own, as an effort that sustained and consumed itself. Such action, therefore, spells out its own time. Certain characters, of course, are there to carry it out; but, in turn, it conditions them to the logic of its trends and the necessities of its duration. As we read, we realize how the succession of events is kept in focus. Everything seems to find its place in a forward movement which does not admit deviations or intervals: the characters have no existence outside the action, the action no scope outside the present perspective; and all emotion, all thought is the reflection of what is actually happening.

This isolation in time appears all the more striking if considered, as it were, from a metaphysical point of view: not only in relation to other ages or events, but in the light of what the characters themselves believe concerning their destinies and, more particularly, their future state. For such beliefs might, by their very presence, attenuate the purport of what is at stake in the present. Thus, for instance, in the *Oresteia* of Aeschylus crime and counter-crime appear as stages toward a happier state conceived in conformity with human or divine morality, and Pindar's heroes know about a glorious future in the Elysian isles. In Homer, on the other hand, there is no idealization of existence, let alone any future reward. In his age the Mycenaean centers had long been destroyed together with those local pieties which (as the remains show) perpetuated the lives of kings and heroes beyond the grave; and a new sense of death as an all-encompassing doom had now risen, Hades gathering the whole world's dead in an inane survival which was nothing but regret for the warmth of life. The practice of incineration seems the outer symptom of such an idea. "This is the way of mortals whenever they die," explains Anticlea to Odysseus, "no longer do the sinews hold the flesh and the bones, but the might of burning fire subdues them . . . and the phantom flits away like a dream" (*Od.* 11. 218 ff.). Hence an elusive thinness dissolving into nothing: Achilles would embrace the ghost of Patroclus, but it vanishes like smoke under the earth. A dream, smoke—before such images the living are abandoned to their fond delusion, to their human solitude. They are firmly set on their feet for a moment, but on the edge of a void. For the Homeric heroes this permanence in the world is, literally, a matter of today and tomorrow; the full momentary experience has for them a sort of absolute finality.

But this is not all. There exists among men another form of sublimation—that which consists in posthumous glory. It also provides, in a different way, a compensation for what seems so elusive in the present—especially so when it is concerned with the destiny of a whole people or with a cause that must be upheld at all costs. This is notably so in a poem like the *Aeneid*. But, again, in Homer we find no such diversion. In the *Odyssey* the struggle of Odysseus is very much a personal issue, however loaded it may be with a sense of right and wrong. The situation in the *Iliad* is similar. Troy has no future, its doom a dark foreboding even at the moment of the fighting. As for the Achaeans, they do not really strive for any cause (it cannot be the revenge on Paris which is not treated as a fundamental motive); their tribes do not cohere into a single nation whose fortunes are extolled; there is no national pride; there is no city-state to honor them when they are dead. It is important, in this respect, that the reasons of the war should be so paltry—a question of robbery, almost. This leaves the individual quite to himself. What concerns him is something immediate: a boon to be presently won or lost, a sudden escape or annihilation.

Seen in such a light, each deed appears mercilessly bared of all superstructure. Its recognition is not the glory enshrined in future history, but an immediate report or impression. Fame here comes quite naturally from any remarkable event insofar as it happens and it is witnessed. This is, in fact, the meaning of the word "glory," *kleos*, in Homer. Its etymological sense—"hearsay," "what is told and heard"—seems to cling to it: in several passages it simply means "news" (*Il.* 11. 21; 13. 364; *Od.* 16. 461; 23. 137; etc.)—a meaning which merges into that of fame, as when Telemachus expresses his quest of Odysseus saying: "I am after the wide-ranging renown of my father, if ever I hear" (*Od.* 3. 83). Such is the quality of an action recorded far and wide, made into a tale or a theme for poetry, like the one sung by Demodochus, "whose fame at the time reached the sky" (*Od.* 8. 74); or, again, a similar repercussion may come from any significant object when observed and admired, as in the words of Hector: "One day some of the future men sailing on his well-benched ship over the wine-dark sea will say: 'That mound over there is of a man that died long ago, one of the bravest whom valiant Hector has slain.' So shall someone say; and my glory shall never die" (*Il.* 7. 89 ff.). The "glories" of men, the *klea andron*, are nothing but accounts of their deeds. Such accounts, transmitted from age to age, become a pale reflection of what once happened in all its fulness: an "echo" we might say; and even so we might translate the word when the poet, appealing to the Muses for help in the record of past events, says: "for it is only the echo we hear and we know nothing" (*Il.* 2. 486).

Similarly the synonymous word *kydos* implies a "glory" which is one and all with the achievement itself or with the object which suggests it. It is the victory granted by a god (as in the typical phrase "Zeus gave him *kydos*"); or it is a matter of pride, an object of delight such as the headpiece of *Il.* 4. 145 which is "an ornament for the horse and *kydos* for the charioteer." Likewise it may be a certain spell or prestige visible in a man, in the living and not in the dead, as when Hecuba says over the corpse of Hector: "You were *kydos* to the Trojans while you lived, but now death is upon you" (*Il.* 22. 435). In this last sense it is no other than the aura surrounding a god when enthroned in his majesty, rejoicing in his glory (*kydei gaion*).

The fame or splendor of persons and things is thus never hypostatized. A sense of immediate evidence always sustains and justifies it. It follows that events yield instantly their message. We have before us a comprehensive presence: nothing happens but has its repercussion, just as an image has its shadow. So the wrath of Achilles is at once set forth in itself and in its fateful effects; the mere appearance of a character, or a word from his lips, is enough to stir up tremendous wonder, or hope, or discomfiture, as the case may be. All value judgments, all reasons for regret or gratification are here the direct outcome of a concrete occasion, not terms for a distant future reference.

Even the gods seem to underline this human moment. For their chief concern is what happens to a hero in some crucial moment of his life, not the destinies of cities and nations nor any holy place or any particular sphere of the natural world. Being quite anthropomorphic and humanized, they are made into characters and detached, therefore, from their ancient associations with nature or with tribal cults. Neither a royal abode nor a shrine can now retain them any longer. They have become wanderers in a world of unpredictable events, moving far and wide in response to a human need. Such is Thetis when she mourns for Achilles; such is Zeus when he sheds tears of blood for Sarpedon; such is Apollo when he must abandon Hector to his fate. What will they do, once the human drama which they took so much to heart is past, once their favorite heroes are dead? We are not told. Back in Olympus they must indulge, we presume, in their timeless revelry, or find others upon whom to bestow their care. For they have nothing to say about the future of an age or a people. Their immortality appears at times as a mere absence of death, an inability to die. All the more complete, on the other hand, is their absorption in a present issue. We are made aware of it at the opening of both the *Iliad* and the *Odyssey:* the attention of all the gods—and thus, in a way, the attention of the cosmos—seems riveted upon a scene of passion and upon the return homeward of a lonely man. Other parts of the world hardly play a role, other experiences of other times are almost ignored; and, in such a perspective, the action stands out massively, gaining in present relevance what it loses in temporal extension.

In no other work of literature that I know of is there such a concentration of human and superhuman powers upon single acts. In Greek lyric poetry, for instance, individual experiences are strongly portrayed, but they evaporate into idealizations of love, time, and other human values. In Greek tragedy the power of fate all but submerges personal initiatives which are viewed within the compass of broad sweeping vicissitudes. In the Latin poets the glory and destiny of Rome impinge on the subject matter introducing a perspective of centuries which is like an outline of human history. And then Christianity brought into poetry and life a transcendental vision, a pervasive subjective craving for what is not, a view of things *sub specie aeternitatis*. In all such instances different worlds are conjured up in which the single everyday acts lose their immediate physical relevance, merging into a synthesis and concurring to make up a sublimated image of life, whether as an ideal in itself or as serving some supernal purpose.

In Homer, on the other hand, the human event is never idealized. If anything, it is stylized—that is to say, it is caught in a native rhythm of its own, in a form which it most consistently takes, in a typical pattern, quite apart from the circumstances and quite apart from its greatness, nobility, worth, dignity. What matters is the way it affects a man in body and mind. It is treated as an occurrence in nature, having its own inevitable duration; and, as such, it is essentially the same in one or the other hero, essentially the same in man and other animals—whence the many similes drawn from animal life. Its intrinsic dimensions cannot, therefore, be altered—shortened or broadened to fit into a superimposed design; and time is nothing else but the measure of an actual process, identical with it, not mentioned as a separate entity.

This is true not only of the single acts, but of the plot as a whole. For the story itself is conceived as a concurrence of simultaneous or successive acts which, by their own dynamism, draw to a natural conclusion. Various efforts are thus gathered into one massive tension which hastens to spend itself. Such a forward movement appears irreversible, inevitable as soon as it is set loose. As a reply follows hard upon a question or a summons, so deed follows hard upon deed by a logic which is embedded in the nature of things. It was the genius of Homer thus to isolate the human action and to see it in its dynamic pattern—as a self-existing phenomenon emerging from the stress of interrelated moves and maturing as quickly as the human organism might allow, unhampered by alien circumstances or by secondary motives.

It is, therefore, the cumulative impact of separate moments which here spans out the whole lapse of time. In the *Iliad*, for instance, the interval between the withdrawal of Achilles and his return is made up by a series of strokes and counter-strokes leading to the defeat of the Achaeans. Reduced to a strictly chronological sequence, such happenings are nothing but a flimsy episode of war taken out of its historical context; but, represented as they are in the full stress of each effort, they seem to set forth from moment to moment the occasions of the same vital process. What strikes us is here the very act of resistance or attack, the very dynamics of movement. And, as the action goes on, we are made aware how this mechanical interplay is imbued with a continuous purpose, how the sum total of all these instances traces out a cycle of experience—from agony to recovery, or the reverse. Time is then the heartbeat of the effort at hand; and, in its wider ranges, it is the indispensable cadence whereby an undertaking can achieve its own end.

A simple act caught in its climax and anticlimax—such, then, seems the kernel whence the Homeric poems drew their first movement. But it is an act which rebounds in its human implications as well as in its volume. As it gathers momentum, it prefigures a whole world of complex values; and yet we cannot forget that everything hangs together on the strength of one sweep that drives to its conclusion. Hence the story bears a clear human message; and, at the same time, it appears curiously self-contained, homeless, and ageless. It is as if time resided in the vortex of that action, and of that action alone.

2

We may wonder, now, at this isolation of the action. How far is it possible or conceivable? Can any story be told as if its incidents took place entirely by themselves, in their own time, out of relation with any definite period? This is possible, obviously, in a fairy tale: its suggestion of "once upon a time" establishes a start-

ing point for any train of events. It is so, again, in a myth: there is
a timeless permanence in its images, not the transience of human
characters that live out their experience; a mythical account often
takes the form of an apologue, of an allegory, of an example whose
significance is symbolic. What is recorded as a true event, on the
other hand, naturally falls into a historical perspective, as part of a
general process.

But Homer does not seem to fit into any of these modes of representation. His story lacked the wayward fancifulness of a tale,
or the bulky imagery of a myth, or the temporal dimensions of
history. It presented itself as pure action, as an event in itself and
by itself. And yet it could not be abstracted or conceived in a void.
Acts so powerfully perceived had to be solidly implanted upon the
ground and under the sky. It could not be enough to show them in
their own solitary development. Like everything else in the world,
they too had to fall into their relative positions, subjected to an
inevitable "here" and "there," "now" and "then," "before" and
"after." In default of myth or history or a fantastic illusion, it was
nature itself that provided here the necessary measure of duration,
spelling out the succession of the single separate days that break
out upon the world as well as upon a particular action.

We are touching here upon a different aspect of time—not the
inner measure of each individual act, but a broader measure that
contains all acts, deeds, events as they occur at a given moment.
Such is in Homer the time of nature. Its basic unit is the day.
Everything in the *Iliad* and in the *Odyssey* must happen on a certain day (or night), finding in it its necessary span. This term of
reference marks the stages of the action and binds it to the world.
Without it the single moments of human experience might seem
to pass into a sphere of their own, as in a vision. No such need is
felt in a history or a novel: time and life are here surveyed as in a
bird's view, and only a few scenes are treated dramatically as
taking place on a certain day. It is the opposite in Homer: the
single scenes make up the whole, relying on their own strength;
and, in order to be enacted, they need the surrounding day as a
breathing space.

It thus happens that a certain number of days frames the action of both poems; and these days can actually be counted. In the *Iliad* the plague, occasioning the action, lasts nine days; on the tenth Achilles summons the assembly; here the scene of the wrath flares up instantly; he withdraws, and the response of Zeus to his need comes twelve days later; then a week of intensive battle leading to the defeat of the Achaeans and Achilles' return; finally Hector's death, his ransom after twelve days, and his funeral on the tenth day from thence. Similarly in the *Odyssey*: the first five days are covered by Telemachus' quest for his father; on the dawn of the next the gods decide to speed up Odysseus' return; it takes him five days to build his raft and make ready in Calypso's isle, another twenty to sail and reach Scheria; he stops there three days; taken to Ithaca on the following morning, he wins back his household and this action lasts six days. (Cf. *Il.* 1. 54, 493; 2. 48; 7. 421; 8. 1; 11. 1; 19. 1; 23. 226; 24. 413, 695, 785; *Od.* 2. 1; 3. 1, 404, 491; 4. 306; 5. 1, 228, 263, 279, 390; 6. 48; 8. 1; 13. 18, 93; 15. 56, 189, 495; 17. 1; 20. 91; 23. 347.)

Such a series of days might seem quite arbitrary, conventional. It might, in fact, be increased or decreased, and the change would not affect the significance of the plot. What matters is not so much the number of days and nights as their presence. The poet reminds us of it constantly—not for the sake of chronology, but because his representation of the action requires it. A happening must be visualized in its full contours—taking into account its span of natural time just as much as the bare ground on which it takes place. The day is the light, the atmosphere which makes it possible. Nothing can live without it.

The day and the night are, therefore, often named as divine presences. Every reader is familiar with the rose-fingered, saffron-robed Morn or with the immortal Night. Daybreak and nightfall come as a heavenly counterpoint to wakefulness and sleep, activity and rest. They do not so much measure the length of time as the company which the elements bear to the human action. Darkness and light become signals, not mere phenomena. What matters is not only their succession, but their actual coming and going, their waxing and waning, whence the picture of passing time appears as concrete as that of an hourglass and as encompassing as the air or the sky.

In several passages this relation between the time of nature and human acts is dramatically rendered. Thus in *Il.* 11. 84: "As long as the Morn was lasting and the sacred day was growing, so long the spears were alighting and the men were falling; but at such time as the forester prepares his meal in some mountain-glen, weary in his arms . . . surfeited in mind, his heart beset with desire for sweet food, then the Danaans broke the opposing ranks." Or in *Il.* 8. 485: "Down in the Ocean sank the bright light of the sun, drawing black night over the nourishing earth. Unwished came the sunset to the Trojans, but most welcome, much implored the dark night fell on the Achaeans." (Cf. *Il.* 8. 66; 16. 777; 7. 433, 465; 18. 241; *Od.* 4. 574; 12. 439.)

The day thus contains the action, holds it in suspense, sways its course, while the night bids it pause. In this respect both night and day are divine powers. They impose a measure that cannot be broken. "Cease fighting," says the herald to Hector and Ajax, "the night is now falling, the night must be obeyed" (*Il.* 7. 282; cf. 11. 194; 17. 455; 18. 267; *Od.* 12. 291).

Time so conceived is visualized rather than thought of. Embodied in the stars and in the sun, in darkness and in light, it covers impartially the actions of men, and nothing impairs the regularity of its rhythm. So at each closing stage of Telemachus' journey, "the sun sinks and shadows fall on all the streets" (*Od.* 2. 388; 3. 487, etc.); so as the suitors put an end to their daily pursuit "dark evening falls upon their merry-making" (*Od.* 1. 423; 18. 306). The passing moment thus seems gathered into a pervasive presence; and time acquires, as it were, a spatial dimension. So we read "to walk through the divine night" instead of "at nighttime"; and, similarly, "to sail together with the night," "to come, to go together with the rising or the setting sun." Night, in particular, is felt as a swift, deep, encompassing mass. Hector, for instance, is said to have turned back "when night enshrouded him" (*Il.* 10. 201); Apollo attacks the Achaeans with his arrows advancing "like the night" (*Il.* 1. 47).

We might, now, still wonder at this extensive stress on natural time. It marks, as we have seen, the place and moment of each event; but the poet seems to linger on the presence of these days and nights, suggesting their influence and power, not only underlining their inevitable recurrence. They belong to a sphere of their own, extrahuman and changeless: why, then, are they a constant theme in a poem which is so deeply concerned with a human action? What is their general relevance to the poem as a whole? Here again the reason lies in the very way of apprehending time and existence. Just as the single scenes had to take place on a certain day or night, so the whole action of the poems had to fall into a basic world-wide rhythm. For the days and nights compose the seasons and the life of nature. To Homer they must have had this full significance. He could not treat them as a matter of course. The Homeric poems thus point to an existence which runs on a deep elemental level. Its smooth, constant flow is wholly different from the fitful drift of human actions, and yet it is an indispensable premise to all personal initiative.

Homer makes us constantly aware of such a fundamental condition. Indeed we have sometimes the impression that the whole human action is something secondary, happening on the surface, fed by a vital source that lies deep in the very entrails of nature. Bearing this in mind we may better appreciate the many Homeric scenes which over and again stress the moments of eating, drinking, sleeping, waking. In the same way as we are presented with the recurring sensuous scenery of night and day, we are also told the punctual, rhythmical occasions whereby man's life is harnessed, renewed, restored for its continued subsistence. No dramatic urgency can dispose the poet from emphasizing such fundamental needs. "Let us obey the dark night, and make ready for the meal," Nestor tells the routed Achaeans (*Il.* 9. 66), and they lay their hands upon the laid-out victuals till they have their fill of food and of drink. It is so throughout the poems. The often repeated Homeric phrases seem to echo the phases of a natural cycle; and, out of their particular toils, men are thus cast back into a native state that is common to all. Likewise, at night, sleep falls upon them irresistibly, plunging them into a sphere of its own which is like a wonderful region rather than an interval of time. Presently, in the morning, they wake and dress up to their tasks— as if roused for no particular reason, but simply because of the way things are in the order of nature.

This strong feeling for the days and for the life which they enclose accounts for the perfect stillness and almost timeless atmosphere which we find in the poems whenever the moments of tension subside and people, or things, simply exist in themselves and by themselves. Men and women seem then immune from all hazard, as solid and whole in their natural life as a full-grown tree. It is so especially in the *Odyssey*. Nausicaa when visited by Athena, Nestor with his people, or Menelaus with his kinsmen when approached by Telemachus, Alcinous with his elders when called upon by Odysseus—all these are caught unawares, as it were, and introduced to the reader in a casual moment of their daily lives; and yet they are ever represented in one of the aforesaid essential natural functions, sleeping or banqueting and libating as they are about to retire for the night. Once introduced, they pursue their natural existence to the next morning, when again they bestir themselves to their allotted tasks. That is to say, they do not appear at random or whimsically, but immersed in the life of the world, in the life of each and all, which is real, compelling, immediate, and yet also ageless, ever true to itself.

Life so viewed seems religiously inspired. Each one of its stages comes solemnly, inevitably, as in a ritual. The lustral water, the banquet with its sacrifice, the libation, the omens which occur— all this reminds us of the gods. And accordingly the day is sacred (cf. *Od.* 9. 56; *Il.* 8. 66; 11. 84); the night is very often divine, immortal, ambrosial (*Od.* 4. 429, 574, etc.); Zeus sends the days over the world (*Od.* 12. 399; 15. 477; 18. 137); and to Zeus belong the seasons, the years (*Il.* 2. 134). Under this influence things happen and the fruits of the earth come to ripeness (cf.: *Od.* 24. 344).

We might retrace this sacred aspect of time to the Creto-Mycenaean religion of nature. For what suggested this sacred quality was a feeling for the primordial rhythms which govern the course of existence. Hence emerged day and night with their constant spell; and a corresponding picture of human life, with each of its characteristic moments assuming a destined and ever-recurring form. Homer, at any rate, could still feel the wonder of these natural phases and see them in a vital relation with experience.

3

The natural aspect of time is in Homer quite fundamental. But over and against it there is the human action which breaks out in its dynamic development. Here then we find an unavoidable contrast: on the one hand the smooth uniform passage of the days and seasons, on the other the lapses and stresses of a drama which runs to its conclusion.

This contrast, it is clear, yields two distinct notions of time: the time of nature objectively perceived and the time of individual subjective experience. But in Homer such a basic distinction is never emphasized for its own sake, never carried over into a theme of conflicting ideas and emotions; for the day is like a physical element keeping the action in focus, and even the most soaring human visions remain bound up with a material occasion. Since Homer, on the other hand, human introspection has worn out the natural foundations which conditioned the sense of time. Our very mode of thought, in this respect, has taken a new turn: opposing the ephemeral to the eternal, the particular to the universal, the finite to the infinite, we have overlaid experience with metaphysical values; and, in so doing, we have come to translate the immediate into a transient feeling, nature into a dream of eternity, transfiguring the one and the other with a metaphorical glow. It is remarkably so in the narrative art: while giving an accurate description of succeeding events, we may freely ignore them for a while and submerge them in an imaginative vision stretching far beyond them into the past or the future. Already in Pindar a lyrical strain seems to suspend the heroes in the arms of a destiny which runs from age to age; and the characters of Greek tragedy, once they have played their role, appear quite transposed by the Chorus and presented in a different sphere alongside with the images of ancient myth. Even more, through the Bible, a sense of human history has replaced the patterns of nature, casting its shadow across the world, so that even the most factual epics of modern times seem but phases of a greater and universal drama.

Now, in Homer, the sense of the transient and of the permanent are quite steeped in the actual picture. For these two aspects of time are like different rhythms running through each Homeric scene—the one imparting the quick movement of action, the other fixing it as a point in the perpetual natural flux. Being hardly decipherable in conceptual terms, they are all the more ingrown into the subject matter. It could not be otherwise, the Homeric characters being what they are—images that speak or act *there* and *then* powerfully implanted in their present state, while at the same moment a human passion carries them far along the paths of memory or of hope. "Would that I were ageless and immortal through the length of all days, exalted like Athena and Apollo, as truly as this day is bearing woe to the Achaeans," cries Hector (*Il.* 8. 539 ff.); and a craving for eternal happiness can only be expressed, indirectly, through the fervor of a triumphant moment. "Would that on the day my mother begot me, an evil blast of wind had carried me away . . . before all these things could have happened," says Helen (*Il.* 6. 345 ff.); and her bright presence seems to carry in itself the shadow of her past. It is always so in Homer. His heroes, but recently removed from a mythical setting and still partaking in the life of nature, seem suddenly made articulate. Their recollections and premonitions are not occasional wanderings of the mind, but signs of their coming alive, tokens of a discovered identity under the compulsion of a present instance.

The sense of natural time is thus continually suggested by the way the characters are presented within the compass of a certain day, in successive scenes which proceed without interruption just as the morning turns to noon and the evening to night. Each scene is a frame; but the human acts enclosed within it bubble with all the movements of life—with a sense of development, of beginning and ending, of climax and anticlimax. Here the measure of time appears quite different. As we consider what is actually happening, the hour or the day does not matter; everything seems to take place in an absolute time of its own, and we wonder: can such transitions of victory and defeat be so quickly realized? Can the chances of life and death be met so suddenly, with all they entail of hope and despair, of suspense and constancy? In point of hours or days, each scene is most brief, out of proportion with the magnitude of the issues involved; and yet it presents the full reality of what is happening: vital organs exhausted or restored, a rise and fall of bodies and spirits, a deed just realized or a word just uttered, and yet both decisive, fateful, irrevocable.

How shall we account for this illusion of a long-sustained effort within the fraction of a day? Why is it that Homer did not feel the need to prolong the action in accordance with what we might call chronological probability? It is that the human drama appeared as a phenomenon to his concrete vision. It had to have its daylight evidence. All tension was thus contained in the visual and tangible occurrence, suggested in a sort of immediate wholeness. Rather than a story that proceeds step by step in its probable course we have then a series of separate scenes, each one rehearsing the same essential theme; and their cumulative movement produces a massive effect, as of an event whose rhythm could be endlessly pursued beyond any chronological limit.

This is true of the fighting scenes which make up so large a part of the *Iliad*. The battling which intervenes between Achilles' withdrawal and his return only lasts three days; but, except for a few peaceful episodes, it runs through books two to seventeen of the *Iliad* with such an encompassing alternation of fortunes that it suggests a whole cycle of experience. For the succession of advances and retreats is so persistent in its rhythm as to become almost symbolic: that interplay of motion against motion seems to give an abstract of what happens in the vicissitudes of life. But the scales of Zeus shift impredictably; it is some remarkable individual effort that at some unforeseen moment forces a change and initiates a new movement. This interdependence of opposing forces thus ceases to be mechanical, the battle sways with all the energies at a man's disposal: victories and defeats are instances of recovery and failure, of resistance and frustration. Only through such crucial stages does the reversal take place that finally leads to Achilles' return.

Now, how long can such tensions endure? Homer gives us no realistic reckoning. An attack which is checked, a rout which is retrieved, an effort which is sustained to the point of exhaustion—such events are portrayed for their own sake, unrelated to anything else that might show how long they last. Their only term of reference is the day, the light of day which must necessarily shine upon them as they occur in a full visual display; and that day, though real, becomes an imaginary point of time strained to the utmost by its human load.

The imagery of the battle scenes enhances this want of realistic chronology by riveting our attention to the act in itself and by itself. Hector's rapid appearances are like those of the dog-star fitfully appearing through the clouds (*Il.* 11. 62 ff.); his impact is that of a full-blown storm (Ibid. 297 f.); Ajax's advance evokes that of an overflowing river (Ibid. 492 ff., cf. 5. 87). Similarly the Achaeans move forward "as when on the resounding shore the waves of the sea surge one after the other under the stir of the wind" (*Il.* 4. 422). Later the Trojans rally with Ares steeping the battlefield in the shadow of night (*Il.* 5. 506); and the Achaeans resist "like clouds which Zeus in the windless air sets upon the summits of mountains, motionless" (Ibid. 522 ff.). Such examples are numerous. The natural phenomenon seems to transpose the action into a timeless sphere. The blast of a storm, the surge of a wave, the flood of a river are things both momentary and eternal, instant happenings and permanent images; so are these human efforts when seen in their own native power.

We have the same impression when it comes to the minor clashes between warrior and warrior. The long sequel scattered throughout the *Iliad* is thus introduced: "First Antilochus took a warrior of the Trojans, brave amid the foremost, Echepolus son of Thalysius; him did he first strike on the horn of his horse-haired helmet, pierced his brow, and right in through the bone passed the bronzen spear-head; darkness encompassed his eyes, and he fell, like a tower, in the strong combat" (*Il.* 4. 457 ff.). Again and again, with many variations, the same event is repeated: the clash, the blow, the fall. Each case may be a matter of minutes; but, represented as it is in its essential brutality and bareness of form, it seems to stand outside the pale of transitive happenings which combine to trace an outline of duration. A single doom, a single destiny is thus expanded in volume; we see the condition of a whole world standing between life and death. Again, how long can this tension last? It lasts a moment, and yet it lasts forever.

Often, moreover, the single encounter brings about a larger movement: a warrior is killed; a friend, standing by, is struck with unbearable grief; he instantly moves to take vengeance (cf. *Il.* 4. 491 ff.; 5. 608 ff.; 11. 221 ff.; 13. 363, 384, 402, 417, 576 ff., etc.). Many similar dramas thus reflect the major drama of Achilles returning to revenge Patroclus. Each time passions which transcend the moment are brought into play; and, through recurring occasions, we are caught in the logic of human emotions that perpetually rebound and answer one another. Once more, we may wonder at the fleeting occasions of such shaking experiences: how instantly everything is realized—the fateful chance, the reaction, and the encompassing sympathy. Instantly, and yet constantly. What we have before us in every instance is essentially the same drama. It sustains the whole poem, like a keynote which is vitally present and yet carries with it the echo or the premonition of an enduring destiny.

The time of the *Odyssey* is similarly conceived, notwithstanding the obvious differences. Take, for instance, Odysseus' account of his wanderings. It is supposed to cover three years, up to the landing in Calypso's island. How is this duration suggested? Not by the story of a crew sailing on a lonely ship, as in *Moby Dick*. No, in the *Odyssey* that period is contained in the recurring images of a storm darkening sky and sea, or of a bright stillness encompassing the waters, of men bent wearily on their oars, or of the wind blowing the sail. Here time is the continuous interplay of the elements, condensed in some essential moments. On the other hand, at certain vantage points of the journey, it is Odysseus and his crew that spring into sharp relief. What are these vantage points? They are like islands in time and space where a different reality opens up to the inquiring human eye—places to be lived in, to be loved or hated for some vital reason. Here the human action becomes quite central. What counts is then a moment of resistance or indulgence, of decision or oblivion, a pursuit or an escape lighting up a possible future. Such is the meeting with the Lotus-eaters, or with Circe: no mere adventure, but an experience carrying with it basic alternatives of life.

Again, these human scenes are brief, intense, realized as they are before our eyes. The swaying battle with the Cicones must be completed in one day, like an excerpt from the *Iliad;* the fruits of the Lotus-land are no sooner tasted than given up through the imperious will of Odysseus; we can almost count the hours of the escape from the Cyclops' cave; the great visit to Hades is really made up of a few visions and conversations in an hour of the night; the song of the Sirens, the dread appearance of Scylla and Charybdis are matters of a few moments. Even where the stay in a place is longer (in Aeolia, Aeea, Thrinakia) it is always a self-contained scene, the occasion of a day or a night, which impresses us with a sense of human complexities.

Days, nights—but how charged with their burden! Even more than in the *Iliad* do we realize here how poignantly they impinge upon the even stretch of eternity. For these two aspects of time are dramatically set the one against the other. On the one hand the defiance of Odysseus; on the other, powers of nature, gods, demigods suddenly confronted with the presence of a bold, intelligent man. The Cyclops in his cave or mountain, Calypso in Ogygia, Circe in Aeea—these mythical beings are eternally bound up with the places which are their abodes, untouched by any searching experience, until on a certain day Odysseus arrives and they feel all the friction of human life. Love, hatred stir them from their divine state. A spell appears to be broken, the human moment is vindi-

cated. So Circe's magic can no longer work; her cry, her amazement mark this revelation; she has become a woman, ready to fall
in love and to feel the suspense of time rather than its revolving
flux.

What happens outside such occasions? We are not told, we
could not be told. Homer cannot but concentrate all passion in a
momentary scene. He does not follow the slow stages of maturing
experiences; and if he has to convey the idea of a long interval,
his expressions inevitably revert to the time of nature. Thus the
year spent by Odysseus and his crew in Circe's dwelling is rendered as a period of days filled with eating and drinking: "There
all the days of a fulfillment-bringing year we remained, feasting
on abounding meat and sweet wine" (*Od.* 10. 467 f.). The life of
Aeolus and his children is similarly described (*Od.* 10. 8 ff.); and
so, in general, all stationary conditions (cf. *Od.* 9. 161 f., 556; 10.
183 ff.). Eating, drinking are in fact natural functions as regular
as the process of vegetation.

It may be questioned whether Homer sums up otherwise a
longer period, giving significant details of a personal history as a
straight narrative and not as the dramatic utterance of a certain
character. I can only think of passages in which the image of a
person is so portrayed that its attitude or bearing is momentary
and yet permanently relevant. What one does or suffers on one
day is thus valid for a whole number of days. Such is Odysseus in
his seven years with Calypso: "during the days sitting on the
rocks and the shores, with tears and sighs and grief gnawing his
soul, he looked weeping over the barren sea" (*Od.* 5. 156 ff.; cf.
83). So Achilles in his bitter isolation by the ships (*Il.* 1. 488),
or Bellerophon as a life-long wanderer hated by the gods (*Il.* 6.
201 f.).

Certain crucial days are thus gathered from the tide of natural
time. Their concentration is made obvious, in the *Iliad*, by an action which is so compact and so centred in one place. In the
Odyssey, on the other hand, the scene shifts to different and distant lands; but even here the rising and the falling day sets off each
happening. As Odysseus wakes up in Scheria or Ithaca, as

Telemachus reaches Pylos or Sparta, the sun lights up a new scene, marking it off in time as well as space. There is no random presentation of different sceneries, there is no abstraction nor any attempt to foster the impression of simultaneous happenings by rapidly summing up the situation here and there. No, each place seems enclosed in the spell of its allotted day, as if it led and independent existence in a world of its own. And yet the same day shines for each and all: it is the selfsame drama that from different ends speeds to its conclusion and Athena, everywhere present, keeps together its scattered threads. There is thus one general time; but, in each instance, it is focused in a tangible, visible point—in the day, or the night, which is its physical transparent mould.

4

It will now seem quite natural that, as H. Fränkel has shown,* it is the word for "day" ($\tilde{\eta}\mu\alpha\rho$ $\dot{\eta}\mu\dot{\epsilon}\rho\alpha$), not the general word for "time" ($\chi\rho\acute{o}\nu\sigma\varsigma$) which in Homer expresses a sense of development. The latter only recurs in the accusative, to specify a long or a short duration; and it can be replaced, as it often is, by an adverb ($\delta\acute{\eta}\nu$, $\mu\acute{\iota}\nu\nu\theta\alpha$) "long," "briefly." Here time is merely a question of length. It does not introduce any idea of an active process or of a qualitative experience (as when we say "a good time," "a bad time"). A sense of duration appears insofar as it is something objectively perceived, like "near" and "far," "here" and "there."

The word for "day" (and also "night," "dawn," etc.), on the other hand, often acquires a human significance. Thus Hector says: "Well I know it in my heart and mind—a day will come when sacred Ilium will fall" (*Il.* 6. 448 ff.). And Achilles to Lycaon: "But, my friend, you also must die. Why moan? Even Patroclus

---

* H. Fränkel, *Wege und Formen frühgriechischen Denkens*, Munich, 1955, pp. 1–22. The essay in question: "Die Zeitauffassung in der archaischen griechischen Literatur" is there reprinted from *Beilagenheft zur Zeitschrift fur Aesthetik und allgemeine Kunstwissenschaft*, vol. 25, (1931), pp. 97–118.

died, a man far stronger than you. . . . My mortal fate is upon me as well: there will be a morning or evening or noon, when a man will take my life with a spear-throw or with an arrow-shot from his bow-string" (*Il.* 21. 106 ff.). Similarly, the story of one's life is made up of decisive days, as that of the same Lycaon (cf. *Il.* 21. 45, 46, 77, 81). Similarly Penelope cries out: "And the night will come when a hateful marriage will fall to my lot" (*Od.* 18. 272 f.). So we always find: "on the day in which" to express the time, the occasion of anything remarkable (*Il.* 5. 210; 9. 253, etc.). Eternity itself cannot be conceived but as "all the days" (*Il.* 13. 826; 14. 235; 16. 499, etc.).

In all these passages the day again contains a human experience, a happening. But such a day is summoned up from the past or the future. It ceases to take its place in the order of nature. By being a theme of memory or premonition, it becomes a mental image. It thus outstrips its physical contours, conveying as it does a subjective idea of time. All the same, it comes to the mind in its reality. The words "day," "night," etc. are here no simple figures of speech. They are still suffused with a feeling for nature. That forecast of Achilles, for instance, is no dark foreboding: he realizes his death in its daylight moment, as an actual vision; and it is as if his sense of future time could not do without such a bright point of reference. It is naturally so. For no current general word like "time," "age," "moment," "occasion" was available; and the Homeric language compresses these meanings into the day, the night, the encompassing hour.

With a similar mode of expression the poet can retrace the life of a character and the course of intimate experiences. Penelope thus describes her life-long expectation: "In the days I have my fill of sighs and of tears, even while I attend to the household . . . then when night falls and sleep seizes all, I lie in bed, sharp cares thickly gather round my inmost heart and stir up my sorrow" (*Od.* 19. 513 ff.). Again and again her daylight wakefulness comes to a breaking-point, and Athena casts sweet sleep upon her eyelids (*Od.* 4. 793; 16. 450; 19. 603; 21. 357). Time seems to waste her away: "Woefully ever the nights pass over her and the days as she sheds tears" (*Od.* 11. 182 f.; 13. 337 f.). The very characterization of Penelope depends on the spell of these hours, with their dreams, visions, omens; and such a succession of waking and sleeping, of night and day, gives the sense of a long and intense experience.

The dramatic impact of the poems thus draws the time of nature into the human sphere. It is especially so in the last-quoted passages. For what now fills the day is a feeling; and, unlike a material event, it is something fluid, pervasive; it cannot be fixed at any one point or moment; it affects and colors the whole course of time, tuning it to a certain mood. Hence the days are seen subjectively, their natural bounds becoming measures of a persistent mental state; and what actually happens—the interplay of fortune and misfortune—passes into the more delicate strains of good and evil, pleasure and pain, happiness and unhappiness, making up the rhythms of individual life.

Some such idea we find reflected in the famous words of Odysseus to Amphinomus: "Nothing weaker than man does the earth nourish. . . . No evil he thinks lies in store while the gods give him power and his knees move nimbly; but when the gods bring woes upon him, he yet bears them though unwilling with a patient heart. *For the mind of men on the earth is such as the day which Zeus . . . draws upon them*" (*Od.* 18. 130 ff.). Here is again the order of nature, the days and seasons which proceed from Zeus. Man lies under their sway. He cannot but accept what comes. But, even as he does so, he imputes a human bias to the elements. The overhanging day will appear bright or dark according to his needs. For this relation between man and nature must work both ways. What affects one term must affect the other; and the Homeric words also imply that the day is such as man makes it out to be.

The periods of nature are thus charged with human suspense, and the life span of man is modulated by an elemental rhythm. What emerges is neither a mechanical interplay of night and day and whatever they bring, nor a simple consummation of experience. We are presented, rather, with a reality which lies in between. What name could we give it? It is time, human time; and yet it is also a primordial natural phenomenon. Here the impartial work of nature seemed to blend with the wayward destinies of men and with the course of individual actions. Homer embodied such complexities in the visual spell of the day, giving full scope both to the massive regularity of its rhythm and to the mystery of its human purport.

We might ask how Homer came to this view. But it is hardly a view at all. It is a mode of representation: the human event is not abstracted from its place in the flux of existence. It was the strong Homeric sense of nature that showed the way—the sense of the physical day as a bright, immediate vantage point that could absorb into its compass any contents, any human value. The Homeric characters seem to taste through it all the good and evil which encompass the ages.

In this connection Homer can represent certain basic conditions of human life by qualifying the word for "day" with a simple adjective. For instance, Hector says to Andromache: "Not the future woes of Troy, not those of Priam . . . matter to me as much as yours, when some Achaean will take you as a captive in tears, robbing you of *your day of freedom*" (*Il.* 6. 455). What the Greek says is literally "free day." We might just say "freedom" quite simply; but Homer thinks of freedom as a mode of being, as a condition which is realized in time and fills the day. Hence comes the force of Hector's words: that loss of freedom is like a total eclipse; and the day itself, the very face of existence, change their connotations.

Other meanings too can be so expressed—"slavery," "evil," "destruction," "death."* In each case, a human experience becomes an attribute of the day. What results is a very compact expression. It gathers in one tangible point a recurring drama. For a sense of time here forces good and evil into the moment of their consummation; and what we would see as a general condition is presented as the burden of decisive occasions, as a stroke of fate, as a catastrophe. That "free-day" or "slave-day," for instance, means of

---

* The full list may be found in H. Fränkel, pp. 17–18.

course "freedom," "slavery"; but it is also a happening, something to be endured at its allotted moment.

Any fundamental turning point of life, no doubt, could be rendered in these terms. Actions and situations coming to a head, or issues that are settled once and for all, point to a crucial instance, to a decisive day. Such a day stands out supreme, gathering the threads of time. It represents a typical vicissitude in the life of a man. Thus in the *Odyssey* the return of Odysseus is a typical, central event. It is no less his own, it is no less a crucial issue in his life for being the very same to the many heroes who came back from Troy. As we read the poem, we become aware of it as of a ripening moment which casts a significance over the whole course of time. It is so sought, so thought of that it becomes an ideal occurrence—νόστιμον ἦμαρ—"the day of return," "the returning day," not simply "the return." A destiny seems to assign it, working from year to year; and it comes as a fulfillment, loaded with all the prefigured fancies of a long hope.

Containing as it does the world's experience, the day thus almost becomes a symbol of human time. Almost, but not completely. For in Homer it never acquires a purely metaphorical value —as when we say, for instance, "day of reckoning," "doomsday," or simply "a better day." No, its sensuous, natural spell is never lost, however it may be broadened into an ideal measure of time. Herein lies, I think, the distinctive quality of the Homeric picture. On the one hand the day (and, therefore, the course of time) marks an epitome of human history; and, on the other, history itself falls into a natural phase, each one of its instances encompassed by the light of day and the darkness of night. The greatest tragedy comes as a knell struck by the elements; but the elements, in their turn, stand affected by the human predicament.

The relation between nature and human acts thus appeared in a basic simplicity. It was characteristic of Homer to show it for what it was, baring it of all mythical embellishments and superstructures. A naive wonder here combined with a historian's insight. For the human day was seen gathering its outline, even as it emerged on the horizons of nature—a marvel to look at; but also a messenger of anything that might happen, a catalyst of feelings and thoughts, a filter of experience.

5

The feeling for the day as an ideal term of reference could not but have a direct bearing on the composition of the poems. Even remote events could be sympathetically drawn into the present daylight hour whenever they appeared instantly relevant. The Homeric scenes are thus often pregnant moments. A poetic synthesis occurred absorbing many elements which a prosaic memory would have left in the background and confined to casual points scattered over the course of time.

It is so, we might say, even in our own experience. Images touching us to the quick gather from different periods of our lives peopling one temporal landscape, one imaginary day which is quite real to the mind's eye. It is so in any narrative which is not a mere record. It is so in Homer, but with a difference: the interval of time seems quite forgotten, and the past moves forward into the present, welded to it by a compact imagery which is not affected by chronology. It is as if past scenes could not be fully realized in their present relevance, unless they were conjured up to share the atmosphere of one common day.

Such a recovery of the past requires of course a powerful motive. Something like it happens at the beginning of the *Iliad*. The wrath of Achilles stirs up a wholesale commotion. His words are echoed by Thersites, the army is caught in the sway of conflicting emotions: tradition has been forsworn, royalty almost forfeited, the reasons of the expedition questioned or rejected. In other words, an inner shock takes place which seems to break the sequence of events; and in that heated suspense past images stream back, much as in a final crisis the initial stages return to the mind with a fresh sharpness. Thus Odysseus evokes the sailing from Aulis as if it had happened "yesterday or the day before" (*Il.* 2. 303); and in this context the rally of the troops looks like the projection of another, distant scene: that of the Achaeans assembling together on the first day of the expedition.

In the text, indeed, these movements of the Achaeans happen according to a certain plan: there is the dream of Agamemnon, his speech which tests the troops by calling for a withdrawal, the subsequent counter-move. But this is a thin thread required to hold the plot together. From a poetic point of view that dream and that strange speech are simply an excuse. Over and above the external texture there is the full reality of the war which presses for recognition on one eventful day. It is as if that burdened moment leaned backward, extending to the first dramatic instances which made it possible.

When later the poet again invokes the Muse (*Il.* 2. 484), it is as if the gates of memory were opened wide—so wide that we can hardly speak of memory in the modern sense. Rather than a digression recalling the past, we find once more a seething present, a cumulative moment deployed in its constituent values. The catalogue of ships is then here at the right place, presenting the great array of the Greeks, their ships, their homes, as if they had just arrived.

Critics have objected to the catalogue; and it does seem strange, placed as it is in the tenth year of the war. But the Homeric mode of representation is here seen at work on a larger scale. The sailing of those ships, the sudden presence of those men on a distant shore appeared as poetic themes in their own right, integrated into this context because of their kindred spell and not presented as a historical premise. The tense, close scene, we may suppose, was seen widening to indefinite vistas in time and space—from the lonely anguish of Agamemnon to the swarming shore and thence to the whole Greek world. The development of the action thus followed the drift of an imaginative thought, whereby people and things could not be confined to an episodic role but had to deliver the full message of their presence. "Those that inhabited Phylake and Pyrasos blooming with flowers, a sanctuary of Demeter, and Iton mother of sheep, and Antron upon the sea, and Pteleos with its beds of grass," we read for instance (*Il.* 2. 695); and times, places advance from the background, so that the occasion at hand seems to be nothing but the slender edge of a complex reality.

The third book follows in the same spirit. The fight between Paris and Menelaus typifies once and for all a permanent feud; the rebuke of Hector and Paris' answer are the clash of ingrained tempers and destined roles; the appearance of Helen by the Scaean gates brings home to the elders a long tale of desire and woe; the Grecian chiefs standing before the walls awake stringent memories that come up like a flood. Each moment here overflows with its silent contents; and each occurrence, as it is portrayed, becomes a theme—a supreme instance rather than a fact.

We are again steeped into a sort of metaphysical day: an indefinite span of experience runs into its compass. And yet it is a real, bright day: the characters are unmistakably lit up by it. As a result, various scenes stand out whose purport is as immeasurable as their outlines are clear, concrete, definite, confined to one moment and one place. We might compare a vase painting in which, for example, the mere juxtaposition of Helen and Paris would be enough to convey their whole story. Homer seems to do no more than to clear the ground for such a specious present. His characters are just as articulate as it is indispensable to their role. They do not linger in any random conversation; and what they say is wholly relevant to their destiny.

It was, as we have seen, a sense of massive movement which suggested placing the catalogue of ships side by side with the rally of the Achaeans in one central moment. Here in the third book the poet touched instead upon individual experience. It was then a grasp of persistent psychic analogies which gathered the past and recast it into the present. The characters were brought to face one another in no casual meeting, but in a moment which seemed to recover the burden of a long experience.

It is so most remarkably in the scene of Helen and Aphrodite, Helen and Paris (*Il.* 3. 383–447). We should read and reread that brief passage to mark its rich texture and its swift transitions. Paris has just escaped from Menelaus, wafted by Aphrodite into his bedchamber; Helen is on the tower in the company of Trojan women; and now the goddess appears to Helen in the semblance of "an aged woman, an ancient woolspinner who used to spin for her beautiful wool back in Sparta, dearest to her than all others." "Come," says Aphrodite, "Alexander bids you come home . . . shining in his beauty and his garments; you would not say that he has come back from the fighting, but that he is going to dance, or that he has just sat down to rest from the dancing." Then suddenly the lovely forms of the goddess flash out; Helen is stirred, amazed; she would reject that summons, resist. "Do not provoke me, o wretch," the goddess pursues, "lest I desert you in my anger, and hate you as much as just now I terribly loved you." Helen follows veiling herself, in silence, unseen, driven by divine power. She goes and sits before Paris; her eyes turn back, and yet she speaks. Shame, wild regret, rage first prompt her words: "You came away from the battle, would that even there you had died." And then, almost immediately: "No, I bid you cease and not fight." It is the new love that wells up replacing the old one. Paris seduces her, takes her in his passion, just as he did the first time. "But come, let us lie and delight in our love," he says "for never yet has love so encompassed my mind, not even when I first took you and sailed from lovely Lakedaimon in the sea-faring ships, and in the island of Cranae I loved you."

The whole scene has something of a mirage. It is so real, it is so present in the moment, and yet like a dream of long ago. As in the second book a sudden commotion brought back the first impact of the expedition, so now this meeting of lovers leads back to their first experience. It is the same instance of love as ten years before in Sparta—the same temptation and resistance, the same flight unseen by other women. The present chamber in Troy might as well be the island of Cranae where they first made love—an unheard of spot just rescued from oblivion, but as real to the imagination as it is baffling to the geographer; and likewise Lakedaimon, the sea, the ships are here again, as scenes that witnessed the love of Paris, impressed once and for all upon his feeling. Certain features of the imagery help to complete the illusion: the impersonation of Aphrodite in the old Spartan handmaid, the appearance of Paris as a dancer such as he must have been in the festive home of his Spartan hosts. But is this really an illusion? Love, so powerfully embodied in the epiphany of the goddess, fills here all the perspectives. It is a force of destiny: past, present, and future are just variations of its spell.

How else could we read the scene? Its movements make up an inevitable sequence which could not be other than it is, now and then, in Sparta and in Troy. What is said, what is done is pertinent to the moment and is also an instance of permanent trends. When Helen cries out to Aphrodite: "O goddess, alas! why still do you want to bewitch me? Will you lead me yet further afield . . . in Phrygia or lovely Maeonia, if there too perchance you have a man whom you cherish?" it is as if different times, lands, people made no difference to the goddess, merely affording instances and occasions for her pervasive spell.

But at the same time this scene is true to life. Its magic is credible. It has its roots in human nature. We may wonder at Aphrodite, and yet understand her: in her transformation as an old woman she rehearses the past side by side with the present. Even so, in the course of our lives, love harks back to some initial revelation: each occasion seems new and yet the same. A beloved image stands out, as if unimpaired by the years; time itself seems to stop, as if absorbed by it; and, in looking back, only the recurring phases of passion seem to count, joining one another and abolishing all intervals.

In actual life, however, such a synthesis is hard to come by, and difficult to keep up, once it is achieved. It comes more often, perhaps, in dreams which draw different images from different occasions and recast them into one picture; but a dream is a troubled, opaque, irrational experience. This Homeric scene, on the contrary, runs smooth and clear. Reminiscence here ceases to be an effort. These terse images account for the past on the strength of their mere presence. Memory does not shake them. What they once were is so compounded with what they are now that the thought of the past, rather than unbalancing them, seems to give them a greater solidity. Their comings and goings proceed with a decisive stride, their questions and answers have a fateful purport; and yet everything is rendered just as it happens, in graphic details which last about as long as it takes to read. It would of course be impossible to retrace the creative process whereby such a scene was conceived; but we may, at least, again observe how the Homeric day encompasses it and bestows a sensuous color even upon the phantoms of the past.

Such passages in the initial books of the *Iliad* are like a keynote. They introduce a foreshortening into the order of years; and the rest of the poem follows in the same movement. Not only does the action gather within the compass of single days; but (what is more important) that action rehearses a mighty theme. Its significance is cumulative rather than narrative. To assemble a great quantity of material within one day, or within single days, might have been quite easy. It would not have required a Homer. The point was, rather, to steep into the day actions which were as pertinent as they were typical—charged with the impact of an oft-repeated movement, coming like a final wave.

We have seen how this is true of the fighting scenes. That synthesis of time which worked so strongly in the first books of the *Iliad* was thus broadened to include all the scattered actions. In its more general terms, it does not concern the lives of individual characters (like Helen), or the history of a certain action (like the rally of the Achaeans); its concern is now the human subject matter as a whole; and different characters are seen undergoing the same destiny, wherever they may be. What emerges is a great single moment common to all, a sort of eternal now which is the sum total of all kindred experiences.

Homer constantly reminds us of such fundamental recurrences. The day of doom, the day of fate hovers over everything. "Not for long will you live, but even now death and the powerful Moira are closing upon you," dying Patroclus says to Hector (*Il.* 16. 852 f.); and Hector, dying, similarly addresses Achilles (*Il.* 22. 358 ff.). "The seven brothers who grew with me in the household, they all went down to Hades in one sole day, all slain by Achilles. . . . Hector, you are for me my father and bountiful mother, you are my brother and flourishing husband," says Andromache (*Il.* 6. 421 ff.). "Me most of all has Achilles plunged into grief, so many of my flourishing children he slew; for all of them I do not so much grieve as for one . . . Hector," cries Priam (*Il.* 22. 422 ff.). Similar are the words of Briseis for her husband and brothers (*Il.* 19. 291 ff.). In the same way the fall of Troy is often foreshadowed, but also that of Argos and Mycenae; for, as we are told more than once, "so Zeus wills it, who has laid low the tops of many cities, and many more will lay low" (*Il.* 2. 116 ff.; 9. 23 ff.).

Nothing casual, arbitrary, capricious could fit into these synthetic perspectives. It would merely occur at random. It would have no significance beyond itself. What is required is something solemn—marking a common destiny, a recurring experience. Only an event of such purport could fill the range of memory and, as it were, bid time revolve around it. So the many deaths of the *Iliad* merge into one great tragic day. But this contraction of time need not always be tragic. Whatever strikes the imagination in recurring occasions presents itself in the same way. The plight of Odysseus during his wanderings, for instance, remains essentially the same in its different moments and places: the sailing, the running ashore, the badly needed rest and repast, the anxious questioning as to who the inhabitants are, the demand for help, the parting to speed back homeward. As we consider the time sequence of his wanderings, we cannot pin it down to any direction. There is really no necessary sequence; the order of the episodes (the Cyclops, Circe, etc.) could be altered without affecting the story. What stands out in our mind, from the viewpoint of coherence in time, are the many instances of sailing and landing. They seem to join one another and compose one great typical day.

Such repetition, such uniformity might seem monotonous. But it is not really so. For Homer fills the basic repetitive rhythm with a sense of life. We find black storms falling from heaven, the bright stillness of calm seas, auspicious winds or gales; and, as a human counterpart to these, the desperate sailing, the joy of touching land, the very sinews restored by food and drink, the tentative approach to a new people, and making sail again to catch the wind.

Weariness here comes to oarsmen with all the burden of indifferent windless skies, buoyancy with all the ease of a full-blown sail, and rest is a complete self-abandonment on some solitary shore, a profusion of earth's fruits to reviving limbs. These recurrences enact moments of full-blooded experience; and a timeless solemnity seems to blend with a day-long urgency.

What first came to the poet's mind was, then, not so much the traditional story of a hero returning home as the very act of returning—a feat many times envisaged, many times attempted, many times rehearsed until its conclusion. For even when Odysseus does finally reach home, his return is presented as yet another landing, yet another venture. It is not casually that he does not recognize immediately his native land. We hear again his anguished cry: "to what land, to what people have I come?" (*Od.* 13. 200 ff.). It is as if he were carried even now by the same rhythm of life and nature as in the previous instances. And the tale of further wanderings echoed by Tiresias seems to confirm this point. Even this return would then be but a stage in a longer series. Finally he will be back for good and live happily until a gentle death will come. But this is of no interest to the poem. What matters is the present moment of arrival and triumph as fresh from the waves he runs to his goal. Is there here another Calypso, another Circe? No, greater values now fall to his lot; and yet they are goods that come to him on the crest of the wave—in the very acts of escaping, landing, setting foot on the earth which he kisses.

The return of Odysseus, the wrath of Achilles, the fighting by the ships—the outcome of these things is well known from the beginning of the poems, decided upon by the gods, foreshadowed in the minds of the characters. If the object of the poet had been merely to tell the story drawing it out at length, it would hardly have been worthwhile. But this was not his way. What interested him was a moment of experience: an action, an emotion, a situation. He visualized it all at once. It presented itself immediately in all its fulness. In other words, it was seen in its own value rather than as part of a narrative. But the human moment then ceased to be a passing instant. Its implications were seen rebounding through the world. It could not but emerge again and again, instance after instance, ever new and yet the same. An accumulation of experience thus replaced the variety of successive details that we might have expected in a tale of war or adventure. And yet the poet could not abstract experience from its time and place. It had to be encompassed by the daylight that shone all around him; and the day became a kernel of time, opening a condensed vision of experience.

6

If the action is gathered in a final synthesis, it follows that the actors are similarly conceived as compact figures. They must immediately stand out as depositories of a recurring experience. We have seen how this is true of Hector, Paris, Menelaus, Helen. They emerge all at once, suddenly and completely, as if to give an ultimate proof of their identity. Agamemnon and Achilles are introduced in the opening scene of the *Iliad;* and yet it is as if we had always known them: the drama which sets them face to face is so primordial, that for all their momentary passion they seem to have the ageless gravity of archetypes.

It is Odysseus that most of all bears the tale of his destiny in his very name and epithets. We see him at different stages of his career, but nowhere do we find an account of his life. It is as if the passing stages of experience had been arrested in his image. Such he appears as soon as we begin reading the *Odyssey:* "Tell me of the man, o Muse—that man nimble in his ways, who wandered." It is impossible to render, in a translation, the immediate fulness of a character emerging out of nothing—how each qualification gathers around the image, builds it up, substantiates it, becoming all one with it. For we have the tendency just to mention a person and then add, as if in brackets, or by way of explanation, whatever may have a bearing on that person's life. But here no such fracture exists. Image, character, biography appear all at once. An indefinite span of time is, again, condensed in the present; but solidified, as it were, and embodied in the actual form of a man.

Odysseus is so firmly set in the opening lines that no need is felt to follow progressively his history. His image, rather, is a pivot upon which present, past, and future seem to turn. Accordingly, he continually appears from different angles, in different perspectives. We see him through the eyes of the gods who know his fate. We see him in his dubious present from the viewpoint of his people at home: where is he? dead? or a forlorn wanderer tossed by the waves? We see him directly in Calypso's island building his raft, and then washed ashore in Scheria. We see him retrospectively, through his own eyes, as he recounts his wanderings. We see him directly again as the Phaeacians waft him back to his native shore and he moves to win back his household. We drift backward and forward, before and after, steadily turned toward him. The traditional length of his absence from Ithaca means little to us. What gives us a sense of protracted time is his persistent image—presented as it is in various moments and places, but always so much itself, always so charged with the load of a given destiny.

All the Homeric characters are first presented as images. That is to say, their presence is immediately transparent, suggesting what they are, what they do. In order to know them we do not have to see them through to the end. As we read on, they do not embark on any novel pursuit, they do not show any new remarkable trait. Whenever they appear, they seem to carry out the same part, deepening its theme, broadening its scope. In point of time, this means that the course of all possible experience is gathered in their immediate function—in a pose, in a gesture, in an attitude which clings to their outline once and for all. Take the first book of the *Odyssey*, for instance: every character that is mentioned—Odysseus, Telemachus, Penelope, the suitors, Phemius —is what he is down to the end of the poem, fixed in a role which is momentary and yet permanent. Henceforward his acts and words cannot be willful or fortuitous, but will closely adhere to a certain form.

The values which make an image must necessarily rebound in time. Though they are recognized in a form whose presence is momentary, they are not momentary themselves. Associations

155

from other times, other ages bring them home to our mind. Odysseus: his very name bears a sense of long adventures. Penelope: her very presence reminds us of endless vigils. Such is always the case. The Homeric characters are so completely contained in the dramatic moment of their appearance, that they become symbolic of what they are actually doing or suffering. Even those who are seen once and no more. So in the first book of the *Iliad* Chryses, Chalcas. They appear suddenly, for a moment; and yet the present occasion tasks their whole being. Here is a priest coming to ransom his daughter, supported by a life-long association with his god; here is a seer advancing to announce a bitter truth, his ancient dignity now jeopardized. A whole life hangs on such issues.

It is the dumb characters that perhaps give out most remarkably this self-contained spell. No words they may utter come in the way. Only the actual presentation conjures them up from their past. It is so with many a warrior of the *Iliad*. Homer lingers now and then on the solitary name of someone who dies and is heard of no more. Ajax, for instance, slays "the son of Anthemion, a youth unmarried, flourishing, Simoeisios—whom his mother descending from Ida bore on the banks of the Simois" (*Il.* 4. 474 ff.). The Homeric words have a natural power of evocation. The adjectives sound like names, lending body to each quality. Whatever is said about a man's life becomes an attribute; it is as pertinent a mark of recognition as a feature of his body. So, in this passage, the youth's name suggests his birth; his birth suggests the river, Mount Ida, and a shepherd's life. Each word, each phrase is thus held in focus; and places, experiences cluster around the image, enhancing it, making it what it is, as closely bound to it as epithets to the name of a hero. Why do we find here these bits of information? We could not read them as an epitaph. They do not bestow any praise, any blame. No, these memories are all one with the image, finally witnessed once more in the moment of its fall.

There are many such passages in Homer, (cf. *Il.* 5. 49, 59, 69, 612; 6. 12, 20; 11. 329; 13. 171, 363, 428, 663; 14. 489; 15. 547, 638; 17. 575; 20. 408). All these instances recover something remarkable from the past—a country, a home, a livelihood, a trade, an art, a birth, a marriage. What is the point of it all? It is that a whole world, a whole age of diverse activities has been out-shadowed by the instant battle; and yet it cannot be kept in complete abeyance, it must somehow stream back into the light of the present day through these momentary images.

Everywhere in the poems we find this teeming present. Things are shown in a penetrating light. Their material becomes transparent. The actual moment which encompasses them seems to open up, revealing its depth. This is true of objects as well as of persons. The same touch draws out the past which they enclose. Thus, in the *Iliad*, we first meet Helen in her hall where "she was weaving a great purple web . . . embroidering into it the many struggles which the horse-taming Trojans and the bronze-clad Achaeans were suffering for her sake at the hand of Ares" (*Il.* 3. 125 ff.). The embroidered web suggests a whole destiny—battles and the long spell of a woman's beauty. There is no heart-searching recollection. Helen only weaves, as if she were weaving her thread of life; and the embroidery gathers into its stillness a sense of long enduring tensions. What does she feel now? Is she proud, sad, repentant? We cannot know. If she told us, her words would be partial, one-sided. What we have instead is a still imagery which fate itself seems to have placed where it is, in a solemn aloofness and a witnessing silence. Again a present moment summons up the past, but in the form of a bewitching object.

We may compare *Il.* 22. 153 ff. Achilles is pursuing Hector. They come to "two fair-streaming fountains, where the sources of eddying Scamander well up . . . and nearby are the broad washing troughs, magnificent, all made of stone, in which the wives of the Trojans and their lovely daughters were wont to wash the bright raiments—long before in time of peace, before the sons of the Achaeans had arrived." Once more the material becomes a vehicle of time. Those waters are the same as ever. Scenes of past life still cling to them; and the fountains, fixed where they are by nature, become age old witnesses. Even so we are often struck by the unchanged presence of some familiar spot known long before in different circumstances. It is as if time had dropped there something of our past. Memories come back as a shock. This Homeric passage, placed where it is, has a similar effect. The unbearable tension of the present moment suddenly dissolves; the fountains conjure up the washerwomen and the years of peace—images of other days coming up most forcibly, out of the stone, as in a daylight dream.

In *Il.* 9. 186 ff. we find Achilles "rejoicing at heart with a shrill lyre—a beautiful thing, cunningly made, with a silver cross-bar upon it, which he took from the spoils after destroying the city of Eetion. With it he delighted his spirit, and sang the glories of heroes." So beautifully represented as Achilles plays it, the lyre also carries with it the story of a destroyed city. The place where it came from cannot be forgotten. Its memory hangs upon it, almost a part of its features, intrinsic to its very notes. We are disturbed out of our contemplation, as the thought of a distant woe merges with the music. The image of Achilles himself is affected. A cruel past is called back: here is a blood-stained lover of beautiful things. The bewildering complexities of the hero's life are made palpable by the presence of that lyre.

Penelope says: "I shall go lie in my bed—my bed full of sighs, ever wet with my tears, ever since Odysseus departed" (*Od.* 17. 102 f.; 19. 595 f.). The bed embodies her long grief. It also becomes, in its own way, a symbol of time. An expression like "life full of sighs" would not have been Homeric. Such a tangible object, on the contrary, provided a striking term of reference. That bed witnessed each night of Penelope, bearing its mark; and it now contains, as it were, the relentless rhythm of her suffering.

Homer often represents objects in this way, mentioning their background (cf. *Il.* 1. 234; 2. 101; 4. 105; 6. 289; 7. 219; 10. 261; 11. 19, 632; 15. 529, 720; 16. 142, 221; 17. 194; 21. 403; 23. 741, 826; *Od.* 4. 125, 227, 615; 21. 11). Such objects are precious gifts of heroes to one another, heirlooms, trophies—all things that have seen distant lands and people. Whatever may be the reason of their being mentioned, the general effect is again the same: they draw out the present scene toward vistas of other times and places.

Elsewhere, in the *Odyssey,* objects or material features become occasions of instant recognition and stir up an intimate realization of the past. Such are the mantle, brooch, and tunic of Odysseus which, being mentioned, bring Penelope to tears (*Od.* 19. 225 ff.); such is the olive stem once worked by Odysseus into a marriage bed (*Od.* 23. 190 ff.); such is the famous scar which overwhelms Euryclea's heart (*Od.* 19. 393 ff.). We may wonder at these antique ways of recognition and find them, perhaps, artificial. But, in this context, they have a special value. The object becomes here a reservoir of pent-up emotions. Remaining what it is through the years, it bridges the widening intervals; and when a coincidence brings it again into focus, it cannot but yield its full message. It is eminently so in the case of Odysseus' scar. As it is uncovered and recognized, snatches of past life instantly return. What a painstaking pen could hardly retrieve is then recalled as if by magic.

We are presented with a world where time seems compressed into images. The scenery is spread out in space, as it appears at a certain moment; but it reveals here and there, as through a film, the phases that brought about its setting. People, things stand out in their full visual relevance, not engulfed or worn away by the hand of time. It is, on the contrary, their imagery which yields a sense of time.

7

The day and the night spread out over the world, actions presented in their typical recurrence, images seen in their full presence— such a picture, however splendid, lacked something that is essential to our feeling for life. It hardly admitted any break between existing things and the mental recollection of their existence. The past and the future hung here on the present, as its penumbra. What we have found so far is an engrossing objective vision rather than a subjective recovery of experience.

A subjective sense of time could only come when a subjective mood had set in. That is to say that, in order to let this happen, a character had to be both implicated in an action and removed from it, casting over it his own perspective and recreating its stages according to the drift of his thoughts. This does not often occur in Homer. Acts, feelings, thoughts, words are so immediately prompted by occasions closely following one another, that the mind does not have the time to realize in its own way the course of things. Let us take a typical example: "And at once from the chariot he sprang to the ground in arms, brandishing the sharp spears he moved through the host all over, spurring them to battle, and stirred up the dread fighting; they turned and stood in front of the Achaeans; the Argives withdrew and ceased from the slaughter, saying that a god had come down from the starry sky" (*Il*. 6. 103 ff.). Everything is here instantaneous. Motives, actions, reactions are immediate, and even feelings come with the directness of physical acts. The particle *de* distinguishes the sentences —that is, the phases of the action. Does it have a spatial or a temporal meaning: "now," "then," "here," "there"? In this compact rendering the two seem indistinguishable, as if each occasion had at once its own time and its own place, outside any sequence traced by human reckoning.

But there are exceptions. At times this continuity is broken. A particular feeling may intervene. Not so much pain, amazement, fear; for such feelings come instantly, as if they were events in their own right. It is so, rather, in moments of doubt, when alternatives are considered. Odysseus, for instance, left alone, thus speaks to himself: "Ah me, what will happen? A great evil it is if I escape in fear of the throng; even worse if I be taken alone after Zeus has scattered in flight all the others" (*Il*. 11. 401 ff.; cf. 17. 90 ff.; 21. 552 ff.). In such passages what happens ceases to be a bare fact or movement in a general rhythm. It is reflected upon, drawn out in its potential developments. The pause in which this occurs is a subjective moment. Elementary as it is, it underpins an imaginary synthesis of time.

Elsewhere the same sort of soliloquy, introduced by the same words, removes us even more from the action: it is no more a question of immediate alternatives, but of vague and far-reaching possibilities. Thus Achilles, wondering at the absence of Patroclus, similarly addresses himself: "Ah me, why is it? Why do the long-haired Achaeans throng again by the ships routed over the plain? May the gods not accomplish the woeful fears of my mind, as my mother once showed me and told me that the best of the Myrmidons would in my lifetime leave the light of the sun by the hands of the Trojans. Indeed he is dead" (*Il.* 18. 5 ff.). As he says this, Achilles scans a distant scene, having remained for days quite aloof from the action. It is as if the range of his remembrances and premonitions were proportionate to this aloofness. For the distance now separating him from Patroclus and from the action becomes a void to be filled, a gap to be bridged by feelings which would recompose the past and mend the present discomfiture. The soliloquy assumes here a wider dimension: what comes to the mind is not an instant blow, but the life and destiny of a friend.

It is through such intervals that a sense of human, subjective time grows and takes shape. Its import is relative, as it were, to the depth of space opening up between the acts. For we have no casual interludes. The very movement of the action breaks at a critical point under a burdening strain; and then the ground is clear for the mind to realize times and places on its own level, in a different scene which has its own silent tension.

The solitude of Achilles is a keynote in this respect. It comes as an inevitable break between actions which have a fateful impact on his life. It provides a vantage ground whence the battle scenes and the war itself can be seen as episodes in an individual's life. For the hero, alone by the ships, broods intimately upon his state; and it is as if all his vitality now spent itself in realizing what happened, what might have happened or still might happen. His reply to those who would have him join the battle again is like a vindication of himself. Memory and hope, those mainsprings of subjective time, run through the whole of his long speech. Let us quote a few passages of it:

> Thankless it was to fight against foes relentless, ever. . . . Nothing accrues to me for the woes I have suffered, ever staking my life in the battle. . . . As a bird that bears to her nestlings every morsel she

wins, but nothing she keeps for herself, so am I for the many sleepless nights I lay out, for the many days of blood I lived through. . . . Why should the Trojans and Argives wage war? . . . Why did the son of Atreus assemble so many men? . . . Now since he robbed me and deceived me, let him not tempt me; I know and shall not be persuaded. . . . Much has he toiled without me . . . but even so he cannot resist the onslaught of Hector. . . . I will not fight against Hector. . . . I shall draw my ships to the sea, and on the third day I shall be in the fair land of Phthia. . . . Many things there await me which I left erring hither. . . . There my soul is all craving to go—and marry a good wife and enjoy old Peleus' possessions. For nothing is worth more than life. . . . Oxen and goodly sheep may be plundered, tripods and tawny horses are there to be bought, but the life-breath of man cannot return nor be taken nor captured again once it has passed beyond the rim of his lips. And my mother Thetis . . . has told me that a twin fate is carrying me on to my doom. If I stay here and fight round the city of Troy, lost would be the return to my home, but immortal fame be my lot; and if I return . . . , lost would be my great fame, but my life would last long. (*Il.* 9. 316 ff.)

A new, entirely subjective sense of time emerges from this speech. The encompassing rhythms of the day recede, quite outshadowed by a vision of things past and future. What sustains this vision is a feeling for life and its values. Good and evil are valued in accordance with a vital personal interest; and on their basis whole years can be summed up. We thus have a survey of time which is not heroic, but simply human. And yet this account, novel as it is, proceeds tentatively. The drift of ideas is not straightforward. Single occasions still retain the attention. It is the outrage suffered which prompts the feeling of the years spent in vain, it is the fond imagery of setting sail which suggests an indefinite time spent at home. The mind moves backward and forward on these themes, until at length the meaning of human life comes up as one comprehensive idea. But even then the words seem to halt, waver in eliciting a general outlook. It is thus the sense of life-breath that first stands out—a precious element dearer than all honors, all glory; but this existential value is then immediately envisaged in terms of time, and the mythical alternative between two opposing destinies is recalled just to stress the enduring good of a long-lasting life. It is as if the ideas so richly suggested throughout the speech forced a new significance on the words. So *psyche* is the life-breath ready to depart and become a phantom, but it is also felt as a value which is ever at stake, ever to be fought for; whence the word *aion* brings out the sense of life as duration. We are far removed from the battle scenes where the spirit is seen in its momentary flight to leave a dying body or as a source of immediate vital power in the living. Achilles' wandering thoughts introduce a new dimension. Life and time can now be envisaged freely, even though for a moment, and merged into one ideal process set outside the limits of the day's natural rhythm.

This speech of Achilles, though a reply, sounds like a soliloquy. He is, in a way, like the other heroes whom we have seen addressing their own heart and revolving in their minds events which overwhelm them. But the scale is here incomparably greater and the purport quite central to the poem. It is as if the whole action came to a head breaking apart, and in that break the shattered threads were recomposed on a mental level. What else could a hero do when left to himself, removed from actions which were like his daily bread? He thinks; and his acts become the stuff of his thoughts. Immediate life thus turns into experience; and experience into a vision of time.

8

A character brooding upon himself must inevitably think of life and time. But his thoughts are likely to stray along their own path. He may end up in a delusion or a dream. So Achilles, in the ninth book of the *Iliad*, is clouded by his wrath; and the life which he pictures for himself is not the one which he has made his own. The very passion which set him scouring over past and future thus becomes an obstruction. We are shown into a private perspective. We lack, in his words, that delicate touch which accounts for the many-sided spell of time. It is, on the contrary, as if time and the world itself became a foil to his incensed feelings.

It is not so when two characters meet, brought together by a movement of mutual sympathy. All one-sided solitude is then given up. From two different poles two views of life converge completing each other. Placed face to face, the images seem to stir out of their daylight stillness. No longer do they stand out like statues, but like characters that give themselves away for what they are, for what they have been.

An appropriate scene was required for this to happen—a secluded spot whence to scan the world and time with human eyes, not only to survey the action and decide upon a certain course. These characters, as they meet, are thus forever associated with certain places—the tower of Troy for Priam and Helen, the citadel for Hector and Andromache, the distant tent by the ships for Achilles and Priam. For Homer, we have seen, does not allow for any casual conversations. His main characters are either present in all fulness, or not at all. He must have thought of them at one with the occasion in which he lets them appear, their vital qualities emerging all at once in the moment of confrontation.

Meeting as they do, these characters cannot bear any longer the constraint of their specious roles. A sudden need of communication seems to break the surface of their self-contained figures, and they elicit from one another the strains of life that went to make them what they are. For they are not delivering a message or saying anything in particular; it is a moment of self-realization, of self-revelation that takes place, and it cannot but come about in terms of time, by conjuring up phases of life.

Andromache's address to Hector (*Il.* 6. 407 ff.) is thus, virtually, one long sentence, one long thought spanning over her life. The days that have laid a waste of death around her now seem to converge upon Hector standing there before her: he is "her brother and mother and father and flourishing husband," as if each successive loss had found in him a compensation, his image made big with time. And Hector's reply, on the other hand, stretches into a future so vividly realized as to become a present scene: Ilion falling, the cry of Andromache led away as a captive, his own love made helpless. So placed face to face, the images grow transparent encompassing one another: life meets with life, and time extends as widely as the scope of a common passion and of a common destiny.

Or consider the meeting of Helen and Priam—how the one sets off the other in a moment that crowns all others, and each one grows upon us from the depth of a secret past. "Come here, sit before me, my child, to see your previous husband and kinsmen and friends; blameless you are in my eyes, it is the gods that I blame who brought upon me this war of the Achaeans and its tears" (*Il.* 3. 162 ff.), says Priam; to which Helen replies: "Awesome you are in my sight, dear father, and revered—would that bitter death had pleased me when hither I followed your son . . . but this did not happen, wherefore I am wasted in tears" (Ibid. 172 ff.). It is the sheer presence of these images which first of all entrances us—a silence that cannot but break into words. For a mutual spell draws them out of one another; and the past which comes to the surface is a destiny seen from different angles, a shared experience, perspectives that blend into one vision.

An imaginative mood of recollection has now set in. When Priam turns to look at the Achaeans marshalled below the walls, his eyes seem to unveil their images and enrich them with a world of memories. Agamemnon stands out in the spell of royalty, stirring up the thought of happy kingdoms, of encamped multitudes seen long ago. Odysseus and Menelaus seem to double into their distant selves, such as they were one day when they came as ambassadors to Troy—congenial speakers and not prepossessing warriors. No summing up, no transition is required. The contemplative moment dispells all enmity, restoring times of peace and recomposing in an instant whole stretches of history.

Even greater are these implications of time in the scene of Achilles and Priam (*Il.* 24. 477 ff.). For it is the sense of a universal human destiny that comes up from this quick exchange of looks and words, as suddenly and powerfully as when a first impression brings home some long-fancied but scarcely realized truth. We are startled and enlightened all at once when Priam enters the casual quietness of Achilles' tent, the wondering gaze of all centered upon him. That wonder clears away all prejudice, all preconceived and static opinions. It is the necessary shock that sets loose the drift of wide-ranging sympathies: the great image of a glorious old man is laid bare, as if an ancient story were now made visible and instantly enacted to its last syllable before our eyes.

But the contemplative suspense can only last for a moment: the bystanders, and least of all Achilles, cannot remain passive, drawn as they are into the meaning of what they see. Priam's words are just enough to set them in tune with a movement that transcends all one-sided perspective. "Remember your father, o Achilles . . . , of the same age as I" (*Il.* 24. 486 ff.), he says. "Remember" is the first word, with all it implies in the Greek—"to think," "to feel," not only "to recollect." It is a summons breaking the bounds of the present moment: parallel existences, parallel griefs are brought together, and one sole fate. The cumulative burden of past times now charges the scene; both Achilles and Priam weep, remembering. In those tears their outward images melt away to make room for a whole world which they carried in themselves unawares.

Character meeting character: it is the occasion in which the course of human time is realized most sharply. This is, of course, quite natural. It is so whenever we meet again an old friend; and any novel, no doubt, could provide us with many instances of the kind. But in Homer this contact is more sweeping. His self-contained figures appear, at first sight, immune from change, almost sacred, qualified as they are by their epithets; all the more striking is their revelation when they are exposed to one another. What they reveal all at once is their growth, their makeup; and time is like a subtle medium holding together the various strains which make them what they are. So subtle, that it is hardly perceptible to them. They do not mention it. It is something that hardly exists separate from themselves; but once they speak about themselves it is implied in everything they say: their whole life and destiny emerge contained in a few decisive events.

A time-value is intrinsic to the very material of the Homeric characters. There is no history outside them. What happens in the external world has no other frame of reference. Not only their own destiny, but that of all others seems to be at stake in their images. We are made strikingly aware of this when one of these characters disappears from the scene. For the death of a hero is not only a loss, but a fracture in the lives of others, a gaping void. So Andromache's dirge over Hector (*Il.* 24. 725 ff.) is a prophecy of annihilation: Troy destroyed, she herself led away on a Greek ship, even the death of the infant son darkly surmised in its gruesome detail. Or take the death of Patroclus: Achilles at once envisages his own death (*Il.* 18. 90, 98; 19. 319). Thetis, in her turn, mourns for him beforehand (*Il.* 18. 54 ff.); and it is as if her immortal life were brought to nought. What in the living image was so suggestive of time and experience is now blotted out. No commemoration, no obituary is possible. Thoughts about life need in Homer a living object to sustain them: they cannot project into unimaginable times, creating a world of their own. What these dirges dwell upon is much more the present despair than the life and character of the fallen hero. It could not be otherwise: the necessary link with posterity is missing and glory offers no compensation. This lack is felt in the last words of Andromache over Hector's bier: "nor did you speak to me a pithy word which I might remember all the days and nights of my weeping" (*Il.* 24. 744 f.).

9

In the great dialogues of the *Iliad* memories (or forebodings) come instantly, intermittently, under the pressure of the present moment. We only catch snatches of time and life. There is no leisurely representation of other times. The presence of the characters is too engrossing to allow for any long-drawn digression. Past and future are like prolongations, reverberations of the present scene. We lack here all vague, wandering survey of far-off things, all the charm of thoughts that recompose distant events. Only the ghost of Patroclus appearing to Achilles can indulge in such a luxury (*Il.* 23. 77 f., 86 ff.).

This indefinite sense of human time cannot come gratuitously, like an idle dream. As everything in Homer, it must be occasioned by material conditions, it must be prompted by a vital need. What is required is a distance between the characters. There must be a man that is cherished or feared, alive but absent, whose destiny is not known. Friends or enemies visualize him far away. Only then can thoughts focus anxiously upon a given object, and yet be free to wander unencumbered by its immediate presence. In such a way the life of an absent character can be mentally realized. His distant experiences are questioned, imagined, tentatively followed in their possible course, and not represented as objective data. The momentary occasion of a day or of a night must be left out of account. Time is here an indeterminate lapse of life, subjectively felt and yet posited in the world at large.

The *Odyssey* fosters this sensibility. We are made aware of it right at the beginning. For Odysseus emerges, as it were, out of nowhere. As he is first presented, his feet do not rest on any ground, he does not stand out in a particular stance, as Achilles and Agamemnon do at the beginning of the *Iliad*. He is unmistakably himself, but only by being strongly entrenched in our imagination. His prominence is due to a certain aura rather than to a single action. Where is he? When will he come? His image is in everyone's mind, remembered, expected, fixed in no given time or place, helplessly out of range.

The first book of the *Odyssey* gathers very quickly various threads of time around absent Odysseus. Telemachus sees him in his mind's eye, imagining the storms that might have killed him. Phemius sings the return of the Achaeans, recalling the destinies of the expedition which carried him away. Penelope hears and bids the minstrel stop, protesting her life-long grief for his absence. The suitors pursue their quest, scarcely concealing how they fear his return. All these characters survey the life of Odysseus in their persistent thoughts; and Odysseus is, in turn, a theme which keeps in unison their moods and their actions. A lapse of indefinite years is thus covered in brief outline.

Such a rendering of time would have been impossible, if Odysseus had been pictured in Ithaca, furthering his cause. His encompassing presence could leave no room for vague expectation or regret. But, as it is, his distance opens up the prospect of things to come and memory fills his vacant place with images from the past. It is as if the poet had no other means to suggest such an extension in time. For it was not his genius to depict changing situations in the manner of a novelist or a historian; and now the radiance of a distant image afforded him an effective medium: here was a man whose spell could reverberate into a whole age.

The distance of Odysseus is essential to the sense of time in the *Odyssey*. Existence thereby recedes more and more from what is immediately visual. It becomes a course of life to be endured or struggled for—a destiny summing up all the days in its own terms. It is so throughout the poem. See how, under the approaching shadow of Odysseus, the quality of each character grows into what it is. Telemachus becomes resolute. The suitors are obstinate. Penelope is faithful. It could not be otherwise: they are weathered by fear or hope, and their feelings have matured into a habit of mind. Everyday business here becomes perfunctory. In Penelope's case, for instance: the daily tasks—which elsewhere in Homer are so self-sufficient—become for her an excuse, a device to keep alive, like the weaving of the famous web which seems to allegorize her long resistance.

Odysseus, on the other hand, thinks of Ithaca. This thought is a driving force, turning his scattered exploits into phases of a long effort. His endurance has a counterpart in that of Penelope: at a different pole of the earth there is a longing which is parallel to his own, affecting his own; and deeply related feelings converge from different angles, gathering all accidental happenings into one great protracted strain.

It is remarkable how this encompassing effect of time ultimately rests, once again, on the spell of the Homeric image—just as in the quick exchanges of the *Iliad*, but much more extensively. For that same spell works now on a larger range, over the distance that separates the characters; and it is the same character that exerts it throughout the poem. Odysseus is πολύτλας, "much-suffering" by definition; and his very name evokes his destiny. But it is as if the burden of his epithet overflowed into his words, into his very features. For his sufferings are his great theme whenever he gives a condensed account of himself (cf. *Od.* 5. 222; 7. 24, 147, 152, etc.). Similarly, they are ever borne in mind whenever he is seen, remembered, imagined by others (cf. *Od.* 14. 42; 1. 161, 195, 235, etc.). As these instances accumulate, they haunt the mind of the reader. It is as if, each time, we saw Odysseus against a deepening background. Insofar as his suffering is expressed in a mere epithet, it is crystallized into his image; and we have no more than a heroic attribute. But, as the poem develops, this suffering is seen in a different light. We become aware of a capacity to suffer, to endure, to strive year after year. The heroic image is transformed into a complex character. Another Odysseus arises before us. Grief and hope have sobered him. His experiences advance in time; and all the dangers or wonders of isolated moments take their allotted place in the large vital movement of his life.

It is, of course, Odysseus himself who gives the full account of his experiences, speaking directly to the Phaeacians. But he arrives from far away. The distance which separated him heretofore from his listeners still isolates him. He is there in their midst; but removed into a world of his own by the legend that has gathered around him, by a past which is all one with the spell of his presence. Here at last a direct contact takes place—not suddenly, fleetingly, as in the scenes of the *Iliad,* but after a long suspense, the intervening distances at last cut short. As the long-suggested image strikes the beholder, the history of a whole lifetime is prefigured even before it is told.

The way in which Odysseus gradually reveals himself to the Phaeacians in the eighth book of the *Odyssey* is visual rather than verbal. He is not simply a stranger saying who he is and recounting his past. His identity seems to transpire, hinted by the wonder of his first appearance, by the wisdom of his words, by the power of his weatherworn limbs. Then the minstrel sings about Troy, and he weeps. His tears offer a glimpse of the actual truth, so that when he finally says his name, it hardly comes as a surprise. It is as if the image of Odysseus hovered in the consciousness of the audience right from the beginning. But what was just divined or known by hearsay is now made flesh and bones, and the timeless suggestion of a distant glory is transposed into the record of a man, legend is turned to self-confession, fame to subjective acknowledgement. The whole Trojan cycle becomes just a phase in a man's life. In that Phaeacian land where gods often consort with men Odysseus insists upon his human character: not only is he a mortal, but the most wretched of mortals. Only with this premise could his story be told in terms of human experience. But, at the same time, he has to rise to the full measure of his own prefigured image, in response to the expectation of those who are there before him questioning and wondering. His past must be elicited from his present spell, and not only from his tales. This is why he does not proceed to give an orderly account of his adventures from first to last. He begins, rather, with the last one—with the journey which brought him there from Calypso's island, as a wanderer, a suppliant. It is his presence there and then which matters most—a wonder for all to witness and account for. And later, when he actually recounts his return from Troy, it is as if his story were a means of self-realization. His past actions are each a parcel of the life which is gathered within him; and time is like the shadow of his image, indefinitely prolonged. He is not only surveying things gone by, he is giving a proof of himself. His relation with the audience is here essential. The listeners progressively contemplate, admire, learn, know; and their knowledge is in turn a new feeling for what they apprehended at first sight. What amazes them is not so much the narrative itself as the narrator who grows upon them as he speaks. His personality, surmised at first, is now recomposed more clearly in its human terms; and we have no chronological sequence of mythical ventures, but the progressive revelation of a man's life—a living process rather than a cycle artificially contrived.

The way in which Odysseus makes himself known in Ithaca is worked out in the same spirit. Again we have the penetrating spell of his image; again the questioning gaze of those who see him, and the distances finally cut short, an interval of absence which must be filled, words which recompose the lapse of time.

Only the circumstances are different than they were in the land of the Phaeacians. Odysseus is now transformed into an old beggar by Athena; and, when the occasion calls for it, again into a young man. These transformations, of course, are required by the plot. But we may also see them in a different light. His appearance as an old man can be justified in an ideal sense. It is an alteration, a disguise worked by the years of absence, a screen which gives way at an even pace with the process of recognition which exhumes the past.

Odysseus seems to emerge more and more clearly out of his rags. He becomes a power in Ithaca even before it is known who he actually is. For his relation with the island becomes more meaningful from hour to hour. He is moving into the circuit of old affections. His bodily presence gradually absorbs them all; and he advances dramatically to take his rightful place, filling the gap of separation and estrangement, retrieving an identity which seemed out of reach. Finally he is made one with the image which had haunted for so long the mind of his people.

His progress in Ithaca is at once a recovery of the past. As he advances, his background is enlarged. For, almost unintentionally, he attracts or challenges whomsoever he happens to meet; and long-standing attitudes are immediately brought into play. Thus Eumaeus is stirred to instant sympathy and impassioned recollection, while Odysseus, standing before him in his rags, participates in the drama of Ithaca with increasing intensity, as if he were drawing new blood from his ancient roots. Now a mysterious familiarity draws them closer to one another. He appears enhanced by an unexpected prestige, so keenly does he realize the true state of the island, so strongly does he judge and forecast the course of events. Who might this stranger be? Even before this is known, he is made to bear the mark of his true character, just as the makeshift story which he composes about himself comes as a preface to the true one, almost an allegory of his life, an intimation of his identity.

His broadening role also means an enrichment of his personality. Here again the element of time is important. For now a more intimate side of his life is opening up, a side of him which had remained concealed so far. Its values come upon him as a distinct awareness of facts and of people in their long careers. Penelope, Telemachus, Laertes, Anticleia now take their pertinent part in his introspection, and a whole portion of his past becomes intrinsic to his being. At a certain point, it is as if the burden of this past could no longer be contained within him, as if recognition were inevitably imminent through some force of its own.

It is extraordinary how his increasing awareness is matched by an increasing transparency of his image to the eyes of others. More and more does the beggar appear like Odysseus, as he meets the taunts of the suitors and of the handmaids, as he endears himself to Penelope; more and more, accordingly, does his life unfold. The climax comes, of course, when Eurycleia, washing him, recognizes the famous scar. But a premonition haunts her beforehand. At that moment her feelings for Odysseus are singularly stirred; and, as in a vision, she says to him: "Woe is me, o son, for your sake; how helpless I am. Zeus has especially spurned you in spite of your goodness" (*Od.* 19. 363 ff.). Then, turning to the beggar: "Even so, I think, the attendants of far-off strangers have scoffed at him, as now these shameless ones were scoffing at you" (Ibid. 370 ff.). Finally a sympathetic insight flashes upon her: "My heart is all astir with your woes. But listen . . . of all the many wretched wanderers that have come in the past to this house, none have I seen so resembling Odysseus as you" (Ibid. 377 ff.).

The feeling of recognition becomes contagious. The sight of the beggar unmistakably evokes the destiny of Odysseus. A little later Philoitios echoes the words of Eurycleia: "O father Zeus, none of the gods brings more woe than you. You do not take pity upon men though yourself you bring them to birth, and you plunge them in misery and grief" (*Od.* 20. 201 ff.). Then turning to the beggar: "I perspire as I see you, tears rise up in my eyes, remembering Odysseus; for he too, I think, is clothed in such rags a wanderer among men" (Ibid. 204 ff.).

Recognition is the key word here. It implies a recovery of wasted times, values made good again, features retraced to their ancient integrity. To see, to know, to rediscover are now all one. The eyes of the characters are endowed with a particular insight which seems to penetrate beyond the surface. Odysseus, on his part, stands transfigured by the impact of attentive looks. The past blends with the present, shimmering through his outlines. The work of memory is wonderfully quickened. Unwittingly he bears in himself his story.

After a long time people are altered, and yet essentially the same. Their lives might be suggested by their features. It is so with Odysseus: his long suffering is witnessed by the wrinkles that disfigure him, while the power of his limbs still betrays his native prowess. All this is quite natural; but the plot seems so designed as to isolate and stress these effects of time. More and more do we realize that Odysseus' transformations at the hand of Athena acquire in this context a meaning which goes beyond that of a mere stratagem. If he appears now young now old as befits the occasion, is not this a way of rendering visually the suggestions of memory and of present awareness? Penelope, at the end (*Od.* 23. 93 ff.), sits wondering. It is of no help that Odysseus should be made to assume again the splendor of his youth (Ibid. 156 ff.). Her silence conceals the effort to realize the unity of these varied appearances, to make the real coincide with its idealization. She must reconcile her long-matured restraint with her present longing. What are these transformations to her eyes? Who is Odysseus? The husband she remembers, the beggar she has just been talking to, the bright metamorphosis now displayed before her? All these are like illusions which time has played upon her baffled consciousness—the dreams and visions which kept her waiting for so long, shreds of her brooding experience which must now be made into one coherent whole. Here is a heart-searching task which Homer does not, cannot retrace in its subjective, passionate phases, but, again, through the glimmer of shifting appearances.

Penelope cannot resist for long. She must reply to Odysseus' entreaty. When she does so, it is as if his transformation into a young man awaked in her the feelings of her earlier life. "I am not proud, I am not disdainful, I am now coming back to myself; I remember how you looked when you sailed away in the long-oared ship," she says (*Od.* 23. 174 ff.). We are reminded of the scene in which Helen is carried back to a past experience by a far different transformation (cf. above p. 148 ff.).

Returning or welcoming back after twenty years is an engrossing experience, especially when those who meet again are an Odysseus and a Penelope. In long regret they have idealized one another; and now they stand out for what they are, weathered by the years. Here is a dissonance between the mental image and the real one. Pent-up feelings suddenly concur to fill up the gap, to restore the harmony. Now more than ever can a long lapse of time be mentally realized. The initial shock clears the way. It was characteristic of Homer to concentrate upon such a moment, to work it up with all the wonder it naturally implies. A miraculous coincidence seemed to occur—destiny joining in with a spontaneous movement of human sympathy. Euripides must have had something like it in mind in his *Helen* when he wrote "to recognize a friend is a god" (*Hel.* 560). Homer could not be so abstract. He brought into play Athena's spell, the transformation of Odysseus.

A long-awaited moment, when it comes, puts everything else in the shade. Our feelings magnify it, gathering into it all that in the past was missed or vaguely anticipated. But Homer could not render it as pure inner experience. He conceived it visually, dramatically. Hence Odysseus' changing image, hence the devious ways of his return to Penelope. There is no passionate celebration, no tender recollection. We have, instead, overtures, approaches, meetings that become more and more pressing, shifting appearances that become more and more significant. All this is carried out as by a divine spell; but the element of wonder is made convincing and forcible insofar as it stresses the human tensions implied in each scene. Thus Odysseus' transfiguration, as we have seen, reflects Penelope's feeling of duration and change, of expectation and fulfillment. It is as if time had discharged upon a visual form the burden of persistent longings.

As in the *Iliad*, the images are suddenly brought before one another and reveal themselves. But here the meeting comes after a long climax; and the crowning moment must be made relevant to a previous story, broad vicissitudes of life compressed into the imagery and action of single scenes. The extent to which this could be done is no small proof of artistic power—of how the bulky epic material could be made to suggest, if not to express directly, the delicate complexities of human time.

10

Memories are stirred up almost unwittingly when people meet again at length. Time gathers spontaneously from many sides: what strikes a common chord comes to the fore, no matter when or where it happened. This is human time, this is life. And yet a survey of one's life is something different. It requires that an individual be followed in the course of his existence. What matters is not so much the significance of single occasions as a sense of continuity, of development, of growth. The idea of time must thus be gleaned from the signs of a vital spark that perseveres in its activity. We shall have to look for it in the notion of existence itself, and not in the self-revelation of characters that meet in dramatic moments.

In fifth century Greek, just as in English, the word "life" means both the fact of being alive and its duration. We easily abstract the sense of time from that of a vital organic principle and, by doing so, we make the word "life" synonymous with experience, history, biography (as when we say "a happy life" or "the life of Shakespeare"). It is not so in Homer. The temporal meaning is only implied. There are no such abstractions as time and life. These are ideal values, submerged as yet in the material which is their source. We find, instead, a stress on those organs or things which make life possible—what nourishes, what breathes, heart, spirit. Herein lies a vital function. By its very nature it yields a sense of time—a common capacity to be, to live, to resist, to endure.

The language of Homer will give us a cue. There are many

words which might be translated as "life"; but not one which normally carries with it a sense of duration. What prevails is everywhere the idea of a vital force or sustenance whose extension in time may be indirectly conveyed by the context, as if the animate vigor were all there waiting to be drawn out. What we mean by "life span," "lifetime" is not something taken for granted; it is a value which is inferred from observing the ways of nature.

A brief survey of the relevant words might help to clear these points. The root *bi-* (cf. Sanscrit *jivas*, Latin *vivus, vita*) is represented in Homer by the nouns βίοτος, βίος, βιοτή. It is βίοτος which is by far the most frequent, with its usual meaning "livelihood," "substance"—e.g. ἀφνειός βιότοιο "rich in livelihood" (*Il.* 5. 544; 6. 14). How deep-rooted this material meaning is in Homer may be shown also by his use of the kindred word ζωή—e.g. ζωὴν ἐδάσαντο "they divided the livelihood" (*Od.* 14. 208; cf. ibid. 96; 16. 429).

A sense of life as duration, on the other hand, only comes up in certain expressions. "If you die and fulfill your measure of life (πότμον . . . βιότοιο)," says Agamemnon to Menelaus (*Il.* 4. 170). "The end of life (βιότοιο τελευτή) would have come upon you, o Menelaus," we read in *Il.* 7. 104; cf. 16. 787. Similarly Poseidon prevents Adamas from slaying Antilochus "grudging him his life" (βιότοιο μεγήρας, *Il.* 13. 563).

The idea of "lifetime" would thus appear to emerge in connection with death. At such a point the material sustenance of life does not matter any more. All that remains is a conclusion, casting the wealth of existence into an irrevocable past. By being so placed in jeopardy or in abeyance, life thus ceases to be a vital enjoyment and possession; at least for a moment, it is viewed in terms of time.

Such glimpses of life running out are characteristic of the battle scenes of the *Iliad*. The *Odyssey* offers more distant perspectives, and the same words draw from it a stronger sense of duration. Thus Athena bids Telemachus set out to learn about "his father's life and return" (πατρὸς βίοτον καὶ νόστον, *Od.* 1. 287). Odysseus' opponents in Ithaca withdraw "craving for life" (λιλαιόμενοι βιότοιο

Il. 24. 536). Eumaeus is told by Odysseus how fortunate is his actual state: "After much suffering you came to the home of a generous man who gives you food and drink with loving care, and you *live a good life* (ζώεις δ' ἀγαθὸν βίον, *Od.* 15. 491). Penelope wishing for her husband says: "O, if only he came and *protected my life*" (τὸν ἐμὸν βίον ἀμφιπολεύοι, *Od.* 18. 254; 19. 127). Menelaus is promised a blessed survival in the Elysian fields "where the life of man is most smooth" (ῥηΐστη βιοτὴ πέλει ἀνθρώποισι, *Od.* 4. 565).

In these passages the sense of life and of its duration is no longer suggested by the shadow of death, but by a positive interest, a need, a desire. Seen in this light, the life span is not simply an allotted period drawing to its end, but an active process. And yet not even here is this fuller meaning quite established. It is evident how a material connotation still clings to these expressions. The quest for Odysseus' life and return, for instance, is nothing more than the urge to know whether he is actually alive (cf. *Od.* 2. 132; 4. 110, 833; etc.). It is so also with Eumaeus' "good life": the context shows how strongly tinged it is with a sense of sheer physical subsistence; for it is linked very closely with the bountifulness of a good lord who affords food and drink. Penelope's βίος is no other—a state of existence, a boon which craves for a protecting hand. All these examples could be similarly interpreted. They all point to a material state; it is the spirit of the poem that gives the words a vicarious sense of time.

There is, however, another word for "life" which contains in its very root the notion of time—αἰών (cf. αἰεί "always," Latin *aevum*). But the Homeric feeling for the immediate is again predominant. Even this word expresses most often the flash of life cut short by death: "short was his life under Ajax's blow (*Il.* 4. 478; cf. 17. 302), "when life and spirit had left him" (*Il.* 16. 453; cf. 19. 27; 22. 58; 24. 725; *Od.* 9. 523). In such passages αἰών is almost equivalent to θυμός, the vital spark in the living animal. Only once does it refer to a long life: Achilles, dwelling on his alternative fates, says: "If I return home . . . , for long will life abide for me, nor will the doom of death reach me soon" (*Il.* 9. 415). But notice the peculiarity of the expression. Achilles does

not say "my life will be long" but "life will be in me for long."
It is as if he meant the vital breath, which can be cut short in an
instant, or subsist for a while.

The word αἰών, like βίος, seems to acquire in the *Odyssey* a more
significant sense of time. It is used for the long years spent by
Odysseus in Calypso's island. He is there yearning for Ithaca "and
sweet life was flowing out of him as he mourned for his return"
(*Od.* 5. 152; cf. ibid. 160; 18. 204). Here again the physical element is uppermost, but how transfigured! It flows; and that flowing is a brooding extension in time. Life is a sweet sap that wastes
away, like sand in an hourglass. It is inherently sweet, though
Odysseus was gloomy. We are not told what a miserable time he
had; we are stirred, instead, with a feeling of languishing hours.

Another group of words approaches the meaning of time and
life from a different angle. These are the words for "spirit,"
"soul," "heart," "life force" (θυμός, ψυχή, ἦτορ, μένος). A phrase like
"the spirit left him as he fell" is typical. "Spirit" is here equivalent
to "life." So for instance: "he lost his life," "he bereft him of
sweet life," "he loosened his might" (cf. *Il.* 4. 470; 8. 270; 10.
495; 16. 332, etc.).

Spirit, breath, power are suddenly stamped out; and this vital
reality is felt all at once the moment it is missed. A sense of time
could hardly be elicited from life so rendered. There is no room for
it in such an instant consummation. But the very breath which
vanishes may convey an idea of life's intrinsic and permanent
value, quite apart from the crushing blow and the fatal moment.
This is evident in the word ψυχή. Like θυμός, it may denote the
spirit as it leaves the body (*Il.* 11. 334; 5. 296; 14. 518); and yet
it is also something self-existing, manifest in its own right and
separable from any organic function. It thus normally indicates
the surviving ghost; but, before being so crystallized, as it exhales,
it is pure breath, an essence in itself and by itself, fit to be depicted
for its own sake. Achilles in vindicating the value of his own life
uses the word most significantly: "They can be plundered the
oxen and the goodly sheep; they can be bought the tripods and
the tawny horses; but the life of a man (ἀνδρός ψυχή) can never re-

turn for seizing or plundering, once it has passed the enclosure of his teeth" (*Il*. 9. 408; cf. ibid. 401, 322; 22. 161, 325, 338; *Od*. 1. 5; 3. 74; 9. 255).

That breath exaling from a man's mouth must no doubt be taken literally; and yet it bears with it all the treasures that life may possess. Self-realization, self-fulfillment are implied, which are things of time, but the Homeric psyche can only suggest them from afar; it is sensuous breath that lies at the source of its meaning, precluding any idea of duration. Achilles, a little further on in the same speech, uses, as we have seen, another word (αἰών) for "life span." The stretch of time and the fulness of life are not welded, as yet, into one notion.

We might expect the word θυμός to acquire the full meaning of "life." For θυμός is not only the spirit leaving the dying body; it is, above all, an animating spark in the living, stirring a man to all manner of feelings, thoughts, actions. But this many-sidedness does not allow it to crystallize into the general meaning of "life": θυμός is continually the mainspring of an inner movement; it can hardly be considered apart from its immediate manifestations. "The θυμός stirred within him," "the θυμός bid him speak," "the θυμός rejoiced in him" we often read; and in each instance "life" is only implied in the vitality of a momentary feeling or act. Very rarely, on the other hand, does θυμός suggest an enduring presence of "life": at the most it is an inner vigor which waxes or wanes in phrases like: "they perish away in their θυμός" (*Il*. 16. 540), which we might render "they waste away their lives" (cf. *Od*. 10. 78, 460–5). Similarly in *Od*. 21. 88, "her θυμός is laid in grief" might be taken as the Homeric way of saying "her life is full of grief." Likewise Telemachus expresses his coming of age: "Now I am full-grown, and listening to the words of others I am learning, and the θυμός is increasing within me" (*Od*. 2. 315).

All these Homeric words present to our mind a sort of rich ambiguity. We have, on the one hand, the meanings of "livelihood," "subsistence," "existence"; and, on the other, the meaning of "spirit." The examples of ψυχή and θυμός seem to be especially important for the concepts they tend to isolate and deliver. Blending into one the meanings both of "spirit" and "life," they cannot express them separately. Neither, for instance, can "spirit" suggest pure intelligence nor can "life" be understood as individual experience developing in time. Idealization here falls short of a purely immaterial notion. What we find is a more primordial identity of breath and existence, but so modulated as to be full of subtle implications and foreshadow the distinctions of a later thought. The rough vitality of action thus refines itself from scene to scene. It is so with the Homeric θυμός which gives one common impact to single, successive instances of intense experience. It is so with the psyche which in Achilles' words almost becomes a symbol for self-existence. Passing emotions, or emotions gathering into states of mind, and breath, or breath quickening into spirit, and spirit epitomizing life—all bring to a head the sense of time as experience; and the premises are set for βίος, "life," to gather up the sum of accumulating significant moments.

11

The word "life" has a complex meaning. It ultimately expresses an idea rather than a condition; and such an idea, once established, lends itself to qualifications which overshadow the sense of time. Thus we may say, for instance, "the life of the mind." The verbs which mean "to live," on the other hand, cannot but point to direct experience. As all verbs, they naturally express something transient, momentary, no fixed condition. They are perhaps more likely to render the elusive and delicate element of time.

"To be," "to exist," "to live"—we use such verbs in giving an account of individuals, people, things. We say: "There lived a man" or "there existed a city" to recall the past; and then, just by changing the tenses, we can point forward. We may further specify: "He lived doing this or that" or "a city existed which prospered." These verbs thus become signals which transpose us to different times and introduce the action. Using them in this way, we hardly realize the intrinsic nature of existing, living. We have somehow loosened it, we have dissolved it into a temporal medium. The tense has overshadowed the actual meaning of the verb, weakened it, subjected it to an ulterior purpose.

Homer does not conjugate the verb "to live" in the same way. He does not use it as an auxiliary, to express successive conditions —now, before, or after. Take the most frequent word, ζώω: it is almost exclusively used in the present, and it means "to be alive" as opposed to "being dead" (cf. *Od.* 2. 132; 4. 833, etc.). Or take the synonymous βιόω which is used in the same sense, but in an aorist form which means "to recover life," "to escape alive," "to save oneself" (*Il.* 15. 511; 10. 174; 8. 429; *Od.* 14. 359).

When Ajax says to his companions: "It is better either to die once for all or to live rather than to wear away at length in the terrible struggle" (*Il.* 15. 511), the element of time is taken into account only to describe the moment of death and the gradual exhaustion ("once for all," "at length"). When one dies or wastes away, he is encompassed in an empty stretch of time. As for the matter of living, it is a function, a pursuit in itself—something to be achieved, won at each moment. The course of time seems all taken up by carrying out this vital role.

There is thus something positive, self-sufficient, absolute about the act of living as expressed in Homer. Its value only resides in itself and cannot easily be referred to other terms than its own. It would be unlike Homer to say: "he lived happily." In such a phrase the word "lived" would only convey a sense of duration, quite subordinate to the idea of happiness. All the vitality of "living" would be lost. In order to express something of the kind, Homer would say: "his spirit was in a state of joy" (cf. *Od.* 6. 155); or else: "the gods gave him good fortune" (cf. *Od.* 8. 413). So we read in a passage: "may the gods grant them happy things to live upon" (*Od.* 7. 149). The verb "to live" here points to an immediate gain, to a vital nourishment; and the idea of duration comes from that of a permanent fortune.

To pass one's time, to conduct one's life in a certain way, to live through an experience—all such meanings seem quite alien to the Homeric verb "to live." Homer would not say "to live in

Mycenae," but "to inhabit." Nor would he say "to live bravely"; he would rather describe in concrete terms a brave course of action (cf. *Il*. 6. 444–6). The nearest example I can find for "living" in terms of experience is *Il*. 24. 526: "for the gods spun out this lot to mankind—to live grieving." But what we have here is a destiny rather than a way of life.

The representation of "living" as a vital activity is deeply rooted in Homer. It does not merely concern the meaning of a few verbs. Homer loves to dwell on the sinewy vigor and native qualities of the living. "Whilst I am living and see with my eyes on the face of the earth," "As long as breath abides in my breast and my knees can stir" are current expressions (*Il*. 1. 88; 9. 609–10; cf. 5. 120; 11. 477; 17. 447; 22. 388; *Od*. 4. 540, 833; 14. 44; 15. 349; 16. 439; 18. 133; 20. 207). The sense of duration is given by the temporal turn of the phrase. "Whilst," "as long as," "until": the imagined stretch of life is filled with a vital exertion. This energy is not only physical. Breath that is spirit, eyes that enjoy the sun, knees that are nimble—these carry out the task of living; and the time of life lies in their continued resilience.

These vital functions have a certain rhythm which is essentially the same from moment to moment. They endure as long as the individual frame makes it possible, remaining what they are from one's birth to one's death. They thus give us a sense of smooth, even continuity: any instant is here typical of a lifetime. We may, therefore, still wonder how Homer conceives the plain fact of living from one age to the other, how he expresses or renders existence in its forward stages, how far he can convey a sense of development in time. The verb "to live" was here of no use. It was too bound up with the immediate striking evidence of a live body. In order to abstract from the present and render the arch of a man's years, a different meaning, a different idea presented itself— not "to live," but "to nourish oneself," "to be reared," "to grow" (τρέφομαι, ἔτραφον). Again the sensuous evidence had to be taken into account. The subtle process of gradual change could only be apprehended as growth, as increase, just as it appeared in the ways of nature, in a form that blossoms and mellows.

Thus bearing in mind the general course of his life then Ajax says to his friends: "no fool was I born and grew up in Salamis" (*Il.* 7. 199; cf. 1. 266; 2. 661; 3. 201; 9. 142, etc.). Again this is not simply a question of vocabulary. Homer, as usual, draws from a physical, natural source his descriptions of the human condition. To be born, to live—or to waste away, to die—are things of the animal and vegetal world; and the feeling for this obvious truth runs singularly deep throughout the poems, implied as it is in the words and the imagery. In this spirit Thetis speaks about the childhood and youth of Achilles: "he shot up like a young branch; I nourished him like a plant on a hill-top" (*Il.* 18. 56). Telemachus is similarly described (*Od.* 14. 175). Nausicaa is a blossom as she enters the dance (*Od.* 6. 157); her beauty is like that of a young palm tree to the eyes of Odysseus (Ibid. 163).

To pass one's life is to vegetate, to bloom, to wither. It is the destiny of what springs from the earth and returns to it. The lives of men in general are seen in this light. We may think, in this connection, of the famous simile comparing men to the leaves of the forest (*Il.* 6. 146 ff.; cf. 21. 464 f.). Odysseus goes even further when he says: "Nothing weaker than man does the earth nourish" (*Od.* 18. 130). We would say, perhaps: "no being that lives on the earth is weaker than man." The phrase of Homer is remarkably different: he does not see men that live their lives in the world, but the earth that nourishes them. Compare in *Od.* 11. 365: "such men as sown far and wide the dark earth feeds in great numbers." What these passages convey is the course of life, but steeped in nature, conceived in terms which are not purely human.

The act of living and the process of growth suggest the work of native energies. What stands out is a common function, a common destiny. Homer gives it prominence, bringing out a uniform consistency. Individual experience is here disregarded. But how could human life be considered as a merely natural activity and development? The life of any one person is something unique. Certain joys and sorrows make it what it is. They are, to our mind, part and parcel of life. We join them with the act of living in one and the same expression when we say, for instance, "he lived with hope," "he lived in despair." How could Homer convey such an essential experience of living?

We might say that Homer would simply leave out the verb "to live" and say "he hoped," "he despaired." But such an explanation would not be adequate. For the Homeric verb is different from ours. While its tenses can refer, as in English, to present, past, and future, they also possess, more than in English, another value —the so-called aspect. They can express an action as continuous (present, imperfect, future), as momentary (aorist), as complete in itself (perfect). Time is here inherent in the action or in the state of being; it does not mark the relative sequences of now, before, and after. We may thus read into the Homeric forms a sense of being, of existence, over and above the specific meaning of each verb.

If we pursued this subject, we would go beyond the limits of this essay. One or two examples will be enough. Take, for instance, the verb "to grieve." Using the present, ἄχομαι (*Od.* 19. 129), Penelope dwells upon her fate as a whole. The sense, therefore, requires "now I am living in grief" rather than simply "I grieve" or "I am grieving" which would seem too weak for such an encompassing experience. Or we find the perfect ἀκάχηται about old Laertes. It indicates a state both past and present, affecting the whole period of his old age; it really means "he is steeped in grief, and he has been so for the last twenty years of his life."

Acts and feelings thus have an intrinsic time-dimension. The mode of their realization is more important than their chronological order. Such a form of expression is symptomatic. It points to a style, to a way of looking at things. For what is stressed is the action itself rather than the career of the actors, and the whole narrative proceeds on these lines. Even a long story is told by stressing certain essential phases rather than by regularly tracing the course of actions and events from beginning to end. It is especially so in rendering the life of a character. Helen, for instance, expresses herself in this way when recounting her past. She says to Priam: "Would that cruel death had pleased me just then, when hither I was following your son, from the moment I left my home . . . but these things did not happen; wherefore I am wasted in tears" (*Il.* 3. 173 ff.). It is impossible to translate the way in which the verbs here mark each essential stage in the way it happened: the instant departure, the protracted journey, the long state of languishment. Nothing about life, living; no account of circumstances and results. Her emotions, her movements have their own allotted duration. Time is internal to them; not a pattern imposed from without. The years thus gather around certain focal points, and a cry of anguish fills the intervals.

Homeric poetry is concise, forcible. Its condensed power partly resides in the way it renders the lapse of time, of life. We could hardly summarize this expressive quality or define its purport: it is one and all with the language itself. We may get an idea of it if we realize how far we have thinned out our expressions of time, spiritualizing existence and refining it into the tenuous threads of subjective experience. The Homeric verb, on the other hand, renders an action of a feeling in its objective contours: what we mean by life and experience is integrated into the meaning of each verbal form, while for Homer the actual fact of living is nothing else but being alive, keeping alive, growing.

12

When we think of a person's life, we unwittingly idealize it abstracting from the living presence of the person itself. Only in moments of poetic insight, or in the recollection of someone we know, do we focus upon the actual image. Otherwise what comes to mind is the hero's distinction and his motives—experiences, works, achievements which we order into a plausible sequence. Our very way of thinking about people is biographical. "What is he doing with his life?" we say; and our judgment makes up for the failure to realize sympathetically the natural process of living.

Homer stands at opposite ends. His words for "life," "living" give us a cue. He cannot turn away from the actual presence of his characters in order to give us an account of their lives. We are presented with prepossessing images whose past or present state is not necessarily considered or even mentioned. Quite apart from their characterization, Homer endows them with a sort of self-explaining birthright. Some idea of what I mean may be gleaned from such expressions as "the sacred might of Alcinous," "the force of Iphicles," "the heart of Pylaimenes" etc. used instead of the proper names themselves (cf. *Od.* 7. 167; 11. 290; *Il.* 2. 851; etc.). What is the original reason of the periphrasis? It is that a man is introduced in a native countenance which belongs to him once and for all. His existence, whatever it may have been in the past, is all gathered there. In his name, in his image, we have an aggregate of power, life, spirit. That vital spark which in Homer continually prompts feelings and actions is now crystallized, as if it were part of a person's name. These men, these heroes are sheer embodiments of life.

A life-story in Homer can only be conjured up dramatically, in the flashes of a dialogue, as in the scene between Hector and Andromache. Characters are never traced back in their long careers. At the most Homer touches upon natural growth, bringing out a blossoming moment which is almost visual. He thus humanizes the drift of nature; and the primitive impulse to live is turned into a phase of self-fulfillment. The process of growing is here spiritualized; and yet it is swift, inevitable, like that of the seasons. A good instance is Telemachus coming of age, in the first four books of the *Odyssey*. A new power seizes him quite suddenly through the agency of Athena, like a human springtide (*Od.* 1. 296–7, 301–2, 320–2, etc.). His father's *menos*, his father's temper, is like a keen substance infused into him and it must give its fruits (*Od.* 2. 271 ff.). At the same time this power is intelligence, a capacity to think and to speak (*Od.* 3. 26 ff.). What is portrayed is a time of transformation. It comes in brief, sharp touches. The image of Telemachus is composed and recomposed accordingly—his brooding loneliness (*Od.* 1. 114–5), his bold outburst (*Od.* 2. 40 ff.), his still-lingering shyness (*Od.* 3. 22 ff.), his self-awareness, will power, resolution *(Od.* 15. 87 ff.). These are only some significant passages out of many. Youth, or early manhood, appears as a state which is immediately present, its gradual stages transposed into the full evidence of decisive moments. Telemachus has something of the rigidity which we find in a primitive *kouros,* and yet also an Athenian suppleness. That suppleness marks the impact of time.

We have, on the one hand, the mighty presence of heroes like Ajax whom we know the moment we first meet them; and, on the other, characters that are caught in an age of growth and self-realization, like Telemachus or Nausicaa. There seems to be nothing in between, no idea of the progressive experiences which make a man, no real biography. The course of life, if at all, is recorded in its natural terms. It is so with the warriors of the *Iliad* whose death calls for a brief obituary. Iphidamas, for instance, "who was bred and grew in fair-soiled Thrace mother of sheep; Kisseus reared him . . . and then when he had attained the full measure of glorious youth, he detained him and gave him his daughter; married he went off from his bed-chamber to join the Achaeans on the track of their fame" (*Il.* 11. 221; cf. 5. 542; 6. 21; 13. 172, 364, etc.). A basic natural pattern underlies these records. We hardly find here any personal trait, but events which affect the world of nature as a whole: birth, childhood, manhood, marriage are like generalized signals of existence, inevitable conditions of life.

The language reflects this outlook. The phrase "to attain the full measure of youth" recurs quite often (cf. *Od.* 18. 217; 19. 532; 11. 317). Measure: that is to say "portion," "allotted time span"; youth is seen as a value in itself, not to be altered according to individual cases. It would be un-Homeric to say "a miserable youth." The meaning of youth cannot admit any arbitrary qualification. It is naturally glorious. Nor can it easily be expressed as a predicate. Homer does not normally say "he is young": the word "young" ($\dot{\eta}\beta\acute{\omega}\omega\nu$, $\alpha\dot{\iota}\zeta\eta\acute{o}s$) is an epithet, an attribute, or a noun, all one with a certain image, not a predicate. We find instead "he has the flower of youth "(*Il.* 13. 484), "he is not lacking in youth" (*Od.* 8. 136). The state of youth is something positive in itself, removed from change. It is the same with old age. The word "old" ($\gamma\acute{\epsilon}\rho\omega\nu$) is essentially a noun, not a predicate. For the predicative "he is old" we find phrases like "old age is upon him," "old age is pressing upon him" (cf. *Il.* 8. 103; 4. 315, etc.).

In these expressions the time of individual experience is hardly relevant. Youth and old age are made visible, tangible. They are displayed in the limbs and features of a person. They are just as actual as blossom or decay. But all the more is their impact remarkable. What is it that produces such alteration at a certain point? It is youth, old age; they are not simply stages in the course of life, but real agents. The cause, the occurrence, and the effect are here all one. These opposing states are influences that exclude each other; and this polarity leaves no room for the intervening period. It is as when we look at two pictures of the same person young and old: the resemblance lies deep down and no comparison enables us to recompose the gradual transformation. What may be explained as a process of experience could hardly be rendered in visual terms.

Hence the people in Homer appear to be either quite young or quite old. So, in the *Odyssey*, we have Penelope, Odysseus, the suitors along with Telemachus and, on the other hand, Laertes, Mentor, Eurycleia. This is quite striking in the case of Odysseus and Penelope. They must, of course, be middle-aged; but all the same they are endowed with youthful vigor and beauty through the agency of Athena. This inconsistency is clearest in Odysseus. The toils of twenty years should have weathered him; and those who knew him and loved him best might have recognized the familiar features grown old. But what we see is quite different: he appears alternately as a disguised old beggar and as a young hero.

This situation, strange as it is, is such as we might expect in Homer. However humanized in the dramatic parts of the poem, figures like Penelope and Odysseus retain a hard traditional core. A beautiful bride who is waiting, a valiant husband who will finally return home—these are, after all, typical images conceived in a permanent form. While bringing out the sense of time and life in a few intimate scenes, Homer could not reduce the fixity of the images.

We therefore do not find in Homer any attempt to survey

imaginatively a whole life-story. Even when a character speaks about himself, the biographical details appear quite colorless if they are set forth with deliberate directness and not conjured up under the stress of a dramatic moment. An example in point is Nestor. He is very old and likes to dwell on his past (*Il.* 4. 318 ff.; 7. 132–57; 11. 670–762; 23. 629–42). He is portrayed vividly— but only insofar as he is a real old man standing before our eyes, with old age weighing upon his native alertness. When he refers to his past, it is not so. "Would that I became young again," he begins; and his youth is just an age of heroic strength, not a formative phase of life. Take, for instance, the longest account (*Il.* 11. 670–762). We are introduced to a chapter of myth and tribal tradition—the battles between the Pylians and their north-ern neighbors: Nestor, the young prince of Pylos, routs whole multitudes, even the monstrous Moliones hardly escape him. Events follow one another quite mechanically, hardly enhanced by exaggeration and overpraise. The old hero speaks about himself as about another person seen and admired long ago. There is no link between his youth and old age. Might we detect a touch of irony in his ostentation? If so, this would confirm my point, as if the poet could not handle these ancient stories in the earnest man-ner which is more nearly his own.

The imagination of Homer, unlike Pindar's, is not at all mythi-cal. What we might call the cyclic time span of mythical events quite escapes him. Or, rather, he is not interested in it. If a great hero appears on the scene, his heroic past is not told. What mat-ters is the moment of his presence. It is so, for instance, with Glaucus (*Il.* 6. 145 ff.). Diomedes asks him: "Who are you?" How can he reply? What he really is, his life, cannot be truly related; and with pity for the generations of men, with a certain scorn and reluctance, he proceeds to give his genealogy. Genealogy, not personal life. Only his ancestor Bellerophon lives again for a moment in his words; he himself is just the last of a famous line. It is as we had nothing in between: on the one hand the living moment of the action, and on the other a genealogy which is like the work of nature in human terms.

It is so whenever Homer traces back the origin of his heroes. The past then seems timeless, placed as it is beyond experience and knowledge. We might compare Diomedes (*Il.* 14. 110 ff.), Aeneas (*Il.* 20. 213 ff.): they also go through their lineage as if it were a tale whose truth cannot be tested, but must simply be accepted to establish who they are in the eyes of others. For they live in the earnestness of the moment and they cannot dwell on far-off things. The account of Homeric genealogies is, therefore, often blurred, colorless; and it contrasts sharply with the bright appearance of a hero. So Theoclymenos, a stranger, appears suddenly before Telemachus, powerfully present (*Od.* 15. 223). He is escaping from his country, he is a seer; but we learn nothing about him, and the story turns to his great ancestor Melampos whose record and posterity are told in a loose, allusive manner. The point of the genealogy is here the gift of prophecy handed down from father to son. It helps to give Theoclymenos his standing. But his personal life is something else. It would have been unlike Homer to follow it up from his birth onward. Nor could the past be summoned back without a compelling dramatic motive. What alone stands out is the immediate occasion. It emerges against a vast nebulous background that cannot be scanned. Between the one and the other lies a wide gap—not so much an interval of time as an incompatibility of values.

The feeling for life, and for progress in life, is given by moments of individual self-assertion. The genealogies, on the other hand, point to the impersonal existence of the tribe—to family ties, family feuds. They are a necessary premise to the presence of a hero whose birth must be accounted for. The past which they recall is something static. The poet mentions them as a point of reference, as a condition which is inevitable and taken for granted, not as history leading to the present moment.

The actual point at which we meet the Homeric characters is significant in this respect. Odysseus is out in the wide world or just back in Ithaca like someone unknown, a stranger; the Greek heroes around Troy are caught in a venture which now has long removed them from their homes; the Trojans are at home, but in a city which is on the eve of its doom. And yet these people are not lightly conceived figures; a host of associations binds them very strongly to their world, to all its traditional horrors and glories. There is, therefore, an obvious break in their lives. The most appropriate point in their general fortunes seems chosen to present this break in its full purport. Everything conspires to make the dispersal as evident as possible. The moment's isolation could not be clearer. All memories are brushed aside; and even the past lives of the chief actors remain unknown. Any full biography, again, would be inconceivable here, something quite alien to the imagination of the poet.

A fresh survey of life may, on the other hand, be favored by these circumstances. A character left to himself—stranded, uprooted by a crisis—is bound to look at the world quite unconventionally and to sum up his career in his own way. Such is Odysseus just landed on the shore of Ithaca. Disguised, alone, facing foes as well as friends, what can he say when asked who he is? He must make up a story (cf. *Od.* 13. 256–86; 14. 199–359; 19. 172–202). The longest account (*Od.* 14. 199 ff.) is also the most significant. It is tantamount to an ideal biography. In his wiles the truth comes up unwittingly. His fiction does not impede, but fosters the essential genuine details. For he is now a man without glamour, a beggar; and what must prompt him in this role is a disenchanted and critical view of things, a necessary lucidity. Even the most valiant deeds must here be retraced to some native quality rather than to the customary prestige of a hero.

Let us hear him speak, at a crucial point of his story (*Od.* 14. 211 ff.). His stepbrothers have just excluded him from the family fortune, trying to appease him with a few gifts and a house.

But I took to wife the daughter of men rich in land, I took her on account of my bravery. Not a dullard was I, not a dastard. Though now nothing is left, even from the stubble, I think, you can see, if you look, what once was the grain. For indeed very many are my troubles. Yes, Athena and Ares granted me once all boldness and strength. . . . Rustic labor was not for me, nor the household virtues that breed lovely children; but the ships with their oars did I love, and wars and arrows and well-polished spears—those sorry things that are frightful to others. All this I held dear that a god perhaps set in my heart.

Then comes the Trojan expedition; "nor was there any means to refuse, invidious was the voice of the people that had us go." After the war he returns to Crete, but passes only one month at home: "my spirit bid me set sail for Egypt—fit out my good ships in the goodly company of friends."

A real character emerges from these lines. The story bears upon it from beginning to end, though it runs quickly through a whole age of epic lore. We find here a man in the making, a self-portrait that grows upon us, a life-story however crude and sketchy. The spirit of instant action which plays so important a role elsewhere in Homer seems here detached from its momentary occasions and deployed through time. It thus passes into a temperament that must be ever true to itself, into a way of life that runs its own course.

Our interest is turned to an imaginary person. The great events of the day are for him mere episodes. The most famous places are stepping stones in his career. Any enterprise becomes an occasion to make the best of what is available. It is the very principle of life that seems to move him—a bid to live in his own way, to survive, to gain, to win. He is clever, resourceful, shifty, bold, restless, curious of the world. No given conditions, no patterns of behavior can hold him. He does not escape, for instance, from the family feud in Crete to ask asylum elsewhere according to custom; he resists and turns his plight to advantage. Conventional existence is only a necessary foothold, a starting point. Over and above it, his spirit flickers on its own, and will do so even to the point of extinction. Now, at the end of his career, he turns back. Is it about life he speaks? He uses the image of the stubble and the grain. We find again the imagery of natural growth, as in Achilles likened to a plant on a hill-top. But there is here also the glorious feeling that, deep down, the fiber has remained as it always was, and that, whatever happened, this coherence of life is something to be proud of.

This fictitious person—Castor, son of Hylacos, as he calls him-self—breathes an Odyssean spirit. He is a rediscovered Odysseus. The hero, even in his makeshift tale, cannot get away from his own character. Unburdened of his name, he is, in a sense, more free to speak about his real human self. Compare, on the other hand, his words to Alcinous: "I am Odysseus, the son of Laertes, by all kinds of wiles a concern to all men. Clear-seen Ithaca is my home" (Od. 9. 19 ff.). How could he dwell upon his genius on that occasion? What then fills the scene is his well-known uncontro-versial image which seems to expect recognition even before he speaks. It stands in the way of any immediate and intimate char-acterization, it can only yield its message gradually. But now Castor is a newcomer, a self-made man, a beggar; and what he says comes first-hand. He grows out of nothing, improvised, composed for what he is.

This is then, in spirit, a life of Odysseus. We may even detect certain significant details which are ignored or only suggested elsewhere in the poems. That disapproval of the Trojan war, for instance, and that reluctance to go might be referred to Odysseus' refusal and feigned madness reported in the Cypria. Similarly that subsequent voyage to Egypt recalls Odysseus' further wanderings after his return to Ithaca, as described in the Telegony. What in other poets must have been a myth or a tale taken literally is here taken up as a passing detail of experience, as an additional feature of the portrait, or even as a simple feeling, a simple thought. The factual material is thus reduced to a minimum; it becomes memory —a matter for regret or for pride.

This ideal life-story could only come in such a roundabout way. It is as if Homer, that lover of images, would naturally express the different sides of one man's life by imagining parallel adventures, parallel adventurers. This is nothing very extraordinary. Does not a novelist often express his inmost feelings through the lips of one of his characters better than he would in an autobiography? Now Odysseus becomes, as it were, his own novelist. "He told many falsehoods in the likeness of truth," we read (Od. 19. 203): that is to say, not mere forgeries, but representations of himself in an imagined setting, what actually occurred being altered by the sense of what might have occurred in similar circumstances.

Such fiction clearly brings out the idea of life as a characterizing experience evolving in time. For, in this fanciful rendering, the burden of single days is swept aside and what comes to the fore is the whole extent of one's life, however imaginary it may be. Invention is here quite temperate, naturally lucid. It stresses an individual strain running behind the changing show of obvious events. By a series of transpositions, by the shifting of scenes and names and episodes, the various perspectives of time and place are treated lightly, just as a foil to one man's continuous activity. Seeing things in this way still means seeing them for what they essentially are, but removed from a setting which was so far taken for granted. Their importance becomes only relative. The time of existence is thus no longer compressed into single moments, no longer felt to be one with the presence of any given object. It is wrenched away, as it were, from its local connotations. Heroes, or cities, cease to be images whose destiny is as native to them as their features.

This fiction might, therefore, be considered as a byway to reach a man's life avoiding the accustomed scenes and the well-established identities which would arrest the stream of time. There is in it a feeling that everything is accidental and might have been otherwise. Another Odysseus might have sailed to another Troy. Hence an *alter ego* emerges, a double, a dream of the other, nimbler, lighter, easier to grasp. He can treat the cycle of myths whence he originally sprang as something casual, adventitious. We can follow him as one whose movements are unpredictable. At the end, his life can be descried all at once, as a course of action whose motives might have seemed too wayward, too moody for the terse language of the earnest moments. In a similar way, at a distance, we picture our past more clearly; getting rid of all self-righteous pose, we can look at our own life as if it had been that of a different person.

13

It is hard to recover one's own former self however briefly; it is even harder to recover that of another person. Biography, insofar as it would render an individual's experience of time, cannot but fall short of its mark. It can give us an adequate account of personal fortunes and achievements; but how could it retrieve the formative moments at any length? The very reconstruction of the facts, external as it is, stands in the way. In fiction, on the other hand, accuracy may be dispensed with, but the difficulties are no less momentous: how to conceive a real character afresh and how to make it live.

It is not enough, here, to account for experiences and ideals; for these may be a theme in their own right. What matters most is the underlying sense of time. A perfect biographer, or novelist, will deal with the values of life as they arise in the very act of living; he will render the sweet or bitter taste of a revealing hour; he will realize the actual process of experience rather than merely dwell upon its contents or its message. Time will be the measure of what is possible, relevant, virtually real; and even incredible deeds will be seen in a sort of intrinsic authenticity, as things that happen, exist, develop in their own way.

A life-story further implies a frame for the action. Whatever happens must focus upon a character that remains coherently itself; or else the story will dissolve into a series of sketches turning the hero into a will-o'-the-wisp. Herein lies a delicate point of balance between the constantly stable self and the varied course of experience. Individual life, insofar as it is realized in time, rests on two opposing values: on the one hand the inevitable adherence to whatever we happen to be; and, on the other, a capacity for transformation. Its representation in art naturally shifts toward either pole. In a very general way we might say that in the course of any age the element of change is progressively stressed and that the primitive image breaks apart, varied facets emerging in place of the original spell. We thus find in Homer stalwart images that but seldom give themselves away as if reluctant to impair their immediate and full-blooded presence; while the characters of a modern novel gradually come into their own gathering shape from successive experiences.

The solemnity of Homer, however, is not at all static. His characters are so presented that their lives seem enclosed within them; and when they stir inwardly on the spur of a revealing moment, they let out a part of themselves. It is as if an inner vibration set in motion the mainsprings of memory. Their past comes up all at once, a deeper layer of their being now suddenly brought up to the surface.

We thus catch in Homer vistas of life which, though fragmentary, are deeply relevant to character. They do not amount to biographies; but they contain the first principles of any imaginative survey of individual life. For the hero is now a man freshly aware of his human identity; and the instinct to exist becomes a thought of existence, self-assurance melts into a feeling of destination, and the present day seems to join with all the others. Here is a kernel of experienced time. The spirit of the poems forces it out of the material contents. In a similar way, as we have seen, the word for "life" acquires a temporal meaning from the physical one of sheer vitality.

Homer thus represents a high point in the rendering of individual life. We see, in the poems, how genuine moments of experience are given free scope and intrude upon the grounds of myth and tradition. Consider, for instance, Andromache surveying her life face to face with Hector. She so renders her past as to make it entirely relevant to her destiny, to her image, to her presence there and then, as if nature itself warranted the truth of what she says. Her words come from her lips, as blood from a wound. The lapse of time which is thus set to view is purely human, personal. No alien interest, no ulterior purpose overlays it. The destinies of the age do not matter. Nor is there any allegorizing or moralistic theme in the presentation.

This Homeric achievement stands out quite solitary. Not until times which are quite close to us could life be viewed again so freely. For the intrinsic truthfulness of the picture could no longer be maintained once the natural feeling for life was lost or blurred by external influences. Soon after Homer, an idealizing trend and a taste for allegories or symbols overshadowed the Ionian perceptiveness. This change—or parallel development—prevailed perhaps on the Greek mainland and we find its signs already in Hesiod. Moral ideas, mythically conceived, still sought an image to which they might cling. The hero or heroine, who had been once humanized by Homer, turned into another figurehead. So, for instance, Helen. A goddess in pre-Homeric times, she only retains in Homer something of her divine being as daughter of Zeus; in everything else she is just a woman who broods with human intensity on her life, neither praised nor condemned for what she is, followed with understanding in her grievous experience. This contrasts strikingly with what happened to her afterwards. An evil genius in Aeschylus, a fake angel in Euripides, the one and the other in turn in Stesichorus, a theme for polemical panegyric in Gorgias, she seems to have haunted in a way or the other the minds of men, her life a sort of parable far removed from that intense excerpt of human experience which we find in Homer. Or take Odysseus: is he not a villain on account of his craftiness from Pindar onward, while in Homer that craftiness is just one aspect of his personality, just one moment in a life which is wonderfully rich?

These examples point to a tendency which prevailed throughout the ages. The moral interest in the life of a character appeared misdirected. It was not focused on the complexities of human nature, but on the issues of good and evil in the existence of man. Opposing forces were seen controlling his destiny. The personal image was thus forced into a symbol. Hence the idealization of Aeneas, or of King Arthur; hence the hagiographies and the invectives, the crusaders and their opponents. Only the stage could, now and then, rescue human nature and show it unimpaired.

A real character, and a real life, can only be portrayed in rare happy moments of free and unprejudiced perception. Inveterate habits of thinking must first be brushed aside, and an instinctive sympathy be allowed to have free play. If is so for the characters of fiction as well as of history. The rise of both the novel and of biography in the eighteenth and nineteenth centuries is no casual coincidence. A novelist often vindicates the spontaneous movements of life against a host of conventions; and, likewise, a biographer tries to recover the private individual life which often lies hidden behind the public scene. In both cases the spirit of the age sinks into the background to make way for a more intimate view of time.

A world of difference separates, of course, the life of a Homeric hero from such as we might find in a modern novel or biography. In Homer the time of life is all one with the pulsations of the heart and the past can only be summoned up, as it were, through the interstices of that basic rhythm. For the moderns, on the other hand, time has become metaphysical; and they can only recapture it when touching upon some vibration of life. While Homer seems impeded by the sheer presence of his characters and by the immediate din of their actions, the moderns feel baffled when looking upon people and things that their notion of time has already transformed into aspects of transience. And yet, from opposing angles, the perspectives meet. In certain instances it is the same experience that stands out. Tolstoy's Prince Andrew and Hector, for example: do they not strike us in the same way when they revive from a deadly blow to see the sky and again acquire a consciousness of time?

What we are dealing with, however, are glimpses, partial views, reflections. For this throb of life, or of time, is hardly a subject matter at all. Though most familiar in discourse, it is most difficult to capture in any form. It is a sort of cadence which is present in everything, but identifiable with nothing. It can only be caught by the wing—in a movement that yields the permanent secret of its charm, in an image whose very stillness is an indefinite suspense. Whatever it is more particularly, it might be rendered in unexpected ways; but writers, when dealing with time, mostly lose touch with it and fall into a descriptive account of current conditions. No wonder. It is so with us every day. Life is usually a routine, time the hour of the clock; and hardly ever do we realize the pure happening of things, hardly ever do we have a real sensation of something that lives and develops within us, around us. Perhaps poets and writers can, after all, give us a better sense of this reality, or of this illusion, than we could ever imagine by ourselves. Homer pointed the way. The words and actions of his characters often seem to convey a sense of sheer existence quite apart from their particular message or purpose; and they carry us into a world, into a time of their own.

14

It remains to be seen how Homer conceives time in its widest terms—not the days and the seasons, not a pregnant human moment and individual life, but the general course of existence. Time in this sense is often given a sublime status. So Pindar (*Nemean* 4. 43) speaks of time bringing to fulfillment all native excellence, and Sophocles (*Ajax*. 646) of "the enduring and uncounted time that brings to light and buries all we see." Time here means change, growth, decay, destruction, or the perpetual flux, the ebb and flow of things seen in their totality. The ancients brought out also its creative and productive force, the moderns have stressed its ravaging hand, as in the beautiful imagery of Shakespeare's sonnets.

Homer stands quite alone in this respect. There is no idealizing of time in the poems. We have seen how the word for "time," χρόνος, is never found as subject of the phrase, but only in some adverbial expressions—such as "for a long time," "for a short time"—to mark an interval between actions, a period of waiting. It would have been impossible for Homer to see in this blank interval the sign of any transcending power. Eyes so keen on the immediate could at best so conceive the day or the night. And yet the Homeric characters often turn their thoughts to the general vicissitudes of existence—to what agency brings them about. Such an agency is then quite different from time; it is some mighty presence, a god or a divine dispensation felt to be close at hand though hailed from afar.

Nestor, in a rout, says to Diomedes: "Do you not see that the might of Zeus sways not on your side? Now to this man does Zeus the son of Cronus give glory, today; and thereafter again to us, if he wills it; a man cannot forestall his designs, not even the strongest" (*Il.* 8. 140 ff.). Odysseus sums up the life of himself and of others "to whom Zeus has given it to wind up the thread of cruel wars from youth to old age until each of us perish" (*Il.* 14. 85 f.). Menelaus perceives in the features of Nestor's son a bright promise for the future and says: "Easy to recognize is the offspring of that man for whom Zeus weaves the thread of good luck at the time of his birth and his bridal" (*Od.* 4. 207 ff.). Odysseus chides Amphinomus on account of his self-assurance, showing him the inherent weakness of men, "for such is the spirit of mortals as the day which the father of gods and of men brings upon them" (*Od.* 18. 137 ff.). Aphrodite, seeking marriage for the daughters of Pandareus, turns to Zeus, "for he knows all things—all that happens and does not happen to mortal men" (*Od.* 20. 75 ff.). Philoitios, seeing Odysseus in rags, exclaims: "O father Zeus, no god is more ruinous than you, you do not take pity upon men after you beget them yourself, plunging them in evil and woe" (*Od.* 20. 201 ff.).

In such passages the idea of time is strongly felt. In certain cases (e.g. *Il.* 14. 85) Zeus is almost an embodiment of it. He does not stand out as a god whose fiat is immediate and absolute. His influence rather blends with the course of the days. And yet he is a real god. We could not replace his name with terms like "fortune" or "fate." They would posit a blind indistinct force. The Homeric picture, on the contrary, is delicately and clearly balanced: on the one hand, the rhythm of existence in its basic moments of rise and fall; on the other, a god that seems to sustain it and justify it. The unpredictable sequence of events is thus not so erratic as to preclude a discerning influence; and the divine will is not so arbitrary as not to come to terms with an order which is inherent in nature.

Religious feeling thus envelops the bare idea of time. Zeus gives the keynote here. He is not, in this context, the impressive image nodding assent to Thetis. His power is scattered over the world, so that the personal physiognomy melts away into a distant but pervasive presence. How does he penetrate so deeply into the general course of events? The reason must lie in the original character of Zeus. For he is essentially a sky-god, a weather-god. He is the father of the days and of the seasons. Natural time emanates from him. If he takes human interests at heart, he will impart to the days and years a human significance. This is what happens in Homer. Zeus becomes an apportioner of good and evil to men in general—to cities as well as to individuals (cf. *Il.* 24. 529; *Od.* 4. 237; 6. 188; 15. 489, etc.). In this generalized function, an indefinite "god" or "the gods" may take his place (cf. *Od.* 3. 208; 11. 139; 13. 45; cf. *Il.* 24. 538, etc.); but Zeus seems more nearly at home wherever the sense of time is keenest—in the day which hangs as a doom or a blessing upon the world, in the moments of birth which seem to have a secret influence upon a whole lifetime.

Religious feeling drew upon nature and at once rose above it fashioning its symbols of eternity. For the wonder of the rising and declining day merged with that of the seasons and the years finding in Zeus a supreme interpreter. Countless ages could, consequently, be imagined as due to his spell. Thanks to his magnetic name, the elusive values of universal time could be given a solid term of reference, a persuasive though mysterious rendering. And yet this god of time never could lose in Homer his primitive character. He was still a weather-god, a god of daylight. He could not become an all-seeing Providence. The same imagination which lifted him up to Heaven and immortality also kept him bound to the earth—to the ways of nature, to the soil that bore daily witness of the eternal flux.

Hence comes a mellow natural piety in all the Homeric passages which touch upon time, destiny, existence. They convey the sense of a chastening harmony which accounts even for the worst happenings. The main characters behave accordingly. They are weathered by a native wisdom. No victory lets them run riot, no defeat deadens them. Hope and despair have here a natural margin; and resignation is not so much forbearance as a knowledge of alternate fortunes which seem as inevitable as the succession of day and night. Friends and enemies can thus be seen in the same light—as waifs in the ebb and flow of existence. Death can be met with a natural courage. It is but the beat of a perpetual rhythm —of the time which passes drawing with it the lives of men.

This religious spirit, pervasive as it is, hardly leads to any act of faith. Zeus does not champion any cause consistently, but simply mirrors and prefigures the ways of nature. Accordingly, the course of time is presented as a mere modulation of existence in its constant terms. It does not contain the promise of a better world—no progression, no forward movement to serve as a pattern of history. The days and the seasons were too essential an element of its texture. They could not be spirited away or attenuated to make room for the idea of a metaphysical time process. The world itself might then have become a mere symbol of transience, and the god of daylight untrue to his very nature.

The very elements which built up the image of Zeus set a limit to his range. Homer, that discoverer of clear outlines, gathered as much as possible into the hands of the god the diffusive influences at work in the world, but he could never forget that natural soil which was the source of all godhead. This is why other agencies appeared here besides Zeus to govern the course of existence. These were powers more deeply embedded in the earth, more closely identified with the process of nature, felt rather than visualized, and all the more penetrating. They might be taken as embodiments of destiny—but of a destiny not at all sublimated, darkly sunk into the patterns of life as an inevitable and unexplained necessity. Time is then at a standstill. It can hardly point backward and forward as when reflected by immortal Zeus. It lies entangled in the conditions of being.

Such ideas as world order, destiny, fate come to our mind. In the Homeric language the words *aisa, moira,* "part," "portion," "lot" are the nearest equivalents (cf. *Il.* 18. 327; 15. 195). These nouns moreover have a suffix which is used to convey the sense of an animate feminine power. The "portion" is also the "apportioner." But there is no personification: the abstract and the concrete are not divorced from one another, and ideas are naturally taken as physical agents.

In certain passages the sense of time pierces through. We might even render the words in question with "time," "lifetime." Thetis says to Achilles who will not live long: "Would that you could remain by the ships without tears, without pain, since your *aisa* is short, of no length" (*Il.* 1. 416). Achilles will not be appeased and refuses the honors promised to him saying: "I think that my honor lies in the *aisa* of Zeus which will keep me by the hollow ships as long as life-breath remains in my breast" (*Il.* 9. 608). The seer Theoclymenos, an exile, tells Telemachus how he is escaping from his country, "since it is now my *aisa* to be a wanderer among men" (*Od.* 15. 276). Odysseus recalls a moment of his wanderings which almost brought him home, "but not yet was it the *aisa* that I should come to my country" (*Od.* 23. 315). Helenus encourages Hector to fight saying: "not yet is it for you the *moira* to die" (*Il.* 7. 52). Proteus tells Menelaus that he can never hope to return home unless he makes a sacrifice on the Nile, "for not before is it the *moira* for you to see your friends and your well-built home and your native land" (*Od.* 4. 475; cf. 5. 41, 114; 9. 532).

In these instances time is reduced to an allotted point. It is distributed, as it were, on the chessboard of existence. As far as men are concerned, it seems to mark in black and white, for good and for evil, the crucial decisive points of their lives. The sense of "portion" fits in quite well, as if time summed up the shares of existence allotted to each and all. This dispensation does not allow for the details of individual experience. What counts is birth, death, or such important occurrences as the return of Odysseus. There is something utterly impartial, elemental in existence so conceived. If a god intervened, he would inject a will which is all too human. This *moira*, this *aisa*, on the contrary, represent the incidence itself—the golden opportunity or the mortifying failure which cannot be accounted for on the strength of any single interest: divine or human. Here is then an ultimate value. It can only be referred to a certain order, to a certain drift in the scheme of things.

Time—or fate, destiny—is sunk into the ebb and flow of matter. The "portion" which marks each phase can hardly be lifted above itself—not even when it is conceived as an active power. Homer does not personify it. A natural limit is set to its characterization. We read, for instance: "He shall suffer all that the *aisa* spun out for him when his mother begot him" (*Il.* 20. 127; cf. 24. 209). That spinning requires an agent, but it is an impersonal task: the days of life are a natural thread in the web of time. Elsewhere the very act of spinning *(klōthein)* is made into an agent, and the "grave klothes" stand side by side with the *aisa (Od.* 7. 197). A power emerges from the material pattern of things; but it is not idealized, it is not a god, its action is inevitable and rhythmical. "Whatever the *aisa*—or the *moira*—spun out for him when he was born": the same solemn words could be used for any person, in any age. We are far removed from Zeus, far removed from a world where hopes and prayers might find a reward. Not without reason Apollo says that "the *moirai* have set a patient soul into man" (*Il.* 24. 49).

Again, this "portion" is actively conceived when it coincides with the fate of a man—most evidently so when he dies. We read for instance: "Him did the ill-named *moira* overshadow" (*Il.* 12. 116; cf. 17. 672; 21. 110, etc.). So the kindred word *moros* is often synonymous with death (*Il.* 18. 465; 21. 133, etc.) or with a doomed life (*Od.* 11. 618). Indeed all the words that have an implication of fate (κήρ, οἶτος, πότμος) bear a similar meaning. "To fulfil one's portion" is to die. By being so frequently identified with death this destiny is again seen in its constant rhythm. Even as a deadly power, it merely underscores something inevitable.

Fate, destiny in Homer are not concerned with the actions of men. A phrase like "the destiny of a man" or "the destinies of a nation" could not recur in the poems. According to the sense of "portion," "lot," the lives of individuals are seen as parts of an indefinite succession. There is no room for history, experience. The course of a man's life does not matter as much as its beginning and ending. At best we may gather a thread that leads from birth to death through the occasions that are most closely connected with these extremes. Here time revolves upon itself; it is an endlessly repeated cycle.

This deterministic view of time and existence is not expounded in the poems, but it is embedded in the language. We may realize it in many ways. Good and evil, for instance, often appear as conditions objectively fixed, lying outside any modifying influence. They are thus equivalent to fortune and misfortune. It is again the idea of "portion" that comes up. "Lacking in one's portion," "evil-portioned" are, interpreted literally, the words which most often mean "unhappy" (ἄμμορος, δύσμορος, δυσάμμορος, αἰνόμορος). Similarly "lacking in what befalls," "evil-fated" (ἄποτμος). So "short-lived" is "swift in one's portion" (ὠκύμορος), a doomed man is someone "due to the *aisa*" (cf. *Il.* 16. 441; 22. 179). It is the same with the meaning of happiness. Priam looking at Agamemnon in his majesty, cannot otherwise render the happy state of that king than by crying out: "o child of the *moira*, rich in fate" (*Il.* 3. 182). It is as if the signal of a blessing or of a curse struck for anyone born, marking him for life. So we read more than once "a miserable man did his mother beget him" (*Od.* 3. 95; 4. 325; cf. *Il.* 21. 84; 1. 418).

What applies to people also applies to events. There is a feeling of destination about whatever happens. A recurring phrase in Homer is: "Thus I tell you, and thus I think it will happen" (*Il.* 1. 204; 2. 257, etc.). The verb for "happening" (τελέεσθαι) really means "to be fulfilled." An event is seen as a fulfillment, as if it traced a certain course from beginning to end filling its place in the order of time. So we find such expressions as "fulfillment of marriage" or "of death" or "of war" rather than simply "marriage," "death," "war." These are not figures of speech. Any remarkable event might be regarded as a *telos*—a consummation. Other striking words, which have an archaic ring, show the same

principle. Such is *tekmor* "goal," "limit"; and we read, for instance: "tomorrow they shall fight until they find the *tekmor* of
Ilium"—which means "the limit set upon Ilium's existence" (*Il.*
7. 30; cf. 9. 418, 685; *Od.* 4. 373, 466). Such, again, is *peirar*,
peirata "boundary," "end," as in "the *peirata* of destruction are
hanging over the Trojans" (*Il.* 7. 402; cf. 12. 79; 7. 102; *Od.* 5.
289). It is as if each happening came to an appointed climax, like a
tide that must attain its full measure.

People and events so conceived are cast in a stark, absolute
form. Nothing seems exempted from its destined role. Here the
spirit of chance, the flighty *tyche*, has not yet made its way. In
such a world there would be no alternatives; a sense of premonition instead of hope, rather than actions inevitable facts, rather
than characters mythical heroes that embody natural forces.

The course of time quite conditioned by natural necessity, individual life steeped in the general rhythm of existence, the gods felt
as impersonal powers lurking in the ways of nature—such an outlook, we may suppose, harked back to something primitive, pre-
Homeric, reflecting world-wide popular beliefs. It must have had
its part in the ancient nature worship of Crete and Mycenae.
Homer could not but feel its pervasive influence even in the very
words which he used. But, over and above it, Homeric poetry developed in an extraordinary way the human character of the gods,
and of Zeus especially. In relation to the idea of time, this means
that the sense of an ideal duration encroached upon the natural
patterns of existence.

There are many signs of this tendency. We find the *moira*, or
aisa, associated with Zeus or subordinated to him (*Il.* 9. 608; 17.
321; *Od.* 9. 52; cf. *Il.* 19. 87, 410; *Od.* 11. 560, etc.). Likewise the
Hours, the *Horai*, are not goddesses of time, but the seasons which
proceed from Zeus; or else the word simply means "appropriate
moment"; so that there is a *hore* for sleeping, resting, eating. If
at all personified, the *Horai* have a very marginal role, as gate-
keepers of Olympus. Again, quite small is the part reserved to the
Erinyes, those ancient nature-goddesses who also, in their own

way, governed the lapse of time according to a fated measure, requiting blood for blood from generation to generation.

No god, however, may be taken for granted. His image, if at all vital, cannot merely rest on a process of syncretism. If his personal influence stretches out beyond the present, it is not just because he replaces ruder gods that presided over the course of nature. What makes him convincing in the first place is his participation in a human action, when he stretches over it an avenging or a protecting hand. Doing so, he seems to derive the very reason of his subsistence from human prayers and curses, from hopes and fears which project beyond the span of individual life. A man can cry out to heaven. A dark foreboding may still oppress his mind; but, for the moment, a vision opens up which has nothing to do with the mechanical dispensation of fate.

Thus Hector knows that Ilium is going to fall, that his own death is near at hand. And yet he tells Andromache: "Do not grieve overmuch. No one will hurl me to Hades against the *aisa*; but no man, I say, shall escape the *moira*, be he good be he bad, once he is born" (*Il.* 6. 486 ff.). This age-old condition of men is taken for what it is, and set aside. Thus he is free at heart. He can laugh, he can be gay, he can utter a prayer for his son and imagine future blessings. He soon must die; but his life is somehow continued in a dream of the future, and Zeus is called to witness.

We find here a sense of time which is human, and yet transcends experience. The actual human drama, intense as it is, provides the first spark. The gods watching over it gather its momentary passions into the paths of indefinite time; and fate is relegated to the background outside the living moment. The interplay of gods and men thus presents itself simply, clearly. The divine influence opens up a new perspective turned on the future.

The very content of the poems seems to force itself beyond the period of time which is allotted to it. We become gradually aware of this. For it is the human action which is quite central. It clears away all irrelevant matter. It fills the scene. As it develops, it acquires a logic of its own. No previous subject matter, no previous history blurs its scope. But, evolving as it does, it necessarily contains in itself a kernel of history—a burden of experience whose value cannot be brushed aside, not even by the doom of all concerned. Thus Hector lives and dies; but his cause is taken up by Apollo in Olympus and Zeus assents. In such a way the gods warrant this enlarged range, this human projection beyond the passing moment. What matters now is no longer the single life, the rhythm of existence, the lot assigned to each. Time is seen yet from another angle—as a prospect in which all interests, all ideals might be included. Not that such an indefinite view of past and future is anywhere set forth or explained; but the bright Homeric day seems to foster it—a day which, so mirrored in heaven, stretches beyond all physical dimension, and also beyond the immediate consciousness of men.

Bibliographical Note

There is today a dissatisfaction with the traditional divisions of knowledge, a desire of fresh perspectives. Hence so many comparative studies. Hence a new interest in ideas and their bearing on life. Greek studies are also affected. "Classical Philology" hardly exists anymore in the old sense. Homer, in particular, offering as he does a comprehensive vision of the world, lends himself to wide-ranging speculation. This is why the Homeric poems are studied in such different books as: Bruno Snell, *Die Entdeckung des Geistes,* Hamburg 1946 (English translation by T. G. Rosenmeyer, *The Discovery of Mind,* Harvard 1953); E. R. Dodds, *The Greeks and the Irrational,* Berkeley 1951; R. B. Onians, *The Origins of European Thought, about the Body, the Mind, the Soul, the World, Time and Fate,* Cambridge 1951; Hermann Fränkel, *Wege und Formen früh-griechischen Denkens,* Munich 1955; René Schaerer, *L' Homme antique,* Paris 1958; H. & A. Thornton, *Time and Style,* London 1962.

The approach of these authors is very appealing to me. It is philosophical, and yet removed from abstraction; it is critical, analytical, and yet broad, suggestive, imaginatively vague. By the aid of semantics it often offers fresh glimpses into history, religion, literature, civilization in general. But at the same time I have felt that such a course of study was somehow lacking in the esthetical appreciation of the material. Snell, for instance, deals with concept of mind and body in Homer by pointing to a certain stage of thought in view of later developments. Enlightening as he is, he leads us to consider Homer as necessarily less advanced than we are. He does not seem to look at the Homeric representation as something positive in itself, valid in its own right, just as appealing to Homer's contemporaries as it is to us.

There are, of course, many books about the poetry of Homer which also deal, in part, with the subject matter of this book—for instance: S. E. Bassett, *The Poetry of Homer,* Berkeley 1938; Wolfgang Schadewaldt, *Von Homers Welt und Werk,* Stuttgart 1959; C. H.

Whitman, *Homer and the Heroic Tradition,* Harvard 1958; G. S. Kirk, *The Songs of Homer,* Cambridge 1962; C. R. Beye, *The Iliad, the Odyssey, and the Epic Tradition,* London 1968.

These books are works of literary criticism and history. They often offer brilliant insights into the characters and the episodes; but when it comes to a general consideration of the poetry and its subject matter, they seem to disregard the individual poet. Thus the mode of composition and the poetic expression are generally referred to tradition or to the technique of oral poetry; the Homeric representation of nature is studied in broad historical terms and compared with that of Cretan, Mycenaean, or Early Geometric Art; man, in general, is considered according to certain patterns of heroic behavior current in epic poetry; or the humanity of Homer is vindicated and opposed to the mythical background, but insofar as it helps to define the image of "Homeric man" as a type which must necessarily belong to a certain age or society. It is likewise concerning general concepts. Basset, for instance, has some very good things to say about time in Homer, but the Homeric conception is regarded as a convenient device to capture the listeners, as part of the "epic illusion."

Homer, however, could be approached also from a purely speculative point of view, as if we were reading him for the first time and trying to discover in the poems themselves the signs of a pervasive thought or of a distinctive imaginative principle. I should like to point, in this respect, to Renata von Scheliha, *Patroklos: Gedanken über Homers Dichtung und Gestalten,* Basel 1943. Also, in a more philosophical sense, Simone Weil, "L' Iliade ou le poème de la force" (published with other essays of the same authoress in *La source grecque,* Paris 1953; (translated into English, *The Iliad or the Poem of Force,* Pendle Hill); Rachel Bespaloff, *De l'Iliade,* New York 1943 (English translation by Mary McCarthy, *On the Iliad,* New York 1962). See also Fernand Robert, *Homère,* Paris 1949.

For my part, I have tried to retrace the poet's touch within certain broad fields of meaning—god, man, nature, time. These, however, are not particular topics, but convenient headings wherein to focus my study. The mode of approach is here more important than the scientific inquiry. The way in which anything is explained or accounted for makes up all the evidence. Any principle which is thereby upheld stands or falls according to whether it makes sense or not; it cannot be proved or disproved on the basis of external data.

Index

Achilles: wrath of, 10–11, 31, 54–58, 125, 146; human identity established, 53–60, 165–67; and Patroclus, 56–57, 58, 59; lyre of, 158; solitude of, 161–63; mentioned, 13, 27, 36, 140, 164

Action: motivation of, 12; present relevance of, 22, 125–26; represented in and by itself, 31; seen from many sides, 32–33; isolation of, 120–21, 123; not idealized, 127

Aeneas: on divine ancestry, 23, 122, 191

Aeneid, 124

Aeschylus, 123, 198

Agamemnon, 13, 30, 206

Ajax, 13

Ajaxes, 39

Alcinous: garden and palace of, 26, 75, 105

Andromache, 164–65, 197

Animals, 84, 85, 105

Anticleia, 25

Aphrodite, 50, 148–50

Apollo: and Hector, 43–45; mentioned, 41, 46, 51, 126

Ares, 51

Argos, 30

Ariosto, 7

Aristotle, 10, 33

Asteropaeus, 122

Ate, 20–21

Athena: and Odysseus, 45–48; characterization of, 63–65

Bacchylides, 22

Basic properties, 6–7, 79–80

Beauty: implications of, 25–27, 63–64, 105, 118–19

Bellerophon, 52, 140, 190

Bible, 135

Biography: implied in the image, 154–57; lack of, 189–90; fictional, 192–95; and sense of time, 196–200 *passim*

Body: oppsition to spirit denied, 35, 37, 42, 91

Calypso: island of, 26, 75; mentioned, 139

Castor, 194

Catalogue of ships, 77–78, 147–48

Characters: out of mythical figureheads, 10, 49, 68–69, 135; both godlike and brittle, 32–33, 122; emotions of, 36; as images, 155; solemn, not static, 197; resignation of, 202–03

Christianity, 127

Chronological probability: disregarded, 136, 137

Cicones, 25, 139

Circe: humanized, 25, 139; island of, 75; mentioned, 48, 109

Cyclops, 25, 109, 139

Cypria, 194

Danae, 107

Dante, 4, 7

Day: basic unit of time, 129; number of, 130; divine, 130; conception of, 130, 131, 132–41 *passim*; as a word for "time," 141; both real and idealized, 142–43; as a term for recurring instances, 151–52

"Day of freedom," "day of slavery," and similar expressions, 144–46